"White and the Esteps have given us a needed probe and overview into the important dimension that curriculum plays in ministry. The theoretical and theological base is sound, accessibles, and practicable. The clear outline, diagrams, explanations, and insights will be clear to seminary, college, or church ministry readers. The age-grouped chapters are written by experts in their respective fields. The result is a text to be used in the area of writing material for Christian ministry."

Gregory C. Carlson
Chair & Professor of Christian Ministries
Director, Division of Biblical, Religious & Philosophical Studies
Trinity College, Trinity International University
Deerfield, Illinois

"*Mapping Out Curriculum in Your Church* is a radical attempt to redirect the focus of ministry curriculum back to the Bible, seeking to ensure that theological concepts and categories inform, shape, and affirm curriculum development, teaching, and assessment. The text is relevant and should be read by all pastors, teachers, and Bible college/seminary students who are involved in teaching ministry."

Jonathan H. Kim, Ph.D.
Associate Professor of C.E.
Talbot School of Theology, Biola University
La Mirada, California

"Christian educators need and will use this long-overdue roadmap to curriculum design. *Mapping Out Curriculum in Your Church* enables the reader to see the complexities without getting tangled in the trivia. Writing from a theologically integrated perspective, the authors guide the reader through the complexities of curriculum design, including an outstanding chapter on learning theory. The references alone will be worth the price of the book. Required reading for anyone responsible for curriculum review or design."

Michael S. Lawson, Ph.D.
Senior Professor, Christian Education Department
Dallas Theological Seminary
Dallas, Texas

"*Mapping Out Curriculum in Your Church* moves beyond viewing curriculum primarily as developing lessons for teaching, which is often based on a tedious process of evaluation, to recognizing the church as God's curriculum to transform human persons and the world. This comprehensive view will prepare Christian educators to develop a transformative curriculum that facilitates spiritual growth and faithful disciples."

Mark A. Maddix, Ph.D.
Professor of Christian Education
Dean, School of Theology & Christian Ministries
Northwest Nazarene University, Nampa, Idaho
President of NAPCE

"Jim Estep, Roger White, and Karen Estep have completed an excellent work to help lay leaders, educators, and local church staff members understand how and why to map out curriculum. They provide an opportunity to understand both theory and practice of identifying and connecting curriculum to the glory of God."

Steve Yates
Associate Dean for Biblical Enrichment, iLEAD Center
Lancaster Bible College, Lancaster, Pennsylvania

"The variety of Bible classes, missions studies, and discipleship groups—spread across age groups and life needs—can produce an incoherent mash of educational efforts and outcomes in our churches. *Mapping Out Curriculum in Your Church* develops both perspective and principles (the why and how) required for local church educators to become "cartographers, making curricular maps for disciples to travel on their way to spiritual maturity" (Preface). Part I unwraps biblical, theological, historical, and psychological foundations for curriculum. Part II addresses practical concerns in the development and evaluation of curriculum. Part III analyzes curriculum development from the perspective of age-group ministries. This book draws from the best Christian Education specialists in the world to strengthen your intentional planning in congregational spiritual formation."

Rick Yount
Professor of Foundations of Education
Southwestern Baptist Theological Seminary, Fort Worth, Texas

JAMES ESTEP

ROGER WHITE

KAREN ESTEP

Mapping Out Curriculum in Your Church

Cartography for Christian Pilgrims

ACADEMIC

NASHVILLE, TENNESSEE

ISBN: 978-1-4336-7238-5

Published by B&H Publishing Group
Nashville, Tennessee

Dewey Decimal Classification: 268.6
Subject Heading: CHRISTIAN EDUCATION—CURRICULA \ BIBLE—
STUDY AND TEACHING \ CHRISTIAN LIFE

Printed in the United States of America

1 2 3 4 5 6 7 8 9 10 11 12 • 17 16 15 14 13 12

VP

This book is dedicated to
the ultimate end of glorifying God
and promoting kingdom movement
throughout the realm of Christ.

It is dedicated to
faithful cartographers
and guides in the church
who assist pilgrims along the way.

This work is dedicated to
fellow travelers and students,
that we may all progress
and abundantly flourish
on the path set before us.

Table of Contents

Section III: Curriculum Theory

Section IV: Curriculum Practice

INTRODUCTION

James Riley Estep Jr.

The history of our world is one of exploration. History is not just written by novelists, historians, or even poets; but by *cartographers*, the mapmakers. The legacy of explorers is captured in the maps, charts, and pathways they leave for those who come after them. They remind us that it is not just a matter of landing on an "uncharted" territory. Rather, it is depicting what they have explored, being able to share their adventure with others, and making it easier for those who follow to complete the journey that makes the exploration worthwhile. The ability to map the journey and chart the course so well that others can follow in your footsteps and along well-trodden pathways, and reasonably know where they are at all times, is priceless for generations to come.

Anyone who has traveled knows what it is like to rely on a map to guide the way. Maps can show the natural contours and features of the landscape, as well as our own additions such as roads, cities, bridges, and rest stops. Maps are also needed to guide us through the journey of faith. We are all pilgrims on a journey. For some, the pilgrimage is new and unknown. For others, the path is familiar. Identifying desirable destinations, pathways that have proven beneficial, and providing a means of navigation along the way are all part of the church's cartography, its mapmaking. Curriculum is a congregation's map through the process of discipleship, providing disciples, new and old, with the means to continue on their way toward Christlikeness, and the Christian educator is the cartographer. This book will equip Christian educators to better use curriculum as an instrument for intentional discipleship and the formation of the faith community.

Curriculum is often misunderstood, and its influence within the congregation underestimated. Some would consider the subject of curriculum more appropriate for a school, university, or other more academic enterprise, but not a congregation. Others see curriculum as no more than the packet of materials a teacher gets every thirteen weeks to use in Sunday school, or the leader's guide to a small group discussion that changes every eight weeks. *Neither of these perceptions is accurate.* Both fail to comprehend the significance of curriculum within any institution. When one fully appreciates the broad concept of *curriculum*, its critical importance to the congregation's ministry becomes self-evident. The curriculum provides the pathway for believers to grow toward Christian maturity. What do believers have to know, experience, and be able to do so as to mature? What do they need along the way to guarantee their continued spiritual growth? With whom should they travel in the journey of faith? The curriculum answers these questions, and gives the believer some direction, some proven paths of travel, so they are not lost along the journey of faith, wandering without direction. Curriculum is a tool of the education ministry to provide for the spiritual formation of believers.

Another aspect of the curriculum's influence within the congregation is that it defines and identifies who we are as God's people. The curriculum is the educational manifestation of the mission and vision of the congregation. If the congregation's vision has an emphasis on evangelism, then the curriculum should reflect that conviction and provide instruction and training consistent with the congregation's commitment. Similarly, what direction the curriculum takes inevitably takes the congregation in that direction. As the curriculum goes, so goes the school, college, institution . . . or congregation. In fact, educational leadership in many respects reduces down to the question, "Who controls the curriculum?" The curriculum, just like a map, is drawn by the congregation, but also directs the decision-making and future destinations of the congregation. In terms of education, there is little more important than curriculum. Overall, curriculum is a tool for ministering and leading within the Christian community.

About This Book

Mapping Out Curriculum in Your Church: Cartography for Christian Pilgrims was born from discussion at the North American Professors of Christian Education (NAPCE) conference in 2009. Drs. Roger White, Karen Estep, and James Estep entered into dialogue while sharing a breakfast at the Brown Hotel (Louisville, Kentucky). The book integrates Christian foundations, educational theory, and practical insights into an approach to curriculum formation in the local congregation. Using the metaphor of cartography, or mapmaking, this textbook addresses the need for curriculum in the local congregation. While some curriculum books focus on schools or theological education, this one identifies curriculum as a means of ministry. Without curricular maps, believers are lost along the spiritual journey, without a clear destination or reliable pathways to travel. This book equips Christian educators to be cartographers, making curricular maps for disciples to travel on their way to spiritual maturity.

The book itself has 16 chapters that are divided into four sections, each contributing to the reader's understanding and appreciation of curriculum in the church (see below).

The first three sections have chapters provided by James Riley Estep, Roger White, and Karen Lynn Estep. The final section gives voice to five new contributors in their given area of expertise. Section I (chap. 1) introduces the reader to the definition and importance of curriculum in the congregation. It answers the question, Why is

| Ch. 1 Intro | Chapters 2-5 Curriculum Foundations | Chapters 6-11 Curriculum Theory | Chapters 12-16 Curriculum Practice |

Structure of the Book

curriculum so important for the congregation? It presents a rationale for the intentional development of curriculum for the fulfillment of the Church's mission.

Section II presents the foundations on which Christian educators base their curriculum design and development in the congregation. It provides an answer to the question, What makes curriculum both Christian and educational? It contains chapters on biblical foundation, theological insights, historical lessons, and insights from learning theory—all of which are essential for building a distinctly Christian curriculum. Only on such a foundation can an educational ministry within a congregation be based.

Section III is comprised of chapters 6–11 and addresses the theory of curriculum. It moves from the basis of theorizing about curriculum toward its design and development, with a focus on establishing curricular purpose(s), goals, and objectives for the congregation's education ministry. The section concludes with two chapters on the evaluation of curriculum and its supervision when the Christian educator assumes the role of curriculum specialist for the congregation. This section answers the question, How does the congregation actually formulate curriculum? The chapters of this section provide a comprehensive overview of the process of formulating curriculum in the congregation, or for a specific ministry within the congregation.

Section IV, chapters 12–16, introduces the reader to the practice of curriculum supervision in the congregation. For this section we invited five individuals to contribute a chapter each, focusing on curriculum in a particular ministry:

1. Holly Allen (John Brown University), Children's Ministry
2. Mark H. Senter III (Trinity International University), Youth Ministry
3. Michael S. Wilder (Southern Baptist Theological Seminary), Adult Ministry
4. Timothy Paul Jones (Southern Baptist Theological Seminary), Family Ministry
5. Brett Robbe (Lifeway/Broadman & Holman), Prepackaged Curriculum

This section answers the question, What would you say about curriculum in your ministry context? We asked these contributors to imagine a student or pastor meeting with them one-on-one to inquire about curriculum in their area of ministry. For this reason, the tone of Section 4 is distinct from the previous chapters. Wanting to preserve the voice of curriculum specialists, these chapters are quite conversational and informal, as if the consultant were having a "coffee-discussion" about curriculum in your ministry.

Conclusion

We are all travelers in this life. As Christians, we are perhaps more than that. We are pilgrims, embarking on a journey of faith. We do not travel the way of the world but have chosen to take a different path in life. In Robert Frost's poem "The Road Not Taken" (1915), the poet asks us to put ourselves in the place of a traveler making a choice of paths:

> Two roads diverged in a yellow wood,
> And sorry I could not travel both
> And be one traveler, long I stood
> And looked down one as far as I could
> To where it bent in the undergrowth.
>
> Then took the other, as just as fair,
> And having perhaps the better claim,
> Because it was grassy and wanted wear;
> Though as for that the passing there
> Had worn them really about the same.
>
> And both that morning equally lay
> In leaves no step had trodden black.
> Oh, I kept the first for another day!
> Yet knowing how way leads on to way,
> I doubted if I should ever come back.
>
> I shall be telling this with a sigh
> Somewhere ages and ages hence:
> Two roads diverged in a wood, and I—
> I took the one less traveled by,
> And that has made all the difference.

As Christians, we do not travel the way of the world, the well-trodden path; but we take the narrow gate, a road less taken, and it makes an eternal difference (Matt 7:13). We recognize the path, know its ways, and can prepare for the journey not because it is the most popular road, but because of the maps and charts provided by our fellow travelers. Curriculum is one way the congregation gives believers a guide, a map, and the resources needed for the journey ahead. May you be blessed for your service within the kingdom for the benefit of God's people.

James Riley Estep Jr.
Professor of Christian Education
Lincoln Christian University
Lincoln, Illinois
2011

SECTION I

Curriculum Introduction

CHAPTER 1

WHEREVER YOU GO, THERE YOU ARE

The Need for Educational Maps in the Church

James Riley Estep Jr.

A re we there yet?" "How much further?" "When are we going to stop?" No parent escapes these perennial questions. Family trips are taken with intentionality; they are not about wandering around directionless or without purpose. They usually include a destination, a desired location to reach at an optimal time with arrangements made for the trip. We are typically not pioneers, boldly going into untamed territory, blazing new trails, charting a course to an unknown destination. Rather, we check atlases and the GPS, map out travel routes, or go online to AAA or another travel service to make sure we are going in the right direction and will reach our destination. We do not want to lose time wandering around aimlessly and getting lost. We need maps.

We are *travelers* in the Christian faith, not *wanderers*. The Bible speaks of people wandering in the wilderness as a chastisement (Num 32:13; 2 Kgs 21:8), rather than moving intentionally toward the land God had promised them. While it may seem that wandering is not bad for a short time, wandering for a lengthy time or throughout life is indeed perilous. In the Bible, wandering is typically associated with unfaithfulness; like the lone sheep in Jesus' parable (Matt 18:12–14), there is implicit danger in choosing to wander from the wisdom of God,[1] usually with disastrous consequences.[2] Jude 13 even describes false teachers as "*wandering* stars, for whom blackest darkness has been reserved forever" (emphasis added). The apostle Paul went on journeys, intentional travels, and was indeed more productive (Acts 13–14; 15:36–21:8, esp. 15:36); just as Jesus had demonstrated intentionality in his traveling through Palestine, moving the disciples through northern Galilee (Jewish), into the Decapolis region (Greek), and into Samaria before entering Judea and Jerusalem as preparation for his disciples' global mission. In short, wandering is not for Christians. We want to be travelers through the Christian life, not wanderers. Exploring and discovery learning have their place, but they supplement the main journey; they do not replace it.

Curriculum is the Church's map to spiritual maturity. It is the intentional direction given by mature believers to those who are new to the Christian faith. It is the lessons learned from 2,000 years of the Christian faith given to the contemporary church as a means of guiding us into a faithful walk and work with Christ. God gave the church as a means of directing people toward himself, and curriculum is the means by which the church maps the travel path toward Christlike maturity. Educational "maps" are simply the intentional plans made by the church for carrying out the task. The plans and their implementation are known as curriculum.

What Is Curriculum?

Defining curriculum is a daunting task. The word itself comes from the Latin *currere*, literally meaning "to run"; it came to mean the components of a course of study, the direction of one's race in life, such as in preparing a *curriculum vita* to demonstrate the path one has traveled through life in preparation for a career. Educationally, definitions are

---

[1] Cf. Prov 17:24; Jer 14:10; 31:22; Isa 63:17; Amos 8:12; Zech 10:2; Jas 5:19.
[2] Cf. Exod 14:13; Job 12:44; 15:23, 18:8; Ps 109:10; Lam 1:7; 3:19.

varied, ranging from curriculum as a packet of materials purchased from a publishing company to all the experiences one encounters in life or in the congregation. Arthur Ellis describes curriculum as prescription (i.e., what you have to know, knowledge-content focused) and experience (i.e., everything from which you learn, learner-child focused).[3] Figure 1.1 expands on this spectrum of curriculum's definitions and is primarily based on the nature of its content and upon what it is centered.[4]

So, how can one define curriculum? In fact, it almost defies definition. Perhaps the most common facet to understanding curriculum is *content*: "What did you teach today?" "Oh, Joshua and the battle of Jericho," or perhaps worse, "Pages 45–61 of the teacher's guide." Content is an inescapable element in understanding curriculum, but not the only one. *Objectives* are another way to grasp the meaning of the curriculum. Rather than focusing on what is taught, this dimension emphasizes *why* it is being taught. When someone asks, "What will I get out of this class?" or "If I participate in small groups for two

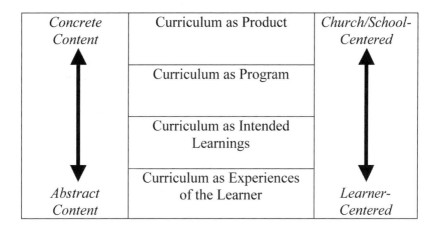

Figure 1.1: Spectrum of Curriculum

[3] Arthur K. Ellis, *Exemplars of Curriculum Theory* (Larchmont, New York: Eyes on Education, 2004), 4–7.

[4] Adapted from Burt D. Braunius, "Orientations to Curriculum Development for Church Education," *Christian Education Journal* 6 (Fall 1985): 52–61. Used with permission.

years, what is the take-away from it?" they are asking about objectives. Whereas the previous dimension focuses on content, this one focuses on the learner's learning—what they get out of it.

The "what" and the "why" are perhaps the two most influential dimensions in understanding curriculum. James E. Plueddemann's seminal question "Do we teach the Bible or do we teach students?"[5] reflects these two primary depictions of curriculum. As a matter of fact, we do both. Curriculum is both what we teach and also the desired objectives we have in the lives of our learners. For example, take the subject of spiritual disciplines. A *cognitive* objective might be stated, "The student will understand the spiritual disciplines," requiring the content to teach them about the spiritual disciplines, such as their history, theology, and definition. An *affective* objective, one that is more experiential or internal, may say, "The student will experience the benefits of the spiritual disciplines," requiring them to practice them for a time and perhaps journal their experience, which becomes the content relevant to this objective. Of course, all this assumes they know how to practice the spiritual disciplines. A more *volitional* objective, such as an ability or skill, would mean the content would have to focus on the how-to, the step-by-step process, rather than just information about spiritual disciplines. Hence, the three basic forms of objectives (cognitive, affective, and volitional) interact with one another to provide a comprehensive approach to learning through the curriculum. If the curriculum is to serve as a roadmap for discipleship, then "the curriculum, as a key or instrument of education, must guide the learner to be and become a 'response-able' disciple of Jesus Christ."[6] This requires the objectives and content to be more than the recitation of head knowledge. Learners need a deeper level of cognitive assent capable of reasoning through life from a Christian perspective, as well as concern for the affective and volitional domains of learning.

However, curriculum is more than just an alignment of content with the intended learning objectives. For example, the definition of curricu-

---

[5] James E. Plueddemann, "Do We Teach the Bible or Do We Teach Students?" *Christian Education Journal* 10 (Autumn 1989): 73–82; reprinted in *African Journal of Evangelical Theology* 13, no. 1 (1994): 44–53.

[6] Johannes Van der Walt, "The Third Curriculum—from a Christian Perspective," *Journal of Research on Christian Education* 9, no. 2 (2009): 163.

lum is also impacted by the assumed relationship shared by the teacher and learners, as well as the preferred or required teaching methods. The "who" and "how" dimensions of understanding curriculum are likewise critical to conceptualizing a definition. The "what" and "why" somewhat determine the "who" and "how." For example, if a congregation wants to equip its members to do evangelism, lecturing them about the necessity of evangelism is probably not the best method, especially since the teachers' relationship to the participants are limited given the lecture method being used. However, if the curriculum dictates a hands-on approach, the teacher is required to assume the role of a mentor (relationship) more than a lecturer, and actually asks the participants one at a time to participate with them in the process of evangelism. Curriculum has implications for the teacher's place in the educational process and the most advantageous instructional methodology.

So, what is curriculum? In short, the answer is *all*. Curriculum is all of this. It is a collectively cumulative matter. It is not any one of these dimensions, but all of them. Curriculum is essentially the plan for how all the lessons, experiences, and relationships collectively nurture, equip, and mentor a learner toward a desired set of objectives; all of which dictates how we do education in the church. It is the tangible representation and incarnation of our educational philosophy. It is the *roadmap* that the educational ministry of the congregation follows. It enables an assessment of the congregation's progress along the faith journey. It informs the education ministry's decision-making process for future direction and development of the teaching ministry of the church.

Education without curriculum is like biblical interpretation without hermeneutics. Without a roadmap, an articulated recognizable curriculum, the education ministry lacks intentionality and creates bewildered wanderers rather than faithful pilgrims. Curriculum is the capstone of education in the church, the expression of the ideal result of the education ministry.

A Tale of Three Curricula

"What we need is a comprehensive curriculum!" A congregation's curriculum is expressed in three ways, and hence a comprehensive curriculum is comprised of three simultaneously interacting layers of curriculum (fig. 1.2). The *explicit* curriculum is the most readily recognized layer. It is what the congregation openly espouses. When a congregation articulates its intended learning objectives for a class, program, or even the congregation as a whole, this is the explicit curriculum. It is perhaps best represented by the content of instruction and the programs comprising the education ministry. For example, if a congregation explicitly states, "We want our members to know biblical doctrine," then we would expect adult Bible fellowship or classroom studies on Bible content, theology, or history of their theological tradition. We would expect to see classes on Romans or Galatians, studies on justification and sanctification, and perhaps even a survey of the church's articles of faith. Unfortunately, most individuals see the explicit curriculum as the only curriculum; they perceive curriculum to be mono-layered, failing to identify the other two layers and their impact on the congregation.

The *implicit* curriculum is best described by what we learn from our experience of the congregation. It is sometimes referred to as the *hidden* curriculum. It may not be explicit, but it is what we learn from our experience within the class, program, or congregation. For example, in a higher education classroom, a syllabus has stated learning objectives (explicit); but if a professor will not accept late homework or counts a tardy as an absence, while it is not part of the explicit curriculum, the implicit curriculum teaches the learner to be on time.

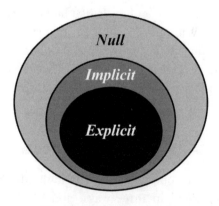

Figure 1.2: Three Curricula

Perhaps the best way to express this difference is what we want people to learn at church (explicit) and what they actually learn at church (implicit), or what they are supposed to learn beyond the explicit curriculum. Suppose a young boy walks into the church building on a Sunday morning wearing a ball cap and someone in the lobby chastises him for wearing it. Then the boy walks down the hall to his Sunday school class and hears a lesson about the unconditional love and acceptance of Jesus—which lesson did he learn best? If anything, the distinction between explicit and implicit compels the congregation to embody what it espouses, to have individuals experience what the church explicitly teaches, to match word with deed. The explicit and implicit curriculum layers work together to help participants learn what they are supposed to learn overtly and covertly.

The third curricular layer dwarfs the first two. The *null* is what is absent from the curriculum. It is what the congregation has chosen not to teach; it is not an experience exemplified by the congregation. In terms of learning, there is more that we do not know than what we can possibly know; so the null curriculum is always the largest layer. For example, if a congregation is not part of the charismatic or Pentecostal tradition, believers in that congregation may never hear about speaking in tongues or be encouraged to experience it; hence, it becomes part of the null curriculum, whereas congregations within those traditions would make it part of the explicit and implicit curriculum. Sometimes prepackaged or published curriculums reflect a particular theological tradition, doctrinal distinction, or take a particular posture toward a social or moral issue that does not fit the congregation's convictions. Hence, such materials must be used intentionally, or they become part of the null curriculum.[7]

A comprehensive curriculum has three layers: explicit, implicit, and the null curriculum. However, oftentimes the determination of these layers may be very intentional or quite unintentional. For example, is the content of the null curriculum determined intentionally or due to ignorance? This is the planned versus unplanned aspect of the com

---

[7] See Joseph Bayly, "Evangelical Curriculum Development," *Religious Education* 75, no. 5 (1980): 539–45.

prehensive curriculum.[8] Collateral learning will always occur, meaning we will learn beyond the explicitly planned objectives and content. Likewise, the implicit and null curriculums may both be planned but are typically unintentional. The call of the Christian educator in this respect is to insure that the three layers coalesce rather than conflict, that the individual's experience in classroom or small group matches expressed learning objectives.

Define whollistic vision
Define objectives

The Church, Education, and Curriculum

Every congregation has a curriculum. It may not be explicit or intentional; but every classroom, program, worship service, and congregation is a learning environment. This learning may be unplanned, unintentional, and may even be implicit or null, but to suggest that churches do not teach something to their members is simply false. The real question is not whether the church has a curriculum, but rather what is the church teaching its participants; what is the congregational curriculum?

More critically, the church as God's people, the community of faith, *must* have a curriculum, a planned, explicit curriculum! The church is not an inert institution, one that exists simply to exist; rather, it is commissioned to fulfill God's mission within the world. The church must be the people of God to fulfill God's commission to the church.[9] Matthew records in his Gospel, "Jesus came to them and said, 'All authority in heaven and on earth has been given to me. Therefore go and make disciples of all nations, baptizing them in the name of the Father and of the Son and of the Holy Spirit, and teaching them to obey everything I have commanded you. And surely I am with you always, to the very end of the age'" (Matt 28:18–20). Decades after Jesus' ministry, Paul wrote to Timothy about his own ministry, "Although I hope to come to you soon, I am writing you these instructions so that, if I am delayed, you will know how people ought to conduct themselves in

---

[8] Cf. Ellis, *Exemplars of Curriculum Theory*, 11–12.

[9] Cf. James Riley Estep Jr., "Ecclesiology and Christian Education," in *A Theology for Christian Education*, ed. James Riley Estep, Michael J. Anthony, and Gregg R. Allison (Nashville: B&H, 2008), 232–63.

God's household, which is the church of the living God, the pillar and foundation of the truth" (1 Tim 3:14–15). For the church to fulfill its transformative mission, it must *be* the church, "the church of the living God, the pillar and foundation of the truth" (1 Tim 3:15) as well as *do* church, "Go and make disciples . . . teaching them" (Matt 28:19–20). Intentional discipleship (individual) and becoming the people of God (corporate) do not happen automatically. These tasks are neither implicit nor null, but rather call the congregation's education ministry to a planned, intentional, and explicit curriculum.

Figure 1.3 depicts the transformative mission of the church. The mission of the church is indeed to transform the people of the world

Figure 1.3: Church on Mission

into the people of God, to build a community of the faithful from the faithless people of the world. This transformation is not instantaneous and is not accomplished through evangelism alone. Maturing in faith, becoming Christlike, no longer being conformed "to the pattern of this world," but "transformed by the renewing of your mind" (Rom 12:2a) is not an automatic or natural occurrence. It is a life-long process of engagement with God through Scripture, by the Holy Spirit. It includes participation within the community of faith, the church. This should not be a haphazard process; it requires an intentional, overt, and explicit curriculum that leads the individual step-by-step toward becoming Christlike and building the community that God desires the church to become. The church not only has a curriculum, but the church *is* God's curriculum to transform the world. D. Campbell Wyckoff says it succinctly:

> The task of Christian education is the nurture of the Christian life. In order that such nurture may be effective in accomplishing its purpose, the church as a rule rejects reliance upon haphazard means and adopts a reasoned and planned teaching-learning process for its education work. A curriculum is a plan by which the teaching/learning process may be systematically undertaken.[10]

Sometimes the idea of curriculum sounds boring and extraneous at best. Classes, lesson plans, materials, content, teaching methods, and learning assessments may appear to be at least a step removed from doing ministry. But this misses the point. That is like describing a family trip with words like car, tires, gas stations, and road signs. If that is all a family vacation is, it would indeed be a boring and undesirable experience. It is the destination that makes the journey worthwhile. It is knowing where we are heading, what awaits us on arrival, and knowing how to get there without getting lost. Then, even all the preparation and travel seem enjoyable. *That is curriculum.* It is the roadmap that leads the Christian toward a life-long journey of faith in the community of the church.

Intentionality in Disciple-making

Discipleship requires curriculum. Disciples are not born, but born again. God forms them through the church. Once again, if we are to be faithful pilgrims rather than wayward wanderers, then curriculum is essential. Disciples are not cookie-cutter images of one another, and curriculum does not imply this, but discipleship has core elements for

---

[10] D. Campbell Wyckoff, *Theory and Design of Christian Education Curriculum* (Philadelphia: Westminster, 1961), 17.

a healthy and growing relationship with Jesus Christ. A map does not dictate to the traveler where to go, but identifies possible destinations and prevents someone from becoming a wayward wanderer rather than a diligent pilgrim. New believers need direction and paths toward maturity—they need a curriculum. In order to be intentionally engaged in fulfilling the Great Commission, congregations need benchmarks for maturity (objectives), core subject matter and experiences (content), as well as more mature believers (teachers) to instruct and methods to match. Discipleship requires curriculum.

This is perhaps the most daunting task of the Christian educator. The roadmap that curriculum becomes in the church is not to a generic destination. The curriculum of the church defines what it actually means to be Christian. What does it mean to be Christlike? To have a mature faith? What does it mean to be the church? The answers to these simple yet profound questions become the goals for the congregation's education ministry, for the Sunday school's learning objectives, and the foundation for the map that describes the path believers take along the journey to deeper faith.

When Paul wrote his second letter to Timothy, he exhorted him to use Scripture appropriately in forming and growing the Christian's faith. In contrast to the false teachers in Ephesus, he instructs Timothy:

> But as for you, *continue in what you have learned* and have become convinced of, because you know those from whom you learned it, and how from infancy you have *known the holy Scriptures*, which are able to make you *wise* for salvation through faith in Christ Jesus. All Scripture is God-breathed and is useful for *teaching, rebuking, correcting and training in righteousness*, so that the man of God may be *thoroughly equipped for every good work*. (2 Tim. 3:14–17, emphasis added)

Paul urges Timothy to continue in what he has been instructed. There is indeed a content, a "what," that has been taught to him. Likewise, there is even a "who," since he was well aware "from whom you learned it." We may not know the instructional methodology, but the passage certainly emphasizes the objectives. Elsewhere Paul affirms the instructional intention of Scripture as God's Word,[11] but

---

[11] Rom 15:4; 1 Cor 10:11.

what are the objectives? How does it intentionally make disciples? First, it aids in the formation of the Christian mind. Scripture makes us wise unto salvation; it leads us to Jesus Christ (vv. 14–15). Second, scriptural instruction likewise is designed to form Christian piety, living "in righteousness" (v. 16). Scripture forms our values, priorities, and relationship with God. Third, Paul tells Timothy that Scripture equips us to serve in the church, "equipped for every good work" (v. 17). All this does not happen naturally or without a plan. Discipleship is holistic, transforming the mind, life, and vocation, the reorientation of our entire existence toward God. Anyone familiar with the domains of learning will recognize these as the cognitive, affective, and volitional domains. Intentional discipleship requires an intentional curriculum.

Curriculum for Becoming the Church

The plural of Christian is "church." What God desires for the individual believer, he likewise expects of the collective experience of believers. We do not *go* to church; we *are* the church. We do not serve *at* the church; we serve *as* the church. Like individual discipleship, becoming the people of God does not happen automatically or accidentally. God desires his church to be a distinctive people. Reminding the churches of Asia Minor, Peter writes, "But you are a chosen people, a royal priesthood, a holy nation, a people belonging to God, that you may declare the praises of him who called you out of darkness into his wonderful light. *Once you were not a people, but now you are the people of God*; once you had not received mercy, but now you have received mercy" (1 Pet 2:9–10, emphasis added). While instantaneous transformation is made by God through receiving his mercy, learning to live in accordance with these re-orientations is not so instantaneous.

Though still in this world, the church is God's new society, and it must be distinct from it.[12] The church is not to mirror the sociocultural segregation of this world, but present to the world a new kind of community. This unity that Jesus desires among his followers is further explained by Paul: "There is neither Jew nor Greek, slave nor free, male nor female, for you are all one in Christ Jesus" (Gal 3:28 Cf.; Col

---

[12] Cf. David S. Dockery, "A Theology for the Church," *Midwestern Journal of Theology* 1, nos. 1–2 (January 2003):13.

3:11–12). Likewise, Paul exhorts the Christians in Rome, a church with an obvious Jewish-Gentile division, to "accept one another, then, just as Christ accepted you, in order to bring praise to God" (Rom 15:7). As Edmund Clowney writes, "The way in which the people of God are joined together by this assembly and presence produces their distinctive fellowship."[13] How does one learn to live in such a new society? How does the church instruct itself on kingdom citizenship? These things will not happen unless the people of God engage one another intentionally, articulate expectations, and plan accordingly. In short, Christian community formation requires a curriculum, a roadmap not only to the community of faith, but through it as well.

What is the rationale for the programs comprising the education ministry within a congregation? Far too often it is couched in fad-based resources or popular figures. Neither of these approaches produces a desirable cumulative effect on the congregation. Curricular intentionality—explicit and planned—makes a tangible cumulative impact on the community-life of the congregation and contributes to kingdom growth. The church is not only God's curriculum for disciple-making, but each congregation needs a curriculum to form a distinctive people.

Conclusion

H. G. Wells concludes his treatment of the rise of civilization by writing, "Human history becomes more and more a race between education and catastrophe," noting that the greatest travesties of contemporary Western culture have been a result of the failure to educate populations and generations appropriately.[14] The same could be said for the church. Discipleship and community formation in the congregation requires a curriculum; an orchestrated, intentional, concerted endeavor to fulfill God's vision for what the church should be and do in the world. Without this curriculum, we abandon new Christians in a spiritual jungle without so much as a map to warn them of dead ends or inform

---

[13] Edmund Clowney, "Toward a Biblical Doctrine of the Church," in *Readings in Christian Theology, Volume 3: The New Life*, ed. Millard J. Erickson (Grand Rapids: Baker, 1979), 24.

[14] H. G. Wells, *The Outline of History: Being a Plain History of Life and Mankind*, vol. 2 (New York: MacMillian, 1920), 594.

them of well-traveled paths. In the journey of faith, the education ministry's curriculum is the congregation's roadmap to becoming the people of God.

Key Terms and Concepts

Curriculum	Null Curriculum
Explicit Curriculum	Planned vs. Unplanned Curriculum
Implicit Curriculum	Discipleship and Community Formation

Reflection Questions

1. How did this chapter change or challenge your understanding of *curriculum*?
2. Think of curriculum as a map, the path for intentional traveling. In what ways is it present in your congregation? Lacking?
3. What is your congregation's explicit curriculum? Implicit? Null (which you could only know by becoming aware of something not taught or experienced in your congregation)?
4. On a scale of 1–5 (1 being low/5 being high), how intentional is the curriculum of your congregation? Explain your rating?

SECTION II

Curriculum Foundations

CHAPTER 2

ORIENTING TO TRUE NORTH

Biblical Perspectives on Curriculum

Roger White

When uncertain about which way to go in life, each of us must check our bearings and determine where we are in relation to some point of reference. The decisions we reach may be instantaneous and subjective, or they may follow long periods of careful reflection. Although the conscious awareness of our decision-making process varies, we somehow come to conclusions such as, "I need to visit a friend," "I would like to start a hobby," "It is important that I begin to volunteer in the community more," or "I am going to start a diet." In the midst of ever-changing surroundings and varied life experiences, we align ourselves with impressions or ideals in which we have some reason to trust and then we set off. After sizing up our situation, we step into a new set of possibilities. The phrase "true north" suggests an ultimate orienting reference and grounding for recognizing reliable direction.[1]

---

[1] In geographic terms true north represents a line across the earth's surface ending at the North Pole.

The Bible is not true north. God is true north. The Bible orients readers to true north from the standpoint of many different times, individuals, and situations. It reveals and proclaims to all, "This is the way, walk in it." As the psalmist says of God's self-disclosing revelation, "Your word is a lamp to my feet and a light for my path" (Ps. 119:105).[2]

The image of a journey is used repeatedly in the Bible to portray life progression and to illustrate choices accompanying it. Guides and mapmakers in the church ally themselves with the biblical heritage of traveling pilgrims to learn from their experiences. The ways to true north as revealed through the Bible include exemplars and models for use in developing curriculum for the church and intentionally planning learning opportunities for the sake of others. Curriculum, therefore, involves making deliberate choices as to what is most worth knowing and learning, thereby determining and planning the way to go in life and education. For Christian educators, the Bible provides numerous illustrations of individuals, families, communities, and nations at various places along their journeys who sought to orient to true north, follow God, and pursue *lifeways* (paths that lead to abundant life). This chapter presents biblical perspectives on curriculum (life maps), including how educators serve as guides to help orient and facilitate learners' responses to God throughout their life journey.

Life as a Journey

In the Genesis account of creation, the first humans were given a path to follow, resources for the journey, and the choices of whether and how to pursue it. As image bearers of God they were to steward the creation on God's behalf and for God's pleasure within the parameters set down by the Creator. A life path was clearly laid out but another was taken, and dreadful consequences followed.

Choosing one's path is a major life theme found throughout the Bible. The alternatives are variously characterized:

1. The way of faith or the way of pride?

---

[2] Cf. John 8:12. Unless otherwise noted, all Scripture quotations in this chapter are taken from the New International Version of the Bible.

2. The way of the wise or the way of the foolish?
3. The way of the just or the way of the unjust?
4. The way of the righteous or the way of the wicked?
5. The way of life or the way of death?

Path travelers are identified by their actions. The book of Galatians lists some of the distinctions. When led along the sinful nature path, the way is characterized by "sexual immorality, impurity and debauchery; idolatry and witchcraft; hatred, discord, jealousy, fits of rage, selfish ambition, dissensions, factions and envy; drunkenness, orgies, and the like" (Gal 5:19–21). When one keeps in step with the Spirit of God, the way is characterized by "love, joy, peace, patience, kindness, goodness, faithfulness, gentleness and self-control" (Gal 5:22–23). The immediate lesson is to choose well and keep on choosing well.

Life is made up of a series of small steps, each with their accompanying direction and consequence. All of our experiences are part of this journey, a multitude of choices arising out of who we are and where we are, what is happening around and to us, and what we feel and think. The stories of Scripture repeatedly use the journey image and related metaphors in this holistic sense.[3] The foundational Hebrew word used in the Old Testament for "path" or "way" is *darak*. It is used more than 700 times in the Bible and most frequently refers to general human activity not actual roads.[4] This prominent imagery extends into the New Testament where we find questioners of Jesus acknowledging and recognizing him as teaching "the way of God"[5] and the early Christian movement being referred to simply as the Way.[6]

The seriousness of choosing and following the way of God is emphasized in Scripture by stressing how life's journeys turn out.[7] Given the all-inclusive nature of our endeavors, the consequences associated in choosing the right way are characterized as life and death

---

[3] For example, see Ezek 18:21–35.

[4] Daniel P. Bricker, "The Doctrine of the 'Two Ways' in Proverbs," *JETS* 38, no. 4 (December 1995): 501–17.

[5] See Matt 22:16; Mark 12:14; Luke 20:21; cf. Acts 18:26.

[6] See Acts 9:2; 19:9,23; 22:4; 24:14,22. This was how the early believers referred to themselves; outsiders called them Christians. Paul identifies himself before Felix as "a follower of the Way" (Acts 24:14).

[7] See how the two ways are described in Psalm 1.

issues. In Deuteronomy, Moses sets before the people of God the options of life and prosperity or death and destruction as his context for giving the direction "to love the LORD your God, to walk in his ways, and to keep his commands, decrees and laws" (Deut 30:16a).[8] He describes how the two ways end with either blessings or curses. Relatedly, the writer of Proverbs warns that certain ways may appear right, but ultimately lead to death.[9] Later, in the New Testament, Jesus echoes this notion when he teaches that the broad road can lead to destruction and the narrow one to life; many enter the former, but only a few find the latter.[10] Given the significance of these kinds of life decisions, Christian pilgrims are urged to "enter through the narrow gate" (Matt 7:13a)[11] and abide in the way of God. The alternative way is characterized by winding paths leading to ruin where travelers frequently stumble.[12]

So like the nation of Israel, like Abraham, Joseph, Moses, and Paul, there is a spiritual journey set before believers.[13] Christians are called to live out their faith amid life's uncertainties and to [purposefully] pursue the right path.[14] Removing things that may hamper or impede progress, they are encouraged to run with perseverance the race marked out for them and not to run in vain.[15]

Educational journeys facilitate life journeys; therefore, teachers must be intentional in their tasks especially with regard to curriculum. The word *curriculum* referred to a racetrack and specifically a lap around the track. It derives from the Latin word for run (*currere*) and in a more general sense suggests a course of action or the race of life. Today the term is used to speak of the plan or course of study that teachers and learners follow in the quest to reach educational goals and progress in life's journey. Thankfully, God has provided the church with direction and guides for navigating curricular journeys.

---

[8] Cf. Deut 30:15–20.
[9] Prov 16:25.
[10] Matt 7:13–14.
[11] Cf. Luke 13:24.
[12] Judg 5:6; Isa 59:9–10.
[13] Cf. Jer 6:16.
[14] 1 Cor 9:24–26.
[15] Heb 12:1; Gal 2:2; 5:7; Phil 2:16.

Guides Along the Way

Basic to all education is God's self-disclosure. Seen most clearly in the person of Christ, God's revelatory communication is foundational to life, meaning, and purpose. Curricular paths ideally align with and advance the Word of God, the divine revelation found generally in creation and uniquely in the Bible. Recognizing and revering who God is and what God does is the beginning of understanding the way and accompanying educational implications.

Education also addresses human response. Teachers serve a partnering role in setting forth God's messages of life and in assisting learners with understanding and responding to God in order to become who they were meant to be. In order to do this, educators need to be intimately acquainted with both God and the individual learner. This involves knowing what God has communicated and also how people come to understand life, develop, and flourish. These are fundamental components of the educational exchange in life: God communicates, people respond, and teachers partner (fig. 2.1).

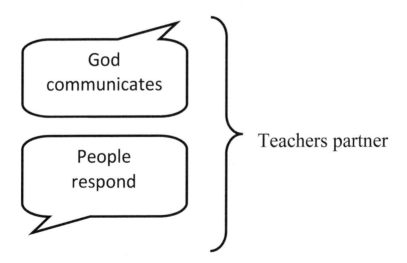

Figure 2.1: Teacher's Role in Education

The Bible includes many accounts of people specially called and equipped to partner in the educational process and to serve as guides on behalf of God and for the benefit of learners. In fact, the word *educate* comes from the Latin term *educit* which means, "to lead out."[16] These guides variously lead, assist, facilitate, interpret, and mediate. In all these ways they share in the learning experience. Educators are leaders, not simply in a pragmatic business, administrative, or political sense, but rather as personally committed guides along a shared divine path.

God is our primary guide. According to Paul, God's law leads us like a tutor to Christ.[17] God directs our steps,[18] and as we trust and acknowledge God our paths are made straight.[19] The prophet Isaiah spoke of the day when many people would go to the mountain of God to be taught firsthand God's ways in order to walk God's paths.[20] Jesus proclaimed himself to be the way and repeatedly instructed listeners, "Follow me."[21] His words and manner are truth and life. While perfectly summing up all that the way represents, Jesus modeled perfect God-honoring responses. His authoritative voice and exemplary character are the basis for using imitation as an instructional approach in curricular practice. By following his lead, we are transformed[22] and the Holy Spirit is our Helper along the way.[23]

The human pattern God established for passing on and instilling the truth of God's lifeway in people's lives is for parents and the covenant community to convey to succeeding generations.[24] They are the specially ordained human guides for the journey. Abraham was cho-

---

[16] In the parable of the good shepherd, the shepherd knows his own sheep and leads them out through the gate. The sheep know the voice of the shepherd and follow him (John 10:2–4; cf. Isa 40:10–11). In Psalm 23 the shepherd leads besides still waters.

[17] Gal 3:24–25 NASB.

[18] Prov 20:24.

[19] Prov 3:5–6.

[20] Isa 2:3; cf. Isa 28:26.

[21] John 14:6; and Matt 4:19; 8:22; 9:9; 19:21; John 1:43.

[22] Even Jesus' "hidden" curriculum on the road to Emmaus yielded a whole-hearted response in his two traveling companions (Luke 24:32).

[23] John 14:26.

[24] Ps 78:1–8.

sen to father and lead a great nation and to instruct his children and household in the ways of God.[25] Descendants were to tell their children who in turn would tell their children and so on.[26] In the covenant community, leaders like Moses passed on the task to subsequent community leaders who passed it on to still others.[27] Later, the way would be illuminated in synagogues and through various educational ministries of the church. Over time when families and churches were unable fully to carry out their responsibility, it was sometimes shared with others; the rise of tutors and formal schools occurred.[28] The role of a guide frequently overlaps with those of prophet, priest, regent, and sage found throughout the Bible.[29]

The initial context for the educational exchange involving God's communication and human response is the family. The book of Deuteronomy records the great commandment, "Love the LORD your God with all your heart and with all your soul and with all your strength" (Deut 6:5) and then immediately follows that with the instruction for parents to impress a whole-hearted application of God's commandments on their children.[30] The educational plan for the task is outlined, "Talk about them when you sit at home and when you walk along the road, when you lie down and when you get up. Tie them as symbols on your hands and bind them on your foreheads. Write them on the doorframes of your houses and on your gates" (Deut 6:7–9).[31] Correspondingly, children are urged to respond with obedience and show honor towards their parents.[32] The importance of guiding children is clearly seen in the proverb, "Start children off on the way they should go, and even when they are old they will not turn from it" (Prov 22:6).

---

[25] Gen 18:18–19.

[26] Deut 4:9; Ps 78:5–6; cf. Joel 1:1–3.

[27] Lev 10:11; cf. 2 Tim 2:2.

[28] On *in loco parentis*, see Gal 4:1–2; cf. the school of the prophets in 1 Sam 10:9–13.

[29] 2 Kgs 17:27; Ezra 7:6–26; Mal 2:7–9; cf. Isa 40:3–8; Matt 11:10.

[30] Deut 6:6–7.

[31] Cf. Deut 11:18–21.

[32] Exod 20:12; Deut 5:16; Eph 6:1–3; cf. Prov 1:8; 3:1; 6:20.

As a collection of families, the covenant community supports and reinforces the educational efforts of parents and community leaders. Old Testament community events like feasts, celebrations, temple practices, and regular readings of God's law were all designed to be specific reminders of God's lifeway.[33] Similarly, in the New Testament, one of the purposes of the church as the visible expression of the body of Christ is the building up of its members. One means for accomplishing this is the regular administration of the Lord's Supper, a further reminder of the lifeway of God. Through the educational ministry of the church and related discipleship activities, believers are helped to walk in the Spirit and follow the Spirit's lead in all things.[34] The curricular mission of following God's lifeway is best undertaken in this broad community of faith in order to combat tendencies toward individualism, narrowness, or exclusivity.

Because of common grace, and being created in the image of God, all people regardless of background can in some ways be a general guide to God's lifeway.[35] As image-bearers, all people have the potential to reflect facets of the nature of God and thereby advance God's self-disclosure. Even individuals who do not believe in God and who choose to walk other paths cannot escape how they were made. Atheism does not erase God's image in their life. Remnants of the divine image, though sometimes hardly recognizable, may remain. While the fall of humankind marred the image of God inherent in men and women, it did not completely remove all semblances of it. In this sense everyone in their mere humanness is still equipped to some extent to serve as a guide and to be a type of human signpost to true north even though they may not be aware of it. (See the Gentiles' condition as described in Rom 2:12–16.)

In the Great Commission of Matthew 28, Jesus specifically commands and gives authority to his followers to teach and help disciples on their way.[36] This responsibility goes beyond simply being image-bearers. It involves actively making disciples and providing direct instruction

---

[33] Deut 31:10–11.

[34] Rom 8:4,13–14; Gal 5:16,18,25.

[35] Gen 1:27.

[36] Matt 28:18–20.

and guidance. Within the church community some are set apart and divinely gifted to teach, being further equipped with an exceptional ability to serve in the role of guides.[37] These individuals usually come to sense this responsibility and life call internally through the Holy Spirit or through the acknowledgement of their special gifting by others in their community. Humans then at multiple levels have a guiding and reflecting role to convey who God is by the witness of how they live and what they say (fig. 2.2).[38]

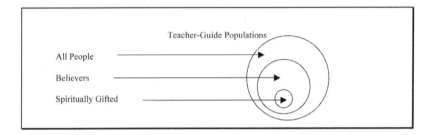

Figure 2.2: Teacher-Guide Populations

The question now turns to how to make our way in the journey of life, sometimes leading and sometimes following. For those who guide along the way, what characteristics can be discovered regarding the nature of the path and the best manner in which travelers proceed? The Bible directs readers to walk by faith on a path of wisdom and provides numerous examples to follow.

The Path of Wisdom

The book of Proverbs affirms the fear of the Lord as the beginning of knowledge and wisdom.[39] Here the fear of the Lord means a healthy reverence for God, not servile terror. It moves individuals from being

---

[37] 1 Cor 12:28; Eph 4:11–13; cf. 1 Cor 12:29; Exod 35:30–35.
[38] 1 Cor 12:27.
[39] Prov 1:7; 9:10.

exclusively self-referenced in their understanding to increasingly seeing all things and especially one's life journey oriented in and around God. The writer of Proverbs instructs, "Trust in the LORD with all your heart and lean not on your own understanding; in all your ways acknowledge him, and he will make your paths straight" (Prov 3:5–6). This is a whole-hearted, whole-being response. Having such a deferential posture toward God and an accompanying intellectual modesty are core elements in the pilgrimage of life and learning.[40]

Humble submission of self to God and intentional immersion in God's activities yields wisdom and the attendant grace for living it out.[41] This holistic involvement and total commitment is the vital human starting point for recognizing true north and pursuing the path of wisdom.[42] As we learn from Proverbs, "A discerning person keeps wisdom in view, but a fool's eyes wander to the ends of the earth" (17:24). The path of wisdom involves the fundamental components of life—God's communication and human response. When awareness and understanding of this dynamic exchange is out of balance, one's ability to stay on the path and guide others is compromised. For example, even though the twelve spies who were sent to explore the land of Canaan saw the same terrain and gave the same initial report, only two had an adequate view of both God and themselves and recommended going forward to take possession of the land.[43] The other ten viewed themselves as grasshoppers and responded by urging the people to reject the proposed path for acquiring the land God had promised.[44]

Maintaining equilibrium when designing and developing curriculum (what we call map-making) is a walk of faith.[45] The challenge for

---

[40] Cf. Matt 5:3.

[41] Prov 2:1–11.

[42] Cf. John Calvin's comment in *Institutes of the Christian Religion,* Book I, Chapter II, 42: "For how can the thought of God penetrate your mind without your realizing immediately that, since you are his handiwork, you have been made over and bound to his command by right of creation, that you owe your life to him?—that whatever you undertake, whatever you do, ought to be ascribed to him? If this be so, it now assuredly follows that your life is wickedly corrupt unless it be disposed to his service, seeing that his will ought for us to be the law by which we live."

[43] Numbers 13–14.

[44] Num 13:31–33; 14:36–37.

[45] Cf. 2 Cor 5:7.

guides and mapmakers is to find the proper balance between promoting
God's communication and nurturing human response; between teaching doctrine and demonstrating piety in life; and between presenting
theory and advancing practice. These dialectics occur along continua,
and attention to them will differ depending on circumstances of time,
place, and persons. For example, some have seen different emphases
between the roles of structure and the freedom of the spirit in how
God's lifeway is taught and presented in the Pastoral Epistles and the
Johannine literature.[46] The first tends to emphasize structure, especially designated leaders maintaining orthodox teaching; the latter
tends to emphasize spirit, especially the Holy Spirit as divine teacher in
the heart of every believer.[47] When curriculum programs overempha-
size structure, they can become characterized by elitist style teaching
where conformity is achieved through coercion, and "new" teachings
are labeled as suspect. By contrast, programs overemphasizing spirit
have faced difficulties related to individualized experience, interpretation based solely on subjectivity, and the subsequent rise of divisions
and disagreements.

Educators seeking balance in their pursuit and promotion of the
path of wisdom must be careful to distinguish between developing
wisdom and acquiring knowledge, between personally and carefully
guiding pilgrims along the way, and merely pointing to locations on a
map declaring them as possible destinations, or stating "you are here."
Knowledge carries with it the idea of possessing ideas, while wisdom
suggests proper use of ideas. The path of wisdom involves an active
engagement of the will, as Herman Bavinck describes in his distinction
between knowledge and wisdom:

> The source of *knowledge* is study; of *wisdom*, discernment.
> *Knowledge* is discursive; *wisdom* intuitive. *Knowledge* is theoreti-
> cal; *wisdom* practical, teleological; it makes *knowledge* subservi-
> ent to an end. *Knowledge* is a matter of the mind apart from
> the will; *wisdom* is a matter of the mind made subservient to the
> will. *Knowledge* is often very unpractical; i.e., not adapted to the

---

[46] See Richard Robert Osmer, *A Teachable Spirit: Recovering the Teaching Office in the Church* (Louisville: WJK, 1990).

[47] Titus 1:5–9, note v. 9; John 16:12–14; 14:26.

common affairs of life; *wisdom* is adapted to life; it is ethical in character; it is the art of proper living.[48]

According to J. I. Packer, the definition of wisdom is "the power to see, and the inclination to choose, the best and highest goal, together with the surest means of attaining it."[49] Wisdom is made manifest in the Scriptures and is best seen in Jesus who "has become for us wisdom from God" (1 Cor 1:30), for in him are "hidden all the treasures of wisdom and knowledge" (Col 2:3). In the following section, a number of curriculum principles found in the Bible and reflecting aspects of the path of wisdom are considered.

Curriculum Principles in Scripture

The Bible is a record of God's self-disclosure and interaction with the world. It includes stories of how people lived, describes their varied journeys, and features Jesus as the central human figure of history.[50] In his letter to Timothy, Paul tells of how the Holy Scriptures make readers wise in regard to salvation and faith in Christ.[51] These God-breathed accounts, he declares, are particularly useful for teaching, rebuking, correcting and training in right living.[52] Travelers pursuing true north are prepared for good work along the way by continuing in the lessons learned in and through the Bible.[53]

A panoramic backdrop for a meaning-filled life is wonderfully displayed in the Bible. The self-expression of God and the personal experiences of human lives are contextualized throughout the Scriptures, providing sweeping vistas of truth and understanding. Each book of the Bible with its particular literary genre and unique place in redemption history is understood in light of the entire revelation. Every part reflects a meaningful facet of the whole. A song can be used to teach

---

[48] Herman Bavinck, *The Doctrine of God*, trans. William Hendriksen (Great Britain: Banner of Truth, 1951), 195.

[49] J. I. Packer, *Knowing God* (Downers Grove: InterVarsity, 1973), 80.

[50] Cf. Gal 3:24.

[51] 2 Tim 3:15.

[52] 2 Tim 3:16.

[53] 2 Tim 3:17.

God's way.[54] A life can be a letter of testimony.[55] A precept can provide a principle to follow. Both in part and in whole the Bible provides a basis for conceptualizing curriculum useful for navigating through life. Sometimes examples may emphasize God's communication; other times they may emphasize human response. The Holy Spirit blends and mediates the two. Consider how the balance is represented in the following introductory survey of curriculum principles gathered from the Bible.

Curricula Are Relationally Meaningful

The early chapters of Genesis describe a life map given to Adam and Eve. They were given a personal curriculum to follow, a way to live and walk with God. It includes God's direct instruction, "Be fruitful and increase in number; fill the earth and subdue it. Rule over the fish in the sea and the birds in the sky and over every living creature that moves on the ground" (Gen 1:28). It also includes explanation: "I give you every seed-bearing plant on the face of the whole earth and every tree that has fruit with seed in it. They will be yours for food" (v. 29). It provides warnings and gives consequences, "you must not eat from the tree of the knowledge of good and evil, for when you eat from it you will surely die" (Gen 2:17). It is purposeful—the curriculum involved cultivating and managing the garden and being fruitful. A particular responsive activity for Adam was naming the animals. In this Genesis account we see God personally involved with the entire educational plan, integral to its delivery, and interacting with Adam and Eve in the midst of their responses. Their curricular map had purpose and was relationally robust.

Curricula Are Contextualized in Community

Later in the Old Testament, God's covenant people receive a curriculum through Moses, the law, and the prophets to guide them in how to live. Their curricular map is an integral part of their unique relationship with God first established through Abraham. It builds on prior learning going back to the beginning of humanity and includes God's

---

[54] Deut 31:19.

[55] 2 Cor 3:2.

promises and commandments to them as God's chosen people. Along with the law of God, there is the experiential learning of leaving Egypt, wandering in the wilderness, establishing and following sacrificial practice, and entering the Promised Land. God's demonstration of power and loving-kindness are displayed in a multitude of ways throughout the narratives. God's lifeway is made clear as the response of the people is described in the history of Israel. The God-guided journey and experience of the Abrahamic people becoming a great nation provides lesson parallels for contemporary life journeys and curricula. The same emphasis on community is mirrored in the New Testament church as described in the book of Acts. Curricular maps are learned and followed in the context of community.

Curricula Incorporate Varied Practices

In the New Testament there is only one recorded instance where Jesus is ever asked by those around him to teach about a specific topic. His response provides another example for mapmakers in the church. Jesus was with his disciples when one of them asked him to teach them how to pray.[56] The disciples knew John the Baptist had taught his disciples such things[57] and they also knew it was Jesus' custom to pray often.[58] This life demonstration and modeling by John and Jesus supplied the disciples with incentive to learn more and want further direction on the subject. Jesus answers the disciples' inquiry by providing a model prayer and a parable, setting forth some direct statements and posing rhetorical questions. These all illuminate the subject and provide direction for practicing prayer. The model Lord's Prayer provides both an actual prayer that may be prayed as well as a pattern and method for how to pray (e.g. adoration, supplication, intercession).[59] The parable of the persistent neighbor and accompanying directives to ask, seek, and knock highlight the importance and accompanying benefits of actively persevering in prayer.[60] Using several questions exaggerating the likelihood of petitioning and children receiving unwelcomed parental gifts,

---

[56] Luke 11:1; Jesus taught about prayer on many occasions. Cf. Matt 6:5–15.
[57] Luke 11:1; cf. Luke 5:33.
[58] Luke 3:21; 5:16; 6:12; 9:18,28–29.
[59] Luke 11:2–4; cf. Matt 6:9–13.
[60] Luke 11:5–10.

Jesus assures his listeners that those who ask will receive the Holy Spirit.[61] God's parental benevolence exceeds that of humans. Through this assortment of methods the disciples are guided into a fuller understanding and deeper experience of the practice of prayer.

Curricula Are Developmental

The author of Hebrews uses a metaphor to illustrate developmental aspects of life's journey. To those who are spiritually immature, who put forth little effort and need re-teaching in the basics, the author compares acquiring the elementary truths of God's Word with a baby's early need for milk. The type of nourishment is particular to the season of life. The writer then applies the image by relating a list of introductory teachings about Christ: "The foundation of repentance from acts that lead to death, and of faith in God, instruction about baptisms, the laying on of hands, the resurrection of the dead, and eternal judgment" (Heb 6:1–2). Alternatively, solid food is said to be reserved for the mature.[62] They have different nutritional needs than the child. Those who receive solid food and the teaching on righteousness exhibit their advanced state by giving attention to the ongoing spiritual discipline of discriminating good from evil.[63] Travelers are at different points in their learning journeys and need curricula uniquely suited to their development.

Curricula Evolve

The disciple Peter lists a progression of characteristics typifying the travels of maturing believers. In his list we see an articulation of overlapping virtues that the traveler is encouraged to pursue. Those established in faith and called to participate in the journey of the Christian life are instructed by Peter to add to this foundation by acquiring and increasing certain qualities in their lives. He lists a series of these qualities, suggesting they evolve in a successive fashion. The sequence reads, "Add to your faith goodness; and to goodness, knowledge; and to knowledge, self-control; and to self-control, perseverance; and to

---

[61] Luke 11:11–13.
[62] Heb 5:14.
[63] Heb 5:11–6:3.

perseverance, godliness; and to godliness, mutual affection; and to mutual affection, love" (2 Pet 1:5–7). Cultivating these virtues keeps pilgrims from getting stuck in their tracks or stagnant on the path.[64] The pattern evident in Peter's words highlights the importance of curricula that evolve in a recursive manner, with incremental phases that unfold in succession, each building upon the other.

Curricula Are Customized

In Titus 2:1–15, Paul provides Titus with several guidelines pertinent to life journeys of different groups in the Christian community. His directives orient his readers to true north and line up with sound doctrine and prior teaching in the church. Old men, old women, younger women, younger men, and slaves are singled out with special mapping instructions. Titus is given the following curriculum guide to follow:

1. Teach the *older men* to be temperate, worthy of respect, self-controlled, and sound in faith, in love and in endurance.
2. Likewise, teach the *older women* to be reverent in the way they live, not to be slanderers or addicted to much wine, but to teach what is good.
3. Then they can train the *younger women* to love their husbands and children, to be self-controlled and pure, to be busy at home, to be kind, and to be subject to their husbands, so that no one will malign the word of God.
4. Similarly, encourage the *young men* to be self-controlled. In everything set them an example by doing what is good. In your teaching show integrity, seriousness and soundness of speech that cannot be condemned, so that those who oppose you may be ashamed because they have nothing bad to say about us.
5. Teach *slaves* to be subject to their masters in everything, to try to please them, not to talk back to them, and not to steal from them, but to show that they can be fully trusted, so that in every way they will make the teaching about God our Savior attractive (Titus 2:2–10).[65]

---

[64] Cf. 2 Pet 1:8–9.
[65] Emphasis added.

Individuals making up these groups are at different places in their journeys and have different life and instructional needs. When used for large numbers of pilgrims, a curriculum plan can never be entirely individualized; however, common trail patterns can be discerned for people who share similar characteristics. Paul details for Titus how certain groups should be led and instructs him to authoritatively encourage and rebuke in this way. Educational plans can thus be specially tailored for groups of co-travelers.

Intentional Mapping

Everyone has a set of unique learning experiences that constitutes their personal life curriculum. Some of these are planned, and some seemingly happen by chance. Yet regardless of what paths individuals arrive on, everyone has a responsibility to orient to true north and travel well. The Bible includes unique life curricula accounts of individuals and how God ultimately directed their learning journeys even though their way was not always clear.

Moses received an Egyptian education and then on the job training as he led the people of God out of Egypt to the Promised Land.[66] In the midst of this we see him praying to God "teach me your ways so I may know you and continue to find favor with you" (Exod 33:13a). We get a sense of Solomon's curricular path through a description of his learning, "He spoke three thousand proverbs and his songs numbered a thousand and five. He described plant life, from the cedar of Lebanon to the hyssop that grows out of walls. He also taught about animals and birds, reptiles and fish" (1 Kgs 4:32–33). He gains through God a degree of wisdom vastly exceeding what was found in "all the people of the East, and greater than all the wisdom in Egypt" (1 Kgs 4:30). Daniel received a Babylonian court education yet God blessed him with "knowledge and understanding of all kinds of literature and learning" (Dan 1:17).[67] In terms of his wisdom and understanding, he is said to have excelled ten times beyond others in the kingdom.[68] And in the life

---

[66] Acts 7:22.

[67] Daniel could also understand dreams and visions.

[68] Dan 1:20.

of the apostle Paul we see a curricular program quite different from the other apostles who had personally known Jesus. Paul was trained in the laws and traditions of Judaism and studied under a Pharisee named Gamaliel, the president of the Sanhedrin (cf. Acts 22:2–3). Yet after receiving the gospel as a revelation from Jesus, Paul spent many years in virtual seclusion before taking up a role of leadership in the church. Each of these characters has a different and individualized life curriculum overseen by God. Even though portions of their learning journeys went through dark passages, God's purposes and plan prevailed.

Teachers must partner with God and learners in the process of orienting to true north. The degree of intentionality may vary due to circumstances, but the foundational nature of travelling remains. Regardless of where a traveler is, he can always reorient to true north. Mark summarizes the essence of Jesus' message, "The time has come . . . The kingdom of God has come near. Repent and believe the good news!" (Mark 1:15).[69] Elsewhere Paul states, "everyone who calls on the name of the Lord will be saved" (Rom 10:13).[70] It is possible for sign-posts of a life map to be uncomplicated—call on the name of the Lord. Beyond this, responsible guides will of course help learners through lengthy journeys to discover more fully who the one being called on actually is and assist them in entering more deeply into the resulting salvation experience. In the previous example, Paul guides his readers into a more complete understanding of his stark declaration when he explains, "If you confess with your mouth, 'Jesus is Lord,' and believe in your heart that God raised him from the dead, you will be saved. For it is with your heart that you believe and are justified, and it is with your mouth that you profess your faith and are saved" (Rom. 10:9–10). Even though the initial message is basically straightforward, its fullness is deepened through further explanation grounded in community, faith, hope, and love. This is why there is a need for intentional curricular maps and guides to partner continually with travelers in orienting to true north.

---

[69] Cf. Matt 4:17.

[70] Cf. Joel 2:32; Acts 2:21; 16:31.

Key Terms and Concepts

True North   Knowledge

Two Ways   Wisdom

Guides   Fear of the Lord

Reflection Questions

1. How do travelers recognize true north and orient themselves to it?
2. In what ways do educators partner with God and learners in the learning experience?
3. How does a traveler know when he or she is on a wrong path?
4. Who are the key participants in the curricular endeavor?

CHAPTER 3

NAVIGATING WITH A COMPASS

THEOLOGICAL PERSPECTIVES ON CURRICULUM

James Riley Estep Jr.

know exactly where we are! . . . We are lost!" We have all been lost, searching for anything that looks familiar, helpful signs, a map, or compass. "Great, I know which way is north, but how do I navigate through this terrain? Will someone help me get my bearings?" Even once you recognize true north, you will need a compass to make real use of any map. Without a compass, your navigation is sometimes perilous. A compass is a human tool that aligns to an unseen force of nature. Theology is a human tool that seeks to align to God. Both provide a reference for determining direction. God is true north, the Bible points us to him, but theology is the human construct of biblical truth, what it says about God and how to reach him.

Theology must inform every aspect of an evangelical's life, ministry, and education—including curriculum. This chapter will provide a Christian perspective on curriculum in four ways: It will (1) explain how educational philosophy influences the definition and depiction of curriculum; (2) describe the specific role theology plays in a Christian curriculum, explaining how theology informs the development of curriculum; (3) provide a theology of curriculum, i.e., what God has to do with curriculum; and finally, (4) illustrate how curriculum reflects the theological tenets of specific theological traditions. From this, the educator can use a distinctly Christian approach to curriculum, its development, and design to give direction. When the relationship of theology and curriculum is not sustained or made substantial, tangible, and integrated, then Christian education risks become dualistic; advocating goals and objectives that are inconsistent with the church's theology. To avoid this, theology must become the compass for curriculum development and a joint venture for the congregation.

Educational Philosophy and Curriculum

Curriculum reflects the worldview on which it is based. No curriculum is philosophically neutral.[1] As figure 3.1 illustrates, philosophies often have an educational philosophy associated with them, which in turn influences the development of an educational theory and ultimately curriculum.

Just as each philosophy has a core focus, that focus is then reflected in the curriculum it espouses. For example, the philosophy of idealism and some world religions are centered on spiritual realms, whereas the philosophy of realism and its associated educational philosophies are more nature centered; and philosophies such as pragmatism, existentialism, and postmodernism are human-centered.[2] These pose dis-

Figure 3.1: Philosophy and Curriculum

---

[1] Cf. Elmer J. Theissen, "A Defense of a Distinctively Christian Curriculum," *Religious Education* 80, no. 1 (1985): 37–50.

[2] Cf. Robert S. Zais, *Curriculum: Principles and Foundations* (Canada: Pearson Education, 1976), 123.

tinctive and divergent approaches to both education and curriculum. Figure 3.2 illustrates this (see pp. 48–50). The first column identifies the root philosophy, with its educational counterpart in italics below, along with its major proponents. The second column gives a brief definition of the basic ideas of the philosophy, its understanding of reality, truth, and aesthetics (morals and value). The third column provides a metaphor for the educational implications of the philosophy, illustrating how the philosophy translates into an approach to education. The final column describes how each philosophy is reflected in the curriculum associated with it.[3]

What is the point? Figure 3.2 illustrates that curriculum is not an isolated endeavor. It does not exist in a vacuum nor is it developed in one. It does not exist apart from a worldview. Just as these philosophies influence the formation of curriculum, theology in Christian education has a role to play in its development.

How Does Theology Inform Curriculum?

Curriculum that is Christian is formed and exists in the context of theology, not independent from it. Randolph Crump Miller, the elder statesman of religious education, argued, "Theology must be prior to the curriculum."[4] It is the compass of the curriculum. Theology impacts

---

[3] Based on information gleaned from the following sources: James Riley Estep Jr., "Philosophical-Historical Foundations of Christian Education," in *Foundations for Christian Education*, ed. Eleanor A. Daniel and John W. Wade (Joplin: College Press, 1999), 34–59; Michael J. Anthony and Warren S. Benson, *Exploring the History and Philosophy of Christian Education* (Grand Rapids: Kregel, 2003), 408–9; Howard A. Ozmon and Samuel M. Craver, *Philosophical Foundations of Education*, 6th ed. (Upper Sandusky River, NJ: Prentice Hall, 1999), 35–37, 75–76, 196–98, 225–29, 266–67, 365–68; Arthur K. Ellis, *Exemplars of Curriculum Theory* (Larchmont, NY: Eye on Education, 2004), 24, 72, 107; J. Allen Queen, *Curriculum Practice in the Elementary and Middle School* (Upper Sandusky River, NJ: Prentice Hall, 1998), 62–64; James Moore, "Philosophy and Its Influence on Educational Practice" (unpublished paper, Trinity Evangelical Divinity School, Deerfield, Illinois, 1994); Allen C. Ornstein and Francis P. Hunkins, *Curriculum: Foundations, Principles, and Theory*, 2nd ed. (Upper Sandusky River, NJ: Prentice Hall, 1988), 34–67.

[4] Randolph Crump Miller, *The Clue to Christian Education* (New York: Scribner's, 1950), 5.

Worldview *Educational Philosophy*	Basic Idea	Educational Metaphor	Curriculum
Idealism • *Perennialism* • *Essentialism* *Proponents:* Plato, Immanuel Kant, Donald Butler, Hermon Horne	• Reality is only spiritual or mental; physical is problematic and distracts from the pure spiritual and mental disciplines (opposite of Realism). • Truth is eternally consistent, accessible through reason and reflective meditation alone. • Ethics are a reflection of ideal humanity; Aesthetics reflect the ideal. Emphasis on classical culture as basis.	*Library:* Idealism places a premium on the ideas of the past. Consider the Great Books curriculum, wherein students are asked to master the content and connections between the great works of the Western world from Plato to present. Think of what a library represents: The sum collection of all knowledge preserved for us through texts.	Ideas are innately valuable because they have the potential to change the students' lives and minds. Curriculum teaches how a student should think. Its aim is to pass on the socio-cultural heritage of a given society. Knowledge or content centered curriculum.
Realism • *Perennialism* • *Essentialism* • *Positivism* *Proponents:* Aristotle, John Locke, Maria Montessori, Jean Rousseau	• Reality is the material world; physical exists independent of the mind or reason (opposite of Idealism). • Truth resides in the material world and can be discovered through observation and reason (e.g., science). • Ethics are reflections of nature or natural law. Similarly, aesthetics are expressions of the natural world.	*Lab:* Realism is the philosophical basis of modern science. As an educational philosophy, it lends itself best to what one experiences in high school or university science classes, e.g., lecture, demonstrations, hands-on lab work, data gathering, hypothesis testing. Education is a dialogue between the instructor and student centered on the facts of nature.	Discovery and adapting new information to the world requires education to be practical and useful. The curriculum is typically dialogical and hands-on activity with the teacher as guide. Curriculum is typically world-centered or society-centered, especially in the case of social reconstructionism.

Thomism • *Neo-Thomism* • *Manualism* *Proponents:* Thomas Aquinas, Jacques Maritain, Karl Rahner	• Reality is created both spiritual and material and known through reason and reflection. • Truth is eternal, coming through revelation (both special and natural), reason, and the institution (Roman Catholic Church, human authorities). • Ethics are the acts of rational individuals based on eternal truths; beauty is expressed primarily through reason.	*Monastery:* Thomism is an innately Christian philosophy of education. Hence, it has a pronounced spiritual dimension and emphasizes the study of theology and philosophy as means of affirming truth through logic/reason. Education is an engagement of life through the lens of a theologically-informed worldview.	Curriculum aims to integrate the intellectual and spiritual, producing a moral individual who serves God through the church and in the community. The content consists of church dogma, traditions, and the classics. The curriculum requires teaching methods to range from informed dialogue (similar to realism) to recitations and memory drills.
Pragmatism • *Progressivism* • *Experimentalism* • *Social Reconstructionism* *Proponents:* John Dewey, William Kilpatrick	• Change is the only absolute in reality. Reality is always in process, known through experience. Truth is situational, pragmatic (i.e., "Whatever works"), and temporal; determined by individuals or society. • Ethics are relative to the demands of the situation; personal choice of the individual in society.	*Factory:* Pragmatism, as the name suggests, is focused on providing a practical education, something that can adapt to the ever-changing needs of the society, i.e., assuming a valuable role and function in society. Individuals need specific skills to work in a factory setting, but must also adapt to the changing needs of the factory. Pragmatism seeks to equip the individual with the skills and abilities needed to change as the need requires.	Curriculum is focused on application, the immediately relevant, and assessed by learning objectives, not the content or the instructional methodology. A progressive curriculum is student-centered and is designed to help address the self-perceived current needs of the student both as an individual and a member of a society.

Existentialism • *Phenomenology* *Proponents:* Kierkegaard, Maxine Green, George Keller, Van Cleve Morris	• Reality is created by the individual's subjective experience; it is perception as reality. • Truth is determined by individual choice and created internally by the individual. • Any liberating idea or principle is considered ethical. Aesthetics are counter cultural, "in the eye of the beholder."	*Café:* Picture a coffee house. Individuals sitting at small tables of their own choosing, and over an espresso or latte, they discuss life's meaning, the most recent book they read, and share their struggles along life's journey. Education based on existentialism is very much like this. It centers on whatever is more relevant to their "existential" quest.	Curriculum is driven by the process of making meaning, with an emphasis on the personal interpretation and appropriation of the humanities as a means of explaining the human condition. Personal engagement of *status quo* to determine one's own identity and meaning.
Postmodernism *Proponents:* Henry Giroux, Stanley Aronowitz, Michel Foucault	• Reality is based on the individual's choices, and no metanarrative, overarching, universal statement of reality, can exist. • Truth is individualistic, relative; open-mindedness toward multiple truths is a major tenant. • Ethics are culturally determined and culturally-based but not bound to one culture, so having exposure to multiple cultures in determining ethics is crucial.	*Wrecking-ball:* Postmodernism is a reinterpretation and assessment of life through individual perspective, and as such it destroys any sense of universal interpretation or meaning placed on history, literature, and language, i.e. *deconstruction.* You have to clear the old to provide space for the new.	Curriculum enables learners to develop fresh perspectives for themselves through the reinterpretations of language, symbols, and cultural icons. The curriculum focuses on power, history, politics, and the hermeneutics of culture.

Figure 3.2: Philosophy, Education, and Curriculum

curriculum in two ways. First, it provides the content. One aspect of a distinctively Christian curriculum is that it engages Scripture, theology, Church tradition, denominational heritage, and other subjects often absent from other curriculums. Oftentimes this is the limit of theology's influence. However, if theology is relegated to only the content of curriculum, it falls far short of one that reflects a Christian distinctive. What if an existential educator taught the Scriptures? An advocate of realism or idealism would certainly make a different use of Scripture in a curriculum. It is simply not sufficient to just have theology as the content; theology must impact how curriculum is developed and formed.

Second, theology informs our theories of education, which ultimately impacts curriculum. If theology shifts, education shifts, and curriculum is eventually impacted. As D. Campbell Wyckoff observes, "A new doctrine of man results in a new idea of pupil and teacher. A changed Christology results in a new idea of the problem and curriculum of Christian education. A revived doctrine of the church results in a new idea of the context of Christian education, while it calls for an explicit theology of the parish, the ministry, and the laity."[5] As such, theology not only provides the core contents of a curriculum, but is the rationale guiding its development and design. Figure 3.3 (p. 52) illustrates the process of integrating educational considerations and a theologically informed worldview into a distinctively Christian curriculum.[6]

As the basis for a curriculum, theology provides cohesion and a unified approach not only to the curriculum, but also to living a consistently Christian life.[7] If theology is expressed as creedal and confessional, then curriculum is concrete and content-centered; students

---

[5] D. Campbell Wyckoff, *Theory and Design of Christian Education Curriculum* (Philadelphia: Westminster, 1961), 51.

[6] Adapted from Issler's revision of the model offered by William Frankena in "A Model for Analyzing a Philosophy of Education," *The High School Journal* 50, no. 1 (October 1966): 8–13. See Klaus Issler, "Theological and Philosophical Foundations" (paper presented at the annual meeting of the North American Professors of Christian Education, 2002). Used with permission.

[7] See Adrian Thatcher, "Learning to Become Persons: A Theological Approach to Educational Aims," in *Christian Perspective for Education: A Reader in the Theology of Education*, ed. Leslie J. Francis and Adrian Thatcher (Leominster, England: Gracewing, 1990), 73–82.

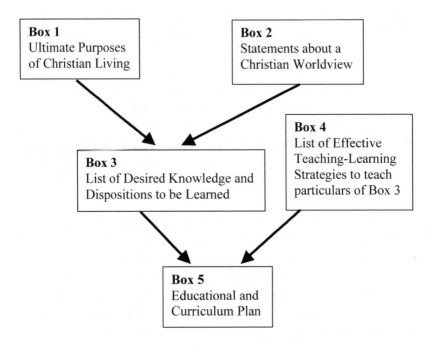

Figure 3.3: Theology and Curriculum Development

being required to master and recite/explain the theological content. Whereas, if theology is expressed as a process of doing theology, then the curriculum is experiential and abstract; students being required to engage in personal theological reflection. Theology is the context in which a Christian curriculum is developed; the greater the strength of their relationship, the more distinctly Christian the curriculum. As such, "The curriculum . . . is the plan for learning that translates what Christians know about God, reality, humankind, and one's calling."[8] Without theology, curriculum loses direction and learners wander without a working compass.

---

[8] Johannes Van der Walt, "The Third Curriculum—from a Christian Perspective," *Journal of Research on Christian Education* 9, no. 2 (Fall 2000): 162.

Toward a Theology of Curriculum

Where is God in the curriculum? This is the most fundamental question when constructing a theology of curriculum. This section describes curriculum from a theological perspective, placing the practice of curriculum development into the broader context of theological enterprise. What is theological about curriculum? Figure 3.4 illustrates that God gave the Scriptures and the church as a means of transforming humanity. God provided humanity two curricula. He revealed Scripture and established the church not only as an interpretive community, but also as a means of learning about him through participating within the body of Christ. The church likewise prepares a guide, its curriculum, as a means of providing direction for believers on their faith journeys.

This makes the process of curriculum development in the church today an extension of the church's historic mission of transformation. God provided both his Word and his church as a means of bring-

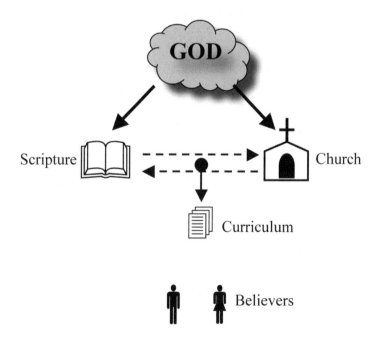

Figure 3.4: Theology of Curriculum

ing humanity back to him; hence, Christian curriculum is the product of God's interaction with humanity through his Scripture and his people. A theology of curriculum can be framed by four tenets: (1) God is the revealer of curriculum, (2) Scripture is God-breathed curriculum, (3) the church is humanity's guide to the curriculum, and (4) humanity is the recipient of the curriculum. Within these parameters, the Christian educator can articulate a theological perspective on curriculum.

God Is the Revealer of Curriculum

The affirmation that "All truth is God's truth" is the hallmark of evangelical theology. All truth ultimately originates with God as revealer. Revelation is the act of self-disclosure, or the disclosure of truth that was otherwise humanly unknowable. God's revelatory acts have been described in regard to its content and means of delivery as being both "special," e.g., the word revelation of Scripture, and "general," e.g., the nonverbal revelation of nature. Because of the nature of the Scriptures, as a special written revelation, it is central in Christian education curriculum.

While God is depicted in a variety of ways throughout the Old and New Testaments, one metaphor used in Scripture is to describe him as a teacher. God was Israel's first "teacher" (Isa 3:8; Job 36:22; Exod 35:34), as well as the church's (Titus 2:11–12; 2 Cor 6:1; 1 Tim 2:3–4). God's revelatory acts, both in deed and word, demonstrate God's role as the teacher of the faith community. Through word, deed, and interventions, God is interactive with humanity for the purpose of instructing and transforming them into a unique people. To do this, God provided a curriculum of Scripture and a community in which to learn the life of faith, the church. God has assumed an educational role through a variety of means. According to Nels F. S. Ferré, God teaches through nature and history, Christian community, theological heritage, imitation of the past [tradition], creative discovery, and participation in the life of the spirit.[9]

God revealed the Scriptures, established the church, and continues to be active in the life of the believers (1 Cor 2:10–16). An indispensible

---

[9] Nels F. S. Ferré, *A Theology for Christian Education* (Philadelphia: Westminster, 1967), 168–71.

part of the teaching-learning process is the involvement of the Holy Spirit in the lives of the student and the teacher. The elements making up a Christian curriculum, its purpose, goals, objectives, content, and prescribed instructional methodology, are subject to the Holy Spirit's guidance in the teaching ministry of the church and in the lives of the teacher and learner.

Scripture Is God-Breathed Curriculum

Though this is implied in the reality of revelation, Paul openly expresses the educational intent of Scripture: "For everything that was written in the past was written *to teach us*, so that through endurance and the encouragement of the Scriptures we might have hope" (Rom 15:4, emphasis added). Later he further expressed,

> But as for you, continue in what you have learned and have become convinced of, because you know those from whom you learned it, and how from infancy you have *known the holy Scriptures, which are able to make you wise for salvation through faith in Christ Jesus*. All Scripture is God-breathed and is useful for teaching, rebuking, correcting and training in righteousness, *so that the man of God may be thoroughly equipped for every good work*." (2 Tim 3:14–17, emphasis added)

God gave us the Scriptures as a means of instruction, equipping us to become mature disciples of Jesus Christ. While Scripture itself may identify other models than just didactic instruction, such as celebration of events and fellowship within the community of faith, it remains the cornerstone of God's educational endeavor.[10] Oftentimes, Scripture is a boundary placed on revelation by evangelicals. We often do not see that within the Bible, additional revelation is mentioned (e.g., even the revelation of nature is independent of the Bible, but is revelation nonetheless). Scripture is the watershed issue in evangelical education and the church's curriculum.[11] We should make use of all that Scripture says is

---

[10] Gerhard H. Bussmann, "A Three-Fold Model of Religious Education Based on the Nature of Revelation," *Religious Education* 72, no. 4 (July-August 1977): 400–408.

[11] Cf. Kenneth O. Gangel and Christy Sullivan, "Evangelical Theology and Religious Education," in *Theologies of Religious Education*, ed. Randolph Crump Miller (Birmingham, Alabama: Religious Education Press, 1995), 73.

beneficial to the Christian life in developing a curriculum for the congregation. Scripture must have a prime position within the curriculum.

For Christian educators, the curriculum must be concerned about the Bible as *content* and as *process*. For example, 2 Tim 3:15–17 describes both the content of Scripture ("All Scripture is God-breathed") and the process of making use of God's revelation ("able to make you wise for salvation . . . useful . . . so that the man of God may be thoroughly equipped for every good work"). Scripture is not only considered a revelation of God, but also *inspired* by the Holy Spirit, referring to God's special provision and oversight in the writing of Scripture. Only when both the content of Scripture and the proper use of Scripture are equally emphasized is education genuinely Christian. Hence, the Scriptures serve as the only sufficient rule for faith and practice within the Christian life and community—not only because of the revealed-inspired nature of the biblical text, but also the relevance the Scriptures have for today.

Nevertheless, Scripture requires interpretation. Likewise, while Scripture can be read and studied individually, it should be studied and interpreted within the context of the community of faith. Scripture was meant to be used by the individual and the corporate body of Christ. God revealed Scripture to his people, and from it the church develops a plan for systematic instruction and acquisition of the Scriptures, the curriculum. Curriculum that is Christian must advance the transformative aims of Christian education; being tied to the God-centered purpose and transformative learning objectives previously mentioned. The curriculum developed by the church must center itself on the curriculum revealed by God, namely, Scripture. As the Word of God, Scripture is able to contribute to the various functions of fulfilling the purpose, goals, and objectives of Christian education (see chap. 8). Curriculum that is Christian provides significant engagement with Scripture on every level of instruction (as demonstrated in fig. 3.5).

While each approach may make a different use of it, Scripture is the central content of a Christian curriculum. The content-centered approach is aimed at making students master the actual content of Scripture and theology and further developing their theological reasoning abilities. A student-centered approach aims students

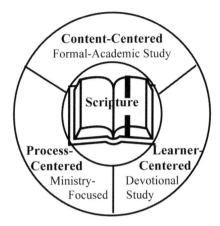

Figure 3.5: Scripture-Centered Curriculum Content

toward making use of Scripture devotionally or as a source for theological reflection. The process-centered approach toward education, designed primarily to equip students with ministry skills, makes use of Scripture to explain the rationale, motive, and "oughtness" of Christian ministry. It would be difficult to assess any curriculum as being "Christian" if it omitted Scripture. Scripture is the essential content of Christian curriculum, but the church is also part of God's curricular plan.

The Church Is Humanity's Guide to the Curriculum

The church is both the keeper of the Scriptures and a God-given curriculum. The curriculum is the expression of the congregation's educational ministry culture. Curriculum must adapt to the faith outcomes of the congregation, the transformative purpose of Christian education. For example, Christians growing through greater comprehension of the Bible requires a content-centered approach to curriculum, matching a cognitive learning objective. Christian piety would require student-centered curriculum to address the affective domain of the Christian faith. Similarly, Christians being most capable and competent to serve the church and community would require a skills-based curriculum to equip the believer to serve. No solo-focused approach to curriculum in the church will provide for the holistic development of the Christian faith; only a multi-dimensional approach can accomplish this.[12]

As the keeper of God's curriculum, the congregation's curriculum must engage the content of Scripture with an ever-increasing depth of study. The continuous study of Scripture at the same depth is insufficient to advance Christian maturity. This is not simply a pragmatic necessity, but one reflected in the biblical foundations of education and in our concept of human salvation and sanctification. Educational theorists have developed taxonomies for knowing (cognitive learning domain),[13] valuing (affective learning domain),[14] and doing (psychomotor or behavioral learning domain),[15] demonstrating ever-increasing depth of learning, requiring a curriculum to facilitate that type of growth. Peter writes, "Like newborn babies, crave pure spiritual milk, so that by it you may grow up in your salvation, now that you have tasted that the Lord is good" (1 Pet 2:2–3). Scripture frequently uses the metaphor of milk versus solid food or meat, often condemning the lack of growth within a congregation (1 Cor 3:2; Heb 5:12–13); but what if a congregation is guilty of not providing anything but milk? Would this not stifle a Christian's growth? Education programs that offer the same level of instruction in a variety of formats are not providing a healthy environment for growth, since people could involve themselves in every avenue of instruction offered by the congregation, but never be fed in such a way as to grow spiritually.

The church is designed to do more than guide believers in their study of Scripture. The church itself is a part of God's plan for instructing His people. As Stanley Hauerwas observes,

---

[12] Cf. James Riley Estep Jr., "Toward a Theologically Informed Approach to Education," in *A Theology for Christian Education*, ed. James Riley Estep Jr., Michael J. Anthony, and Gregg R. Allison (Nashville: B&H, 2008), 266–68.

[13] Benjamin S. Bloom, *Taxonomy of Educational Objectives: Book—Cognitive Domain* (White Plains, New York: Longman, 1956).

[14] David R. Krathwohl, Benjamin S. Bloom, and Bertram B. Masia, *Taxonomy of Educational Objectives: Book 2—Affective Domain* (White Plains, New York: Longman, 1964).

[15] Elizabeth Jane Simpson, "The Classification of Educational Objectives, Psychomotor Domain" (unpublished paper, Urbana-Champaign, IL: University of Illinois, 1966).

> I worry about the idea that religious education is some special activity separated from the total life of the church. When that happens, it makes it appear that what the church does in its worship is something different from what it does in its education. I would contend that everything the church is and does is "religious education". Put more strongly, the church does not "do" religious education at all. *Rather, the church is a form of education that is religious.*[16]

The church as curriculum is not unique to Stanley Hauerwas. Maria Harris described the church as God's curriculum for transforming lives into God's people.[17] As individuals become the church, their experience is within the community of the saved, the body of Christ; and through the process of intentional socialization the Christian learns to be more Christian. For example, churches that practice the "Christian Year" make participation in the life of the congregation an educational experience, celebrating special days such as Christmas, Palm Sunday, Easter, and Pentecost.[18] Based on E. V. Hill's concept of the church, Robert Pazmiño of Andover Newton derived an approach to Christian education based on five aspects of the church, each with specific educational implications:[19]

1. Worship (*leitourgia*)—learning faith, hope, and love in a communal context
2. Fellowship (*koinonia*)—learning love within the body of Christ
3. Evangelism (*kerygma*)—learning faith by sharing one's faith
4. Kingdom Consciousness (*basileia*)—learning hope beyond the immediate community

---

[16] Stanley Hauerwas, "The Gesture of a Truthful Story," in *Theological Perspectives on Christian Formation*, ed. Jeff Astley, Leslie J. Francis, and Colin Cowder (Grand Rapids: Eerdmans, 1996), 97 (emphasis added).

[17] Maria Harris, *Fashion Me a People: Curriculum in the Church* (Louisville: WJK, 1989).

[18] Cf. Vasiliki Eckley, "The Church Year and the Lectionary in Curriculum for the Local Church," *Religious Education* 77, no. 5 (Sept.-Oct. 1982): 554–67.

[19] Robert W. Pazmiño, *God Our Teacher* (Grand Rapids: Baker, 2001), 114–15; id., *Principles and Practices of Christian Education* (Grand Rapids: Baker, 1992), 94–95.

5. Service (*diakonia*)—learning to love through serving others and the world

But where is teaching (*didache*)? Is it absent? Unimportant? Life in the community of the church *is* the instruction. Teaching is in each aspect and between them; it informs the content of each of these five areas and how they interrelate.[20] Pazmiño's model shows the interactivity between these five aspects of the church, requiring "teachers to foster a vital connection for Christians through the explicit curriculum or content of Christian education . . . These links also provide a means by which to assess the educational diet of any particular community and to discern particulars of the explicit, implicit, and null curricula that need attention."[21] Instruction within the congregation is accomplished by experience within the life of the congregation (socialization) as well as through the intentional instruction provided by the congregation (teaching).

As Christians in the twenty-first century, we often underestimate the authority and position of the church in the life of the early Christian. We assume that believers have long enjoyed easy access to the Scriptures, and that they were capable of reading it for themselves for their own spiritual nurture. However, this has not always been the case. Until the Protestant Reformation, private access to Scripture was not common, and literacy rates in the early and medieval church were quite low; so even if they had access to the Scriptures, they were probably not able to read it. Even after the educational efforts of such men as Martin Luther and John Calvin, literacy in Western Europe was still limited. The average Christians could not read Scripture for themselves. From where did the Christians prior to the modern era receive spiritual direction and instruction? It was through their involvement within the community of faith (socialization) and the instruction of the church to its members (curriculum). God not only provided the Scriptures to his people for guidance; he gave a community, the church, to instruct further and nurture their faith.

When one begins to grasp the idea that the church is the people of God, the development of a curriculum specifically designed for a con-

---

[20] Pazmiño, *God Our Teacher*, 114–15.
[21] Pazmiño, *Principles and Practices of Christian Education*, 94–95.

gregation becomes all the more needed. While congregations may share a common theological understanding of the nature of the church, every congregation is unique in its individual character or path in adhering to the pattern described in Scripture. Strict reliance on prepackaged or "canned" curriculum alone cannot suffice for congregations. While congregations should make use of prepackaged materials, they should be used in alignment with their stated purposes, goals, and objective, not just for convenience or to follow faddish curricula. Within each congregation, a team must be responsible for identifying learning purposes, goals, and objectives and assessing how well the congregation's curriculum content adheres to those aims, thus giving ownership of the curriculum to the teaching ministry of the congregation.

Humanity Is the Recipient of the Curriculum

When writing about the unique relationship shared by the Holy Spirit, Scripture, and Christian education, Rachael Henderlite asserts,

> Because it believes that the Spirit of God acts upon the human heart by means of Scripture, the church can build its curriculum upon a specific piece of literature without thereby being bound to the transmission of a stagnant heritage. The Bible is inseparable from Spirit. Without the work of the Holy Spirit to illuminate the words of Scripture, the Bible is a mere relic of antiquity, a book to read but in no sense a book of life. Without the Bible the Holy Spirit is left without a medium through which he can bring to man's heart all that God has done in Christ for our salvation.[22]

Curriculum content must aid the student in building a relationship with Jesus Christ. Curriculum also possesses an often-neglected personal dimension. While it is easy to regard curriculum content as nothing more than the selected topics of study being taught in sequence to an increasing depth, curriculum that is Christian ultimately aids in building a relationship with Jesus Christ. Relationships are between people, not things. The curriculum in many respects is aimed at introducing Jesus to the student and building a relationship with him

---

[22] Rachael Henderlite, *The Holy Spirit in Christian Education* (Philadelphia: Westminster, 1964), 82.

throughout their lives. Regardless of the subject matter, the curriculum must point individuals to Jesus Christ and help them establish a lasting and meaningful relationship with him. While this principle is most readily applicable to the affective learning domain, personal piety and character, it is likewise necessary for the other domains as well.

Theological Traditions and Curriculum

Curriculum is a tangible expression of theology. Curriculum is as diverse as the theologies and traditions constituting the church today. With the advent of each significant theological development in the church came the production of a curriculum to complement it. D. Campbell Wyckoff, when summarizing the theological shifts of the twentieth century and assessing their impact on Church education, notes that these shifts were manifest in the curriculum of congregations and denominations. For example, when speaking of the advent of neo-Orthodox theology in the United States, Christian educators such as E. G. Homnighausen and later Paul H. Veith developed educational theories that reflected this new theological orientation; "this led to a new concept of the curriculum."[23] Just as each of the root philosophies had its own distinct educational philosophy associated with it, ultimately represented in a curriculum; so each distinct approach to theology within Christianity results in its equally distinct curriculum.

Within the contemporary church, numerous curricula have been developed that reflect the diverse theological landscape of the twentieth and twenty-first centuries. The following is a brief survey of the contemporary theological landscape and the curricular developments associated with them:[24]

---

[23] D. Campbell Wyckoff, "Theology and Education in the 20th Century," *Christian Education Journal* 15, no. 3 (Spring 1995): 18.

[24] The following is based on insights and information from several sources: Mary C. Boys, *Educating in Faith: Maps and Vision* (San Francisco: Harper and Row, 1989); Harold W. Burgess, *Models of Religious Education: Theory and Practice in Historical and Contemporary Perspective* (Wheaton, IL: Victor/BridgePoint, 1996); and Harold W. Burgess, *An Invitation to Religious Education* (Birmingham, AL: Religious Education Press, 1975).

1. *Classical Liberalism*—associated with religious education, and advocates a child-centered curriculum, very inclusive and humanistic. The curriculum gives less attention to creeds and confessional statements; the content, and hence the Bible, is regarded as a resource, but not the definitive source of the curriculum.[25]

2. *Neo-orthodox*—associated with Christian education, it advocates that Scripture and doctrine are the contents of the curriculum. Unlike classical liberalism, it is more proclamational and transmissive,[26] but describes the Bible as a record of revelation, not the revelation itself.[27]

3. *Evangelical*—associated with Christian education, it advocates a curriculum of content mastery and application of Scripture. It centers on Christ and Scripture; focusing on the content of instruction, but unlike neo-orthodoxy, evangelicals value Scripture as God's revelation, not a mere record of it.[28]

4. *Fundamentalism*—associated with indoctrination, its curriculum is revivalistic, aimed at the salvation of individuals. The curriculum centers on Bible literacy, teaching as transmission of beliefs/doctrines.[29]

5. *Roman Catholic*—associated exclusively with education in Roman Catholicism, its curriculum is centered on the appropriation of tradition, and advocates the affirmation of the church's tradition. The principle curricula are catechism and the sacramental life.

6. *Process Theologies*—advocates a curriculum that is not centered on content, but on the student's own experience, utilizing Scripture as interpreter of experience through personal reflection.

---

[25] Boys, *Educating in Faith*, 94–95; Burgess, *Models*, 75–107; Burgess, *Invitation*, 73–76.

[26] Boys, *Educating in Faith*, 76.

[27] Burgess, *Models*, 109–44; Burgess, *Invitation*, 105–10.

[28] Burgess, *Models*, 145–85; Burgess, *Invitation*, 35–41.

[29] Boys, *Educating in Faith*, 34.

7. *Social Science*—although not formally a theological tradition, there is an approach to education in the church that promotes the exclusion of theology from theorizing about education in the church; education in the church is solely a social science. Theology would be relegated to the curriculum's content at best, focusing more on the appropriate instructional methodology and assessment of learning than anything else.[30]

8. *Special Interest Theologies*—segments within the church, often perceived as marginalized or minimized, such as African-American, feminist, Hispanic, or Asian theological traditions, each impact the formation of curriculum within their own denomination. Curriculum reflects not only their theological distinction, but also the Christian diversity they represent. Hence, curriculum uses Scripture and theology to address the unique heritage, experience, and social status of the specific group.

Previously in this chapter, a theological-curricular spectrum was presented, ranging from creedal to process orientations. Figure 3.6 illustrates how the curricular approaches listed above align throughout the spectrum, demonstrating the breadth of curriculum present in today's church.

Theology, Curriculum and the Christian Educator

Christian educators must be more than theologians and curriculum specialists. They must be both. Theology is the compass for curriculum

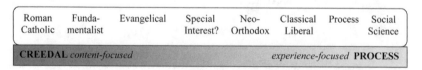

Figure 3.6: Educational Traditions along the Theological Spectrum

---

[30] Burgess, *Models*, 187–221; Burgess, *Invitation*, 134–51.

development. Failure to recognize the intimate relationship between theology and the development or selection of curriculum leads to a pastoral dualism, with theology in one hand and our curriculum in the other; existing independent of one another and leading to teaching one thing while believing another. The integration of theology and curriculum development provides the congregation with a consistent direction, as the curriculum directly reflects the congregation's theology, not only in regard to content, but also goals and objectives. Without theology, the curriculum cannot orient learners to true north; without a curriculum, the congregation is lost.

Key Terms and Concepts

Theology	Curriculum vs. curriculum
Integration	Content and Process
Revelation	Creedal vs. Process

Reflection Questions

1. How strong is the connection between theology and curriculum in your congregation?
2. What does someone "learn" by being part of your congregation? What does the experience of your church teach them?
3. How would you describe the integration of theology and curriculum?
4. What could you do as a Christian education pastor to integrate theology and curriculum more intentionally?

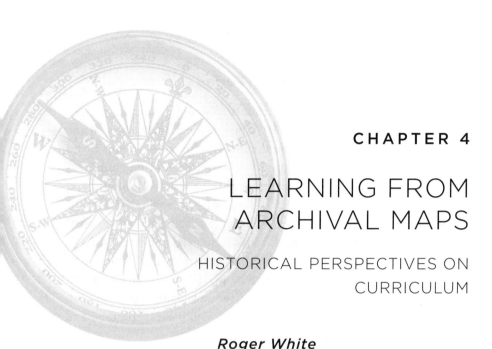

CHAPTER 4

LEARNING FROM ARCHIVAL MAPS

HISTORICAL PERSPECTIVES ON CURRICULUM

Roger White

Today's church has not been left to develop educational plans and maps from scratch. With the God-orienting witness of the Bible and the directional bearings of theology, the church has thousands of years of developmental programs and educational maps from which to gather ideas and inspiration. By attending to ways the Holy Spirit led people of God in the past, educators are able to consider common themes found in church educational plans of earlier periods, discern the wisdom they reflect, and integrate aspects of them into present day curriculum. This chapter provides an overview of curricular maps and approaches used in selected epochs of church history and highlights curricular trends and resources that may bear fruit with further examination.

Early Church Period

One of the first indications of an educational and curricular plan in the church is found in Acts 2:42, "They devoted themselves to the apostles' teaching and to fellowship, to the breaking of bread and to prayer." Community life naturally revolved around ongoing connections to the risen Christ as experienced in the Lord's Supper and through unity with other believers—especially those who had personally known him. The early church went on to practice the educational customs and conventions received from the apostles and handed down from the church's first generation of believers, much of it mirroring what had been done in the Old Testament period. Intentional plans for helping individuals mature in faith and for advancing church growth continued to be administered primarily through parents, pastors, and teachers.

In the church community, an informal consensus developed regarding the essential aspects of God's message. The rudiments of this message are evident in the sermons recorded in Acts and the didactic portions of the New Testament letters. This distilled essence of apostolic preaching came to be called the "kerygma."[1] Its focus is the life, ministry, death, and resurrection of Jesus the Messiah, while looking back to the nation of Israel and forward to a new eschatological age ushered in by the return of Christ. In the kerygma the role of the Holy Spirit is prominently featured as is individual repentance, forgiveness, and salvation in the midst of a believing community.[2]

These themes present in the kerygma were central to the instruction provided to new believers prior to baptism and entry into the church. It is not known to what extent planned curriculum and catechism were formalized, but the New Testament does include elements that may have been present in the faith community in the form of hymn fragments and primitive creeds. For example, 1 Cor 15:3–5,

For what I received I passed on to you as of first importance:

---

[1] This use of the term goes beyond the more common use of the Greek word meaning simply "proclamation" or "preaching."

[2] C. H. Dodd, *The Apostolic Preaching and Its Developments* (London: Hodder & Stoughton, 1944), 21–24.

> that Christ died for our sins according to the Scriptures,
> that he was buried,
> that he was raised on the third day according to the Scriptures,
> and that he appeared to Cephas,
> and then to the Twelve.

Or, 1 Tim 3:16,

> Beyond all question, the mystery from which true godliness springs is great:
>
> He appeared in the flesh,
> was vindicated by the Spirit,
> was seen by angels,
> was preached among the nations,
> was believed on in the world,
> was taken up in glory.

Other New Testament excerpts read as concise teaching summaries such as passages on Christ's humility (Phil 2:6–11), the supremacy of the Son of God (Col 1:15–20), or the prologue of John (1:1–18).[3] These would all have likely served as primary elements of a new believer's educational journey.

As personal accounts and collected teachings regarding the Christian faith circulated by word of mouth and in written form, certain stories, versions, and explanations became more widely used and recognized than others. The gospels and letters that now make up the New Testament were particularly well accepted, thus advancing their circulation, educational value to the church, and eventual canonical recognition. Various aspects of the message of the kingdom of God were also present in other writings of the first few centuries, but they did not gain the status of Scripture even though they were widely used for instructional purposes.

The best known of these other manuscripts is the *Didache* also known as *Teaching of the Apostles*.[4] It dates from the latter half of the first

---

[3] See also Eph 2:14–16 and 1 Pet 3:18–22.

[4] Another piece of Christian literature that found some popularity during the early church period was called *The Shepherd of Hermas* and is a series of visions, mandates, and parables. See also the letters of Clement of Rome, Ignatius of Antioch, and Polycarp of Smyrna.

century and enjoyed widespread use in the church as an instructional manual. The *Didache* begins with a short essay on the two ways of life (cf. chap. 2 and appendix 4.1 on p. 85) and also includes instruction on baptism and the Lord's Supper.

Over time, oral transmission and verbal expression of select content found in New Testament writings and instructional manuals like the *Didache* developed from everyday conversational exchanges occurring in small groups into a recognized teaching style of question and answer utilized increasingly in formal settings. This approach, with its similarities to the Socratic method of discussion practiced by the Greeks, came to be known as catechesis and the standardized questions and answers were called a catechism. This instructional approach grew and was practiced more widely in the Middle Ages and is still used in parts of the church today.

As the core of Christian teaching formalized, there arose a constant need to sharpen and identify the orthodox teaching of the church, to discern the central message of God. When those who knew Jesus and the apostles were gone, the original accounts of these witnesses took on greater importance. When false teachers arose and began to introduce alternative and destructive ideas, their teaching had to be distinguished from the true message. When intellectual challenges to the truth of Christianity arose from segments of society, arguments were formed to respond to them.

Among those who wrote to refute false teaching was Irenaeus of Lyons (c. AD 140–202) who wrote *Against Heresies* (c. AD 180), also known by its full title *On the Detection and Overthrow of the So-Called Gnosis*. In this writing the way of Gnosticism and its emphasis on salvation through knowledge and belief of physical matter as evil is contrasted with the way of orthodox Christianity. Irenaeus provides a comprehensive five-volume response to the Gnostics, appealing regularly to the authoritative nature of the writings that would later make up the canonical New Testament. The map he provides to readers is extremely thorough and an early example of how maps for the church will continually need to be supported by the norm of sacred writings.

The work of early apologists who defended the faith to the world are also of use in the church today because of the clarity and extent to which they spell out how the Christian path does or does not overlap with similar ways advanced by the world. One of the earliest of these works, *First Apology* (AD 150–155), written by Justin Martyr (AD 103–165) is addressed to the head of the Roman Empire, Emperor Antoninus Pius (AD 86–161). It provides a clear exposition of Christianity and rational arguments for the faith's validity and distinctiveness. Tertullian (c. AD 160–220), an apologist who wrote *The Prescription Against Heresies* and one of the earliest writers to use the term Trinity, warns Christians of the paths associated with pagan philosophy and literature as he famously asks, "What does Athens have to do with Jerusalem? What does the Academy have to do with the Church?"[5] In a work on idolatry he includes a section called *On Schoolmasters and Their Difficulties* where he urges Christian teachers not to teach in pagan schools, but allows that Christian children may attend. Christian teachers, he explains, would be perceived as advocating the false ideas associated with such a setting, whereas students would be attending merely out of a general necessity to learn. In Tertullian's arguments, he advances the idea of a "rule of faith," an authoritative tradition passed down through the church and represented in its Scriptures and doctrines, similar to the consensus evident in the early church's kerygma (see appendix 4.2).

Perhaps no individual did more to advance Christian education in the early centuries than Augustine of Hippo (AD 354–430). Among his numerous writings are educational works that touch on curriculum in many ways. In his work *On Christian Instruction*,[6] he explains an approach for studying and understanding the Scriptures and addresses how learning should be communicated to others. In *On the Teacher*,[7] he recounts a conversation with his son about what can be learned from human teachers given the epistemological difficulties related to language, and he expresses how the "inner teacher" Christ provides the ground for true knowledge. In *On the Instruction of Beginners*,[8] he

---

[5] *Prescription Against Heretics* 1:7.

[6] *De Doctrina Christiana.* Also translated as *On Christian Doctrine* or *On Christian Teaching.*

[7] *De magistro.*

[8] *De catechizandis rudibus.* Also translated as *On Catechizing Beginners in Faith, On Catechizing the Uninstructed* or *The First Catechetical Instruction.*

responds to an inquiry from a teacher about the best way to catechize beginners in the faith. In this teaching manual Augustine not only provides general theory and advice for guiding learners, he also supplies two sample curriculum maps outlining Bible and church history. In *Enchiridion on Faith, Hope, and Love,* he provides another manual on the basics of Christian living. This handbook was requested by a layperson wanting to have a summary of Christian teaching. Augustine frames his response around the virtues of faith, hope, and love and illustrates these through brief expositions of the Apostles' Creed and the Lord's Prayer and by appealing to the grace and love of God. Throughout all of his educational writings there is an acknowledgment of the place of human learning and the liberal arts as judiciously selected aspects of a Christian curriculum (see appendix 4.3 on p. 86).

During this period, as the church sought to define more clearly what it believed and taught, several themes emerged related to faithfully following the way. In order to address the absence of apostles and eyewitnesses, rising heretical views, and intellectual challenges from the world, a pattern of appealing to authoritative writings, church community tradition, and reason began to be established. These combined with the arrival of the well-known Apostle's Creed (AD 180?), the Nicene Creed (AD 365 and 381), and Jerome's Latin Vulgate translation of the Bible (AD 405) provided the church with important educational and curricular tools for leading the way through the Middle Ages (see appendix 4.4 on pp. 86–87).

The Middle Ages

By the time of the fall of the Western Roman Empire (AD 476) Christianity had become the officially recognized religion of the state, and the church provided much needed stability for the rest of the empire during the Middle Ages (476–1500s). During these thousand years the church institutionalized, and while the communication of Christian principles and practice continued naturally in homes and through daily social interactions, the intentional curriculum of the church's educational initiatives became increasingly formalized. This formalization is seen in the development of corporate worship practices and the establishment of new settings for the educational ministry of the church. Each of these developments illustrates several examples of new approaches to curricula.

First, with regard to corporate worship, a number of changes occurred through which the laity were helped to understand God's message and to respond to God's claim on their lives. Because many were illiterate, the use of symbols and memory aids were offered to assist them on their faith journey. Beginning with the Eucharist (the Lord's Supper), the church came to emphasize events from the life of Jesus and also redemptive history, featuring the truths of God's revelation associated with those events and setting apart certain days and seasons of the year for worshippers to reflect on their significance. This was an extension of Old Testament practice where feast days and other sacred events were viewed as special times of remembrance (Passover, Day of Atonement, Year of Jubilee). The church had earlier expanded the Sabbath day concept to be a commemoration of the resurrection of Jesus, but now a full yearly calendar of events was developed that included the Christmas and Easter seasons. Church traditions have varied as to the number and nature of special days and seasons recognized, but each has an important curricular value to faith travelers in assisting them to reflect on and respond to the meaning of redemptive history for their personal lives. The days and seasons present in many versions of what is called the church calendar or the liturgical year include Advent, Christmas, Ordinary Time, Lent, Paschal Triduum, Easter, and Ordinary Time (which is included twice).

Like the laity, many leaders of the church had limited education. Common practices and customs relating to corporate worship evolved into prescribed plans to assist clergy and guide worshippers. These plans provided an order for the worship experience, aligned it with the church calendar, and sometimes provided wording (litany) appropriate for the subject and season. Like curricular plans, these plans for worship, or liturgies, helped to provide direction for both the leader and those being led. Guides were also developed directing what doctrines should be preached and taught to laity.[9] One example, from John

---

[9] Marjorie Curry Woods and Rita Copeland, "Classroom and Confession," in *The Cambridge History of Medieval English Literature*, ed. David Wallace (Cambridge: Cambridge University Press, 1999), 376–406.

Peckham (1230–92), then Archbishop of Canterbury, provided outlines for teaching the creed, the Ten Commandments, the Seven Works of Mercy, the Seven Deadly Sins, the Seven Virtues and the Sacraments.[10]

In some cases the liturgical readings existed only in the language of the educated, and ordinary worshippers were not able to understand. In these situations, other means supplemented the primary liturgy (worship curriculum) and provided symbolic representations of God's truths. This would include aspects of the church architecture and the layout of the sanctuary. Many European church buildings were laid out in the form of a cross with high ceilings, drawing the attention of the worshipper heavenward. The placement of the main speaker, the music, the altar area, or the participants, communicated conceptual relationships of form and function. Some church buildings included artwork, statuary or stain-glass windows conveying stories from Scripture so that at least those who knew the stories could tell those who were unfamiliar with them. Other worship spaces conveyed church calendar seasons through the use of select colors used in adorning the building or the worship leaders.

Besides the visual elements used to supplement church liturgy and help Christian pilgrims on their journey to understand and respond to God's message, two other noteworthy communication channels related to corporate worship developed during the Middle Ages. One is the advance of music in conveying religious content and inspiring affective responses to God from the worshipper. The Gregorian chant, polyphony (multi-part harmonies), and organs were developed in this period. The other channel of communication (sometimes used in conjunction with the music) was liturgical or religious dramas where actors would act out stories from Scripture like the Passion, Gospel accounts, or the lives of the saints. Even if language were a barrier, viewers could get some of the meaning from the actions taking place before them.

Second, besides the curricular developments related to corporate worship, there were a number of new settings during the Middle Ages where Christian education rose to prominence and where the accompanying approaches to curriculum are worth considering. These include

---

[10] John L. Peckham, *Archbishop Peckham as a Religious Educator* (Scottsdale, PA: Mennonite Publishing House, 1934).

educational developments associated with monasteries, cathedrals, parishes, and universities. Initially, they all focused on education primarily for those who would serve in the church, but later provided education for others.

Monasticism was a movement for individuals who sensed a call to remove themselves from the distractions of the world to devote themselves entirely to God. Monasteries were communities set up to allow monastics (i.e., monks and nuns) to pursue a contemplative lifestyle by following carefully regimented work programs and devotional schedules. One widely used example of a curriculum used for monastic settings is the *Rule of Saint Benedict*[11] written by St. Benedict of Nursia (AD 480–547). It focuses on how to live a Christ-centered life and on how a monastery should operate. The daily habits and disciplines developed and practiced in monastic settings came to be widely used outside monasteries (e.g., prayer, meditation, fasting, solitude, simplicity).[12] The curriculum inherent in the solitary approach of Christian education present in some monasteries emphasized reading and study, so there was a continual need for books and libraries. To supplement this need, monastic curricula included literacy and writing programs and manuscript transcription. Later, in 1440, the invention of the printing press helped to provide more and less expensive reading materials. Certain aspects of the monastic curriculum were later opened to the wider population in the form of monastic schools.

Another type of church school was set up in conjunction with large cathedrals and local parishes to educate young people about life and faith. These schools became the forerunner for modern day elementary education and grammar schools. The curriculum in many of the cathedral and parish schools was based on the seven liberal arts: the Trivium (grammar, rhetoric, logic) and the Quadrivium (arithmetic, geometry, music, and astronomy), and also instruction in the Scriptures, theology, and philosophy. Recently, the Classical Christian School movement taking its cue from Christian writer Dorothy L. Sayers[13] has returned

---

[11] *Regula Benedicti.*

[12] Richard J. Foster, *Celebration of Discipline: The Path of Spiritual Growth* (San Francisco: Harper & Row, 1978).

[13] Dorothy L. Sayers, *The Lost Tools of Learning: Paper Read at a Vacation Course in Education, Oxford, 1947* (London: Methuen, 1948).

to the richness of this liberal arts curriculum by modifying the Trivium and Quadrivium for use in schools today.[14]

The church was also instrumental in the establishment of universities. As cathedral and monastic schools grew in size and in curricular offerings, some evolved into institutions of higher education with degree-granting programs. Many scholars involved in the universities during the period were heavily influenced by the rediscovery of the works of Aristotle, and a new emphasis on dialectical reasoning was applied to the process and content of the curriculum. This approach came to be called Scholasticism. One of the best examples of how this logic was applied to both sides of theological and philosophical issues is a curricular workbook by Peter Abelard (1079–1142) with the revealing title, *Sic et Non*, meaning "yes and no," where contradictory positions on various theological topics are placed side by side so students could learn and practice dialectical skills. The premiere writing coming out of the Scholastic movement was *Summa Theologica* (1274) written by Thomas Aquinas (c. 1225–1274).[15] Written for beginners, it was an introductory textbook on all of theology; to this day it is still considered a classic work on philosophy and theology.

During the Middle Ages, the church's influence grew and curricular approaches became generally more intentional and standardized for training pastors and educating laity. This was particularly evident in the development of the liberal arts curriculum in Christian education and related Scholastic influences, as well as in new approaches to corporate worship that featured the use of liturgies and symbolism to aid Christian pilgrims.

The Reformation Period

Many of the curricular developments and improvements occurring in the Middle Ages diminished in their influence over time (not unlike advancements of any age). What were new ideas then became tired practices when the original circumstances giving them birth changed. The

---

[14] Douglas Wilson, *Recovering the Lost Tools of Learning: An Approach to Distinctively Christian Education* (Wheaton, IL: Crossway Books, 1991).

[15] See also Thomas Aquinas's *De Magistro* or "On the Teacher."

Reformers (during the Reformation period of 1517–1648) looked at a number of beliefs, practices, and structures in the church (not just those related to education) and called for a major renewal. The emotionally cold and intellectually dry affects of Scholasticism were mediated by a more personal, human emphasis (i.e., Humanism) during the Renaissance. Martin Luther's (1483–1546) nailing of his ninety-five theses to the Wittenberg door in 1517 marked the beginning of a new perspective on the church and by implication on the curricula incorporated to establish, advance, and promote this vision with its new theological emphases. One of the central curricular emphases of the Reformation period was on individual reading and personal interpretation of the Bible.

Martin Luther and John Calvin (1509–64) are two Reformation figures that advocated the development of universal education and the promotion of literacy for the purpose of reading the Bible. They believed that educating all children would help both the church and state. Calvin established an academy for the children of Geneva (1559) that is still in operation today. Both Luther and Calvin developed a catechism for children that focused on the Ten Commandments, the Apostles' Creed, and the Lord's Prayer.[16] Calvin's catechism was the basis for the Heidelberg (1563) and Westminster (1647) catechisms. Contemporary use of the catechetical method as an essential part of church curriculum finds much support and example from this historical period (see appendix 4.5 on p. 87).[17]

Just as catechisms were not new to church curriculum, but found a wider use during the Reformation, liturgies also continued to develop. Perhaps the best-known liturgy of this time period arose as part of the English Reformation and was written in 1549 by Thomas Cranmer (1489–1556) for the Church of England. Known as the *Book of Common Prayer*, it took on a distinctly Protestant character in comparison with earlier liturgies and went through many revisions over the years. It is still used by Anglicans and Episcopalians today and is heavily borrowed

---

[16] Denis Janz, *Three Reformation Catechisms: Catholic, Anabaptist, Lutheran* (New York: Mellen, 1982).

[17] J. I. Packer and Gary A. Parrett, *Grounded in the Gospel: Building Believers the Old-Fashion Way* (Grand Rapids: Baker, 2010).

from by Lutherans, Methodists, and Presbyterians.[18] Besides providing an order and litany for worship and the Eucharist, it includes selections of the Psalms for singing, morning and evening prayers, and liturgies for services such as weddings, baptisms, and funerals. The curricular plans for these important events in the church's life provide direction and structure for worshippers.

In response to the calls for reformation, the Catholic Church experienced a counter-reformation of its own and likewise called for changes from within. Some of the reforms involved curricular matters associated with seminaries, the training of clergy, and returning to spiritual foundations. One key leader of the Catholic counter-reformation was Ignatius of Loyola (1491–1556) who founded the Society of Jesus, the Jesuits. Their work came to be closely connected with education and with schools, universities, and seminaries. The Jesuits would later found hundreds of such institutions around the world including in the United States: Boston College, Fordham University, Georgetown University, and Loyola University just to name a few. Ignatius is also known for developing a curriculum called *Spiritual Exercises* (1548), designed for individuals who are on private spiritual retreat. The handbook of exercises includes prayers, meditations, and other contemplative practices for a four-week time of reflection, but the parts could also be used at anytime. Various editions of this book are still in use today for devotional purposes.

The Reformation period brought new attention to the role of the learner in the curriculum experience. Interpretation of the Bible that had rested primarily with the clergy shifted to include a person's private conscience as guided by the Holy Spirit, making education and well-designed curriculum all the more important. Many new Bible translations soon followed, the most prominent being the King James Version of 1611. The church promoted educational opportunities beyond the confines of church buildings into the broader community. The widespread use of curriculum materials like catechisms, the *Book of Common Prayer*, and *Spiritual Exercises*, provided the backdrop for the enormous growth of curriculum materials that would be produced

---

[18] Charles Hefling and Cynthia Shattuck, eds., *The Oxford Guide to the Book of Common Prayer: A Worldwide Survey* (New York: Oxford University Press, 2006).

up to and including the present day. While there are more than we can survey here, a few pertinent examples will be considered.

The Sunday School Movement

In 1780 an English businessman named Robert Raikes (1736–1811) became distressed by a growing prison population in his city and the number of children working long hours at factories. Since Sunday was the only time the children did not work, he set up a school for that day in a nearby home to educate boys and girls and keep them from turning to a life of crime. This was the beginning of the Sunday school movement, an educational initiative started and primarily supported by laypersons. In this section, we will explore the spread of this movement over a two hundred year period and how it became the catalyst for many of the curricular developments in the evangelical church especially in the United States.

The curriculum of the first Sunday school in Gloucester, England, consisted of learning to read (mainly the Bible), moral instruction, and memorizing the catechism. The school experienced such great success that after a few years the idea quickly spread to other parts of the city, throughout England, and to the United States. One of the factors of the Sunday school's remarkable growth can be attributed to the advocacy of John Wesley (1703–91), a Church of England cleric who adopted the idea of a Sunday school and made it a central element of the Methodist movement.

John Wesley was a great supporter of education and was heavily influenced by the Moravians whose leading Christian educator had been John Amos Comenius (1592–1670) known for developing and popularizing the idea of textbooks and illustrated children's books. In 1748 Wesley started Kingswood School for the children of Methodist ministers and developed an extensive library of curriculum textbooks and resources, most of which he wrote himself.[19] Included among the many items in this library are *Hymns for Children*,[20] *Instructions for*

---

[19] Herbert W. Byrne, *John Wesley and Learning* (Salem, OH: Schmul, 1997), 151–53.

[20] Charles Wesley, *Hymns for Children* (Bristol: Printed by William Pine, 1768).

Children,[21] *Prayers for Children,*[22] *Lessons for Children,*[23] and *A Token for Children.*[24] His support of education and the Sunday school were instrumental in the success of both Methodism and the Sunday school movement.

A second major factor of the Sunday school's success was the formation of Sunday school societies and organizations made up of supporters who supplied books and other learning materials, meeting rooms, teachers, and training conferences. Most importantly for our curricular considerations, these groups also began producing curriculum related materials for use in the Sunday school.

In many communities, Sunday schools partnered with local churches and later were absorbed into the educational ministries of some of those local congregations and into the practice of their denominations. Having started out as one of the most popular and successful parachurch movements of the last two hundred years, the Sunday school led the way for the establishment of hundreds of other independent ministries to follow (youth organizations, campus ministries, study centers, mission groups). Like the Sunday school, many of these parachurch ministries also developed curricula and related materials. Christian publishing companies were established that focused exclusively on producing pre-packaged curriculum materials (see fig. 4.1), while others specialized in publishing books and materials for general Christian growth, education, and study; a few of the larger ones today are Thomas Nelson, Zondervan, Tyndale House, Baker, and B&H.

---

[21] John Wesley, *Instructions for Children*, 2nd ed. (Printed for M. Cooper, at the Globe in Paternoster-Row, 1745). The book is based on a French work by Abbe Fleury and M. Pierre that Wesley translated and adapted. He also added a catechism to the front.

[22] John Wesley, *Prayers for Children* (Bristol: Printed by William Pine, 1772). This work included morning and evening prayers for a week.

[23] John Wesley, *Lessons for Children* (Bristol: Printed by Felix Farley in the year, 1746). A teaching guide of 400 pages for the Old Testament and Apocrypha.

[24] James Janeway and John Wesley, *A Token for Children: Extracted from a Late Author, by John Wesley* (Bristol: Printed by Felix Farley; and sold at the School-Room in the Horse-Fair: also by T. Trye, near Gray's-Inn Gate, Holborn; and at the Foundery near Upper-Moor-Fields, London, 1749). An abridgement of James Janeway's account of the lives and deaths of pious children with a preface warning about dying unconverted.

Over the years many of these publishers have come and gone, merged with other Christian publishers, or, most recently, been adopted by secular publishers.[25]

Publishers of Prepackaged Curriculum	
Abingdon Press	Kidmo!
Augsburg Fortress	LifeWay Christian Resources
Big Idea	One Accord Resources
Christian Reformed Church Publications	Positive Action for Christ
	Presbyterian Church-U.S.A.
Cokesbury	Regular Baptist Press
Concordia Publishing House	Seasons of the Spirit
David C. Cook	Smith & Helwys
Desiring God Ministries	Standard Publishing
Faith & Life Resources	Through the Bible
FamilyWise	Union Gospel Press
Gospel Light	Willow Creek
Gospel Publishing House	WordAction Publishing Company
Group Publishing	

Figure 4.1: Publishers of Prepackaged Curriculum

The combination of Sunday school societies, denominations, and parachurch organizations developing curriculum materials for the church has led to a tremendous increase in choices and resources for use in Christian education. The rise of social science as a distinct discipline of study occurred alongside the growth of these curricular partners of the Sunday school movement. The application of social science theory and research to the formal curriculum development of the church has been the major influence of the present age.[26] This, combined with the post-reformation decentralizing of church curriculum

---

[25] The Evangelical Christian Publishers Association is a trade organization formed in 1974 and made up of many of these publishers. See *www.ecpa.org.*

[26] Robert W. Lynn and Elliot Wright, *The Big Little School: 200 Years of the Sunday School* (Birmingham, AL: Religious Education Press, 1971, 1980). Cf. William Clayton Bower, *The Curriculum of the Religious Education* (New York: Charles Scribner's Sons, 1925).

planning, creates the challenges and opportunities for Christian educators and curriculum developers for which this book was written. In the next section a few concluding points drawn from this review of curricular maps and approaches throughout history are offered as a starting point for the educational mapmakers of today as they consider the curriculum task before them, a task that will be further explored in the chapters to follow.

Learning from Historical Perspectives

One of the difficulties in learning from history is being able to gain sufficient objectivity for considering the significance of the past. In the grander scheme of church curriculum history, it is too soon to know where all the present day educational maps and approaches will ultimately lead the church as a community. New media channels and Internet connectivity provide the latest challenges for curriculum development, design, and delivery. Any attempts to analyze, survey, learn from, and utilize historical curricular maps, trends, and approaches require the long view. The observations on curriculum made in each section of this chapter have attempted to follow this principle.

One history of Protestant curriculum theory written by Mary Jo Osterman identifies four areas of curricular struggle over the last two hundred years. These include (1) the scope of curriculum (doctrine vs. Scripture, content-as-knowledge vs. content-as-experience, Bible-centered vs. life-centered), (2) the grouping used in curriculum (uniform lessons for all ages vs. graded lessons), (3) the focus of the curriculum, the nature of its aims (curriculum aims vs. religious education aims, religious life now vs. preparation for tomorrow), and (4) the teaching-learning model assumed in the curriculum (catechetical vs. expository vs. experiential).[27] Osterman's analysis reveals how quickly best practices and curricular theory can change in one short span of church history.

---

[27] Mary Jo Osterman, "The Two Hundred Year Struggle for Protestant Religious Education Curriculum Theory," *Religious Education* 75, no. 5 (September-October 1980): 528–38.

One place for curriculum developers and mapmakers to start is with curricular approaches and archival maps that have proven themselves beyond the two hundred years of curricular history associated with the Sunday school movement. "Top ten" types of lists are generated periodically in our society as an entertaining way to indicate popularity of items in a category. In a sense, curriculum developers are interested in top ten lists of church curricula to identify what has stood the test of time, not just curricula on the current bestseller list. What curricular materials and approaches has God seemed to bless and the Holy Spirit seemed to use beyond just a short season? For example, a number of books are considered Christian classics because many people in many ways over many time periods have found them useful in their Christian life. Books like St. Augustine's *Confessions* (AD 398), Catherine of Sienna's *The Dialogue of Divine Providence* (1378), Thomas à Kempis's *The Imitation of Christ* (c. 1427), John Calvin's *The Institutes of the Christian Religion* (1536), John Foxe's *Book of Martyrs* (1563), St. Teresa of Avila's *The Interior Castle* (1577), St. John of the Cross's *Dark Night of the Soul* (1586), John Milton's *Paradise Lost* (1667), John Bunyon's *The Pilgrim's Progress*[28] (1678), Jonathan Edwards's *A Treatise Concerning Religious Affections* (1746) are just a few. Attempts to list the best books or curricula inevitably leave out the favorite titles of some and reflect the inevitable limitations of finite compilers. Nevertheless, items on these lists are a good place to start as are the many other works mentioned throughout this chapter.[29]

There are many more examples of classic curriculum materials and approaches than could possibly be mentioned in a chapter of this length. Others have also provided helpful analyses and histories of curricular themes in the church's educational ministry that are useful in addressing and struggling with the historical limitations all curriculum

---

[28] For educators called to help one another on our respective journeys, much can be gleaned from the travel accounts of other pilgrims on the trail. Is it any wonder that one of the most read books in all of church history besides the Bible is *Pilgrim's Progress*, the story of a traveler on a journey?

[29] Collections of time-tested sermons, devotionals, and prayers serve a similar purpose.

developers face.[30] The examples in these works and those given above provide a starting place for identifying the best and most widely used curricula materials and approaches in church history. From these sources ideas, examples, direction, and inspiration can be drawn for current day use in curriculum planning.

Key Terms and Concepts

Kerygma	Liturgy
Didache	Scholasticism
Catechism	

Reflection Questions

1. Why are new believers often directed to the book of John as a starting point for their curriculum journey of faith?
2. Why do pocket Bibles of the New Testament sometimes include Psalms and Proverbs?
3. What are timeless and essential components that every curriculum should include?
4. Which of the time periods was most interesting to you? Why?

---

[30] See John H. Westerhoff and O. C. Edwards, eds., *A Faithful Church: Issues in the History of Catechesis* (Wilton, CT: Morehouse-Barlow, 1981); J. I. Packer and Gary A. Parrett, *Grounded in the Gospel*; Gary A. Parrett and S. Steve Kang, *Teaching the Faith, Forming the Faithful: A Biblical Vision for Education in the Church* (Downers Grove, IL: InterVarsity, 2009).

Appendices

Appendix 4.1

Excerpts from the *Didache*[31] [latter half of the first century/early second century AD]:

There are two ways, one to life and one to death, but the difference between the two is great. (1.1)

Do not be the sort of person who holds out hands to receive but draws them back when it comes to giving. (4.5)

Let everyone who comes in the name of the Lord be received, and then, when you have taken stock of the person, you will know—for you will have insight—what is right and false. If the person who comes in is just passing through, help as much as you can, but the person should not stay with you more than two or three days—if that is necessary. (12.1–2)

Appendix 4.2

Excerpt from *On Schoolmasters and Their Difficulties*[32] by Tertullian [early third century AD]:

We know it may be said, "If teaching literature is not lawful to God's servants, neither will learning be likewise;" and, "How could one be trained unto ordinary human intelligence, or unto any sense or action whatever, since literature is the means of training for all life? How do we repudiate secular studies, without which divine studies cannot be pursued?" Let us see, then, the necessity of literary erudition; let us reflect that partly it cannot be admitted, partly cannot be avoided. Learning literature is allowable for believers, rather than teaching; for the principle of learning and of teaching is different.

---

[31] Based on the translation of Kurt Niederwimmer, *The Didache: A Commentary* (Minneapolis: Fortress Press, 1998), 59, 103, 183, 185.

[32] Tertullian, "On School Masters and Their Difficulties," in *On Idolatry*, chap. X, translated by Sydney Thelwall. Online: http://en.wikisource.org/wiki/Ante-Nicene_Fathers/Volume_III/Apologetic/On_Idolatry/Of_Schoolmasters_and_Their_Difficulties.

Appendix 4.3

Excerpt from *On the Instruction of Beginners*[33] by Augustine [fifth century AD]:

If this discourse, in which I have supposed myself to have been teaching some uninstructed person in my presence, appears to you to be too long, you are at liberty to expound these matters with greater brevity. I do not think, however, that it ought to be longer than this. At the same time, much depends on what the case itself, as it goes on, may render advisable, and what the audience actually present shows itself not only to bear, but also to desire (*De catechizandis rudibus*, 26.51).

Appendix 4.4

Excerpt from *Letter to Laeta* (*On a Girl's Education*)[34] by Jerome [fifth century AD]:

Let her begin by learning the psalter, and then let her gather rules of life out of the proverbs of Solomon. From the Preacher let her gain the habit of despising the world and its vanities. Let her follow the example set in Job of virtue and of patience. Then let her pass on to the gospels never to be laid aside when once they have been taken in hand. Let her also drink in with a willing heart the Acts of the Apostles and the Epistles. As soon as she has enriched the storehouse of her mind with these treasures, let her commit to memory the prophets, the heptateuch, the books of Kings and of Chronicles, the rolls also of Ezra and Esther. When she has done all these she may safely read the Song of Songs but not before: for, were she to read it at the beginning, she would fail to perceive that, though it is written in fleshly words, it is a marriage song of a spiritual bridal. And not understanding this she would suffer hurt from it. Let her avoid all apocryphal writings, and

---

[33] Translated by S.D.F. Salmond, in *Nicene and Post-Nicene Fathers*, First Series, vol. 3, ed. Philip Schaff (Buffalo, NY: Christian Literature Publishing Co., 1887). Online: http://www.newadvent.org/fathers/1303.htm. Revised and edited for New Advent by Kevin Knight.

[34] Robert Ulrich, ed., *Three Thousand Years of Educational Wisdom: Selections from Great Documents* (Cambridge, MA: Harvard, 1950), 168–69.

if she is led to read such not by the truth of the doctrines which they contain but out of respect for the miracles contained in them; let her understand that they are not really written by those to whom they are ascribed, that many faulty elements have been introduced into them, and that it requires infinite discretion to look for gold in the midst of dirt. Cyprian's writings let her have always in her hands. The letters of Athanasius and the treatises of Hilary she may go through without fear of stumbling. Let her take pleasure in the works and wits of all in whose books a due regard for the faith is not neglected. But if she reads the works of others let it be rather to judge them than to follow them.

Appendix 4.5

Excerpt from the *Heidelberg Catechism*:[35]

Question 1. What is thy only comfort in life and death?
Answer: That I with body and soul, both in life and death, am not my own, but belong unto my faithful Saviour Jesus Christ; who, with his precious blood, has fully satisfied for all my sins, and delivered me from all the power of the devil; and so preserves me that without the will of my heavenly Father, not a hair can fall from my head; yea, that all things must be subservient to my salvation, and therefore, by his Holy Spirit, He also assures me of eternal life, and makes me sincerely willing and ready, henceforth, to live unto him.

Question 2. How many things are necessary for thee to know, that thou, enjoying this comfort, mayest live and die happily?
Answer: Three, the first, how great my sins and miseries are; the second, how I may be delivered from all my sins and miseries; the third, how I shall express my gratitude to God for such deliverance.

---

[35] Online: http://www.ccel.org/creeds/heidelberg-cat.html.

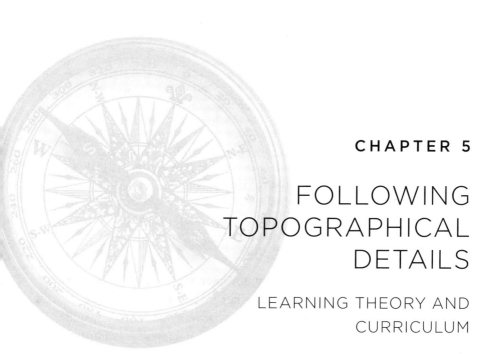

CHAPTER 5

FOLLOWING TOPOGRAPHICAL DETAILS

LEARNING THEORY AND CURRICULUM

Karen Lynn Estep

Traveling through the American southwest, one can see the topography in the bluffs and buttes lining the interstate highways. The best roads follow the topography of the land, bending and curving with it whenever possible, making the trip far more enjoyable and easier to navigate. Topography is the observation, study, and mapping of surface land features and their interrelationships. It includes features that are both naturally occurring as well as those intentionally constructed. Topography is useful for the engineering of roads. In this chapter, topography is a metaphor for the use of learning theories, because like topography they came about through the study of learning and learners. Theorists have used observation, study, and mapping to understand how various individuals learn naturally and in intentionally constructed environments. Understanding major learning theories prepares us for curriculum journeying with the church.

This view of preparing for a journey by ascertaining the topography is like the story in Numbers 13 when the spies instructed by Moses set out to explore Canaan:

> Go up through the Negev and on into the hill country. See what the land is like and whether the people who live there are strong or weak, few or many. What kind of land do they live in? Is it good or bad? What kind of towns do they live in? Are they unwalled or fortified? How is the soil? Is it fertile or poor? Are there trees on it or not? Do your best to bring back some of the fruit of the land. (Num 13:17b–20)

When God's people were preparing to enter Canaan, they set out to observe the land. Joshua and the other spies, in an effort to prepare, looked at the people and the land, what was both naturally and unnaturally occurring. In the same way that topography is helpful in the preparation and engineering of road construction, educators use learning theories to understand the best curricular route for learners.

Understanding the relationship between human development and environmental influences on learning prepares us to teach to the diverse needs of individuals as well as cultural groups within the church. When Christian educators are prepared in this way, they are able to make adaptations and accommodations to the curriculum that ultimately affects cognitive (knowledge), affective (disposition), and psychomotor (skills) learning. Using the topography metaphor, this means educators should have an understanding of the learner's needs and may find themselves building bridges, tunnels, and such to accommodate them. In this way, topography is similar to a discussion of how people learn.

Learning theories are the focus of this chapter. They have proven essential for creating and developing curriculum. This chapter includes sections on the capacity of learning, theoretical approaches to learning, and its significance for Christian education. Both capacity and theoretical approaches help shape our understanding of diverse students within the context of culture and congregations locally and around the world. Thus, along with learning theories or psychological understanding, educators need to recognize the effect of socio-cultural influences on learners and their learning environment. It is essential to Christian educators to build a curriculum that can survive multiple terrains, as the church must have a multicultural and global approach to education (Acts 2:1–21). Thus, the topography for the church is the observation of learners, the study of their diverse and changing needs, and the mapping of what they need to know and how to teach.

What Do Learning Theories Have to Do with Curriculum?

The development of curriculum is dependent on understanding the learner. Thus, educators have been studying and recording their observation of learners for years and creating various theories. As a result, a number of learning theories guide educators in curriculum development. The use of social science research is critical for teaching the curriculum of the kingdom. Often the findings of social science are formalized statements of commonly observed phenomenon. Scripture itself imparts such observations that shed light on effective learning, and some of the same insights are echoed by the social science research findings. These observations include:

1. *Who should teach:* Passing wisdom to the next two generations is the responsibility of parents (Deut 4:9–10).
2. *What are the ideal outcomes and objectives:* To grow in wisdom and stature, and in favor with God and men (Luke 2:52).
3. *What are acceptable methodologies:* Memorization of the law, routine observances, practices and celebration of the feast days, and sacraments such as prayer (i.e., Exod 20:8; Deuteronomy 16; Dan 6:10; Acts 2:46).
4. *What are ideal learning environments:* The integration of teaching in the application of daily living (Deut 6:7; 11:19; Ezra 7:10).
5. *What should the content consist of:* Practical instructions on living life for God come in the form of entire books, such as the five books of the Pentateuch, Proverbs, and James.

Based on various learning theories, curriculum development and design describe how learners actually learn and prescribe a terrain-sensitive path for learning. The learner is only a piece of the terrain, and the study of the entire terrain is topography. The study of the learner directs the approach and development of the curriculum. How we accommodate the learner is like accommodating mountains, hills, rivers, and canyons where topography guides our decision to build tunnels, inclines, bridges, and alternative routes. In educational terms, learning theories guide our teaching, allowing us to use differentiated teaching methods to reach every learner. Learning theory, like topography, studies the features of the learner and determines the path for their educational journey. The development and design of the map is curriculum development and design. This is how learning theories relate to the curriculum.

The art of teaching is both a God-given gift (Rom 12:7; 1 Cor 12:28; Eph 4:11) and a scientific achievement. Achievement through the study of the social sciences has resulted in a body of research we have come to call learning theories. John Santrock notes that research knowledge applied to your teaching situations improves when you make judgments based on your skills, experiences, and accumulated wisdom from the community of educators.[1] The theories provide an understanding of how to teach various individuals. James Loder writes,

> Good theory in Christian education, then, like good theory in science or good theatre, or, more archaically, like envisioning and participating in a festival for the gods, is an on-going disclosure and articulation of a hidden higher order of things in relation to and in light of the Truth of God's self-revelation. It thereby invites our faithful holistic participation in God's on-going redemptive transformation of all creation.[2]

These theories are foundational to building a curriculum that meets the needs of every learner within the church, as practical theories are the result of the reflective observation of educators during their teaching experience. Educators must ask themselves if learning theories can aid them in the ministry of education, in particular with developing the curriculum. As Loder indicates, our use of this research is not without the discernment provided by the Spirit of God.

---

[1] John W. Santrock, *Educational Psychology*, 3rd ed. (New York: McGraw-Hill, 2008), 5.

[2] James E. Loder, "Transformational Christian Education: Educational Ministry in the Logic of the Spirit," ed. Donald Ratcliff, 8 [cited 31 January 2012]. Online: http://loder.ratcliffs.net/prefaceandchapterone.pdf.

Understanding the Capacity of Learning

Learning theories look at the capacity of the learner to acquire new information. In order to do a good job in educating, educators need to understand what influences a learner's capacity to acquire new material. Such understanding should also guide us in church curriculum decisions, though presently the definitions and descriptions of learning are not universally recognized, nor can they adequately address every situation of learning. Still, learning theories guide our understanding of individuals. Learners bring a set of unique attributes to the classroom and when we understand them as individuals, we can serve them better.

When we talk about developmental factors, there are three parts: the process of development, periods of development, and issues of development. Social science research has helped us understand each of these separately and, in doing so, identify the needs of individual learners, thus helping us develop a psychological understanding of individual learners. Figure 5.1 expresses the general tenor of contemporary learning theory.

Learning theory is influenced by several psychological factors (as will be described in the next section), the study of which provides the topography for the development and design of curriculum. When students participate in the curriculum, it affects the factors influencing how they learn, which once again cycles back to engage the factors that influenced the formation of learning theory.

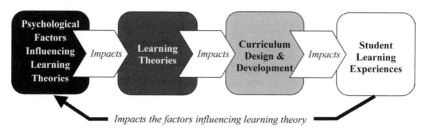

Figure 5.1: Learning Theories and Curriculum

Factors Influencing Learning Theory

Though there are many approaches to listing human developmental processes, Greg Carlson lists six separate processes of development as identified by theorists: physical, cognitive, social, affective, moral and faith/spiritual.[3] Likewise, while we endeavor to understand the process of development by separating each for discussion and exploration, we must also realize they do not occur or develop separately. The same is true in a survey of land. Topography considers both individual details of the terrain and how they relate or work together as a whole. Several processes of developmental factors influence learning theory.[4] For example, Klaus Issler and Ronald Habermas contend that there are three learning families, a concept based on the work of Craig Dykstra: conditional learning, social learning, and information-processing.[5] While all of these families pertain to any developmental age group, Issler and Habermas note that there are certain needs at the developmental age level of children, youth, and adults.[6] Thus, human development, particularly the stage of life in which one lives, lends itself toward an optimal theory of learning, namely conditional learning for children, social learning for youth, and information-processing for adult learners.

Influential Issues in Forming Learning Theory

While a number of developmental issues affect the capacity to learn, educators generally recognize seven:

1. *Nature versus Nurture.* The question this developmental issue raises is this: which of the two plays a more dominant role in education? The answer to this question will impact one's understanding of the teaching-learning process and also the transformation process. The

---

[3] Greg Carlson, "Adult Life Cycle," in *Evangelical Dictionary of Christian Education*, ed. Michael J. Anthony (Grand Rapids: Baker, 2001), 32.

[4] See James Riley Estep Jr. and Jonathan H. Kim, eds., *Christian Formation: The Integration of Theology and Human Development* (Nashville: B&H, 2010) for a comprehensive survey of human development theories.

[5] Craig Dykstra, "Learning theory," in *Harper's Encyclopedia of Religious Education*, ed. Iris V. Cully and Kendig B. Cully (San Francisco: Harper & Row, 1990).

[6] Klaus Issler and Ronald Habermas, *How We Learn: A Christian Teacher's Guide to Educational Psychology* (Grand Rapids: Baker, 1994), 55.

church must realize that learning is not only affected by one's natural ability but also by one's experience and circumstances. If churches only focus on natural development and expectations of growth, how will they minister to those who have been affected by the sins of the world? Therefore, the church cannot assume that believers will by nature mature and grow in their newfound faith. It must seek to nurture its learners by capitalizing on current and past experiences and helping the learner understand how these life experiences ought to conform them to the image of Christ.

2. *Continuity and Discontinuity.* Again, the question is which takes precedence? Does human development involve *gradual* cumulative change known as continuity or does it have *distinct stages* called discontinuity?[7] Christian educators should not rely on one over the other in determining outcomes, but should realize that both are present and essential to learning. Otherwise, the education ministry is limited and either will not allow learners time to meet the objectives fully or will believe that the learner's change should be immediate rather than a continual process. For example, an addict makes a commitment to Christ (this is discontinuity in that it represents a stage), yet change may take longer as the addict grows spiritually, having no prior understanding or experiences, versus someone who has lived a fairly pious life attending church (continuity) but is making a commitment to Christ.

3. *Early and Late Experiences.* This third issue is also about precedence and dominance. Some argue that early experiences are essential and late experiences are not. Yet both are important, though not always possible. It is understood that education that does not meet the needs of individuals throughout their lives will not be as effective. Thus, the church needs to plan for individuals at every stage and realize the need for children, youth, family, young adult, adult, and senior ministries. However, it is also understood that at any stage there are new members who do not have the early experiences which allow for more practice, skill building, and time to develop their learning. To meet their needs churches develop new members classes to teach basic bible content and small groups that will meet their discipleship needs.

---

[7] Santrock, *Educational Psychology*, 30.

4. *Individual Variations*. Humans are unique with their individual talents and gifting, and there are multiple theories about these variations as it concerns learning. Robert J. Sternberg argues there are three forms of intelligence: analytical, creative, and practical. Students who dominate in any of the three look different in the education setting. Typically, those with high analytic ability tend to be favored.[8] Because tasks usually require all, it is important that classroom instructions provide learning opportunities through all three types of intelligence.

Howard Gardner developed eight frames of mind or types of intelligences. He postulates that these intelligences are the result of an evolutionary development within humans—that the intelligences were part of the human brain's development to ensure the survival of the human species.[9] His theory argues that, while all intelligences should be used in education, not all should be used for every type of teaching or learning.[10] Gardner initially formulated a provisional list of seven intelligences. The first two have been typically valued in schools; the next three usually associated with the arts; and the final two are what Gardner called "personal intelligences."[11] An eighth one concerning naturalistic thinking has been added, and still others beyond Gardner have proposed additional intelligences about life issues reflecting on religion and philosophy.[12]

John Mayer and Peter Salovey have considered how to guide an individual's thinking and actions. They claim emotional intelligence is "the ability to monitor one's own and others' emotions and feelings, to discriminate among them, and to use the information to guide one's thinking and actions."[13] There are some similarities in understanding what these theories have in common, and Christian educators need to

---

[8] See ibid., 118–19.

[9] Howard Gardner, *Intelligence Reframed: Multiple Intelligences for the 21st Century* (New York: Basic Books, 1999).

[10] Cf. Santrock, *Educational Psychology*, 121.

[11] Gardner, *Intelligence Reframed*, 41–43.

[12] See The University of Oklahoma, College of Medicine, Department of Psychiatry and Behavioral Services, "What Are the Eight Multiple Intelligences?" [cited 31 January 2012]. Online: http://www.oumedicine.com/workfiles/College%20of%20Medicine/AD-Psychiatry/What%20Are%20the%208%20Multiple%20Intelligences.doc.

[13] Santrock, *Educational Psychology*, 121.

consider what contributes to intelligence and knowledge, developing their education ministry to allow for individual differences.

Christian education should be a combination of analytical, creative, and practical instruction, balancing all and using a variety of teaching methods while realizing and taking advantage of the belief that God created us differently so that we might contribute differently to the culture. Educators should go beyond teaching in only one or two of the intelligences. They must pay close attention to what contributes to learning and design programs that instruct in different learning domains beyond cognitive knowledge alone.

5. *Learning and Thinking Styles.* Learning and thinking styles is a reference to how individual preference affects learning. There are two distinctive styles in this area, which are widely discussed among educators: impulsive/reflective and deep/surface. The first compares the impulsivity and reflective nature of student response while the latter explores the approach taken by a student to learn information thoroughly or just on the surface.[14]

The relationship between learning and spirituality has been asserted for some time, but recent studies have further defined and substantiated this relationship. For example, a study conducted by Young Woon Lee demonstrated the positive tendency in the relationship between certain learning styles and spirituality styles.[15] His findings affirm that how an individual learns is a formative factor in how a learner describes or nurtures their relationship with God and others. Because learning styles are not uniform, spirituality will likewise be expressed across a broad spectrum.

For the church, this bears significance within the faith community and has a direct impact on the type of teaching desired by educators, since each teaching type, reflecting a given learning style, will have a different impact on learners and their spiritual formation.

---

[14] Ibid., 132–33.

[15] Young Woon Lee is Assistant Professor of Christian Education at Torch Trinity Graduate School of Theology in Seoul, Korea. Lee's study is an adaptation of a presentation given at the 19th NAPCE Annual Meeting of the North American Professors of Christian Education (NAPCE) held in San Diego, California, in October 1999 [cited 31 January 2012]. Online: http://www.ronnie johnson.info/files/Creative%20Teaching/wong_learning_style.pdf.

6. *Personality and Temperament.* Stella Chess and Alexander Thomas have led the research on personality and temperament. Personality is concerned with five factors: "emotional stability, extraversion, openness to experience, agreeableness, and conscientiousness."[16] Temperament is concerned with behavior and response.[17] There are three basic categories. (1) *Easy child* with a positive mood, has established routines as a baby, and adapts to new experiences. (2) *Difficult child* reacts negatively and engages in irregular routines and is slow to accept changes. (3) *Slow-to-warm-up* has low activity, is negative, and displays a low intensity of mood.[18]

While Christian educators may find any of the personality and temperament traits more acceptable than another, the reality is that the community of the church contains this diversity, and educators need to adapt strategies that will enable them to work with individuals exhibiting all of these diverse traits.

7. *Sociocultural Diversity.* This factor on learning has four components: culture and ethnicity (which includes the various influences of culture, socioeconomic status, ethnicity, and even bilingualism), gender, disabilities, and giftedness. The establishment of a ministry may sometimes focus on one or more of these variations. However, as a community grows, the diversity also increases. Thus, it is important for the ministry to adapt to the context or needs of the diverse learners. Often the education ministry has tried to transfer educational materials made for one context to another without fully understanding socio-cultural diversity. These ministries have failed due to the lack of transferability. The church that serves only part of the population will not reach the world or the neighborhood. Educators are encouraged to broaden their understanding of learning in an effort to reach the various needs of diverse learners, to seek change in the way teaching takes place, and to

---

[16] Santrock, *Educational Psychology*, 135.

[17] Cf. Stella Chess and Alexander Thomas, "Temperamental Individuality from Childhood to Adolescence," in *Journal of the American Academy of Child Psychiatry* 16, no. 2 (Spring 1977): 218–26; A. Thomas and S. Chess, "Temperament in Adolescence and Its Functional Significance," in *Encyclopedia of Adolescence* 2, ed. R. R. Lerner, A. C. Petersen, and J. Brooks-Gunn (New York: Garland, 1991) as cited in Santrock, *Educational Psychology*, 136.

[18] Ibid.

expand their thinking about the capacity of learners in relation to these developmental issues.

Theoretical Approaches to Learning

Behavioral and cognitive theories dominated research in the twentieth century. However, the ancient humanist philosophy became the new trend in the 1940s and 1950s. Humanism aided in the development of a new approach to research involving feelings, attitudes, and hopes and the interrelatedness of these theories, not their independence, with the belief that the best contexts for observing learners are in the complexity of their daily life and environments.[19] This integration of theories resulted in the formation of new approaches to learning theory in the late twentieth century. The terminology has essentially remained the same, dominated by behaviorist and cognitivist theories. However, social and constructivist theories have also been added and integrated to form four major perspectives: Behaviorist, Cognitivist, Social Perspective, and Constructivist.

The remainder of the chapter will focus on a contemporary grouping of the predominant theoretical approaches to learning just identified and endeavor to explain the reason for the grouping while outlining the significance for Christian education. These approaches have changed since the last century as our understanding broadens with new research. The five categories are Behavioral, Social Cognitive, Information-Processing, Cognitive Constructivist, and Social Constructivist (see fig. 5.2).[20]

Behavioral Learning

Behaviorist perspectives "view all behavior as a response to external stimuli. . . . According to behaviorists, the learner acquires behaviors, skills and knowledge in response to the rewards, punishments, or withheld responses associated with them."[21] Key theorists include Ivan

---

[19] Wilma S. Longstreet and Harold G. Shane, *Curriculum for a New Millennium* (Boston: Allyn and Bacon, 1993), 133.

[20] Adapted from Santrock, *Educational Psychology*, 228 (fig. 7.1).

[21] Judy Lever-Duffy, Jean B. McDonald and A. P. Mizell, *Teaching and Learning with Technology*, 2nd ed. (Boston: Pearson Education, 2005), 14.

Behavioral	Social Cognitive	Information-Processing	Constructivist Cognitive	Social
Examination and assessment of experience, especially reinforcement and punishment as determinants of learning and behavior	Interaction of behavior within a specific social environment, and personal-cognitive factors are the driving forces of learning	Elements such as attention, memory, thinking, and other cognitive processes are means by which learners process information	Emphasis on the individual learner's ability to construct knowledge and understanding from information	Emphasis on the individual-within-society, collaborative process of constructing knowledge and understanding

Figure 5.2: Theoretical Approaches to Learning

Pavlov, John Watson, and B. F. Skinner. Behavioral learning focuses on "how external stimuli (S) can cause a reflexive response (R) within a living organism."[22] Dean Blevins notes there are two basic types of learning: classical conditioning (involuntary responses) and operant conditioning (voluntary responses). However, the basis of learning for both is external forces that can manipulate and change behavior. Classical conditioning, a concept developed by Ivan Pavlov, recognizes learning as "a form of associative learning in which a neutral stimulus becomes associated with a meaningful stimulus and acquires the capacity to elicit a similar response."[23] Operant conditioning is a concept developed by B. F. Skinner who built his ideas from E. L. Thorndike's Law of Effect principle, which states "that behaviors followed by positive outcomes, are strengthened and that behaviors followed by negative outcomes are weakened."[24] This is sometimes called instrumental conditioning. According to instrumental conditioning (as explained

---

[22] Dean Blevins, "Learning Theories," in *Evangelical Dictionary of Christian Education*, ed. Michael J. Anthony (Grand Rapids: Baker, 2001), 420.

[23] Santrock, *Educational Psychology*, 229.

[24] Ibid., 232.

by Thorndike) learning is best accomplished through (1) the learner's readiness to learn being psychologically adjusted, (2) repetitive ongoing practice or exercise, and (3) the learner's recognition of the tangible effect of the learning that brings about emotional satisfaction.[25]

Iris Cully, in summarizing the nature of Christian learning, recognizes the value of positive reinforcement in behavioral learning when she states, "When work is rewarded, people are encouraged to continue because of the approval."[26] While there is no reason to restrict our understanding of teaching to rewards, her words echo the importance of rewards as motivators in the realm of behavioral learning. Early research suggests rewards are only external on the part of the educator; further review of the contemporary research suggests that there is more to understand.

Christian educators have recognized the limitations of this learning theory for use in the church. In Christian education, behavior is seen as *more* than a reaction to a given stimuli, but the result of a more holistic view of the individual. Behavior involves more than mere reaction, but can be an intellectual process or even resulting from one's own imagination.[27] For the Christian educator, human behavior is more than an animalistic reaction to stimuli, but a part of being made in God's image (Gen 1:27–28) and the change of behaviors accompanied by transformation in Christ (1 Cor 6:9–11). Likewise, the impetus for change in an individual need not be an external stimuli, but may well be a guilty or repentant heart when confronted with sin, such as in the case of Zachaeus' encounter with Christ (Luke 19:1–9). Behaviors may indeed be the result of stimuli, but not all behaviors are mere responses to stimuli. Behaviorism has some helpful insights, but not the definitive insights needed for a comprehensive learning theory.

Therefore, curriculum within the church that emphasizes behavioral learning theory should broaden the design to account for the three laws of learning. (1) Learners need to be prepared to learn physically and mentally. If not, educators need to focus on the learner's needs,

---

[25] Ibid., 262.

[26] Iris V. Cully, *Planning and Selecting Curriculum for Christian Education* (Valley Forge, VA: Judson, 1983), 86–87.

[27] Cf. T. A. Francoeur, "Behaviorism," in *Encyclopedia of Religious Education* (San Francisco: Harper and Row, 1990), 58.

i.e., food, clothing, rest, shelter, safety, a sense of belonging (thus, the reason for medical mission trips and similar works). (2) Curriculum which has been designed to focus on memorization and the repetition or practice of skills is beneficial to understanding. Examples include weekly memory work and quiz competitions. (3) Educators need to continue to motivate students with a focus on positive rewards for appropriate learning. While there may be some negative consequences, these would be minimal.

Teachers should focus on the Law of Effect, where learning has a positive experience, rather than a negative one of punishment. Educational programs should develop curricular outcomes that are expressed in terms of behaviors. For example, perhaps a congregation identifies behavioral benchmarks for a spiritually mature believer with a curriculum designed to facilitate these behaviors; hence, it measures one's spiritual formation based on positive behaviors. Children's programs should seek to use tangible positive reinforcement to reinforce desired behaviors and practices. For example, some programs for elementary aged students provide awards for Scripture memorization, doing chores at home, or inviting others to church. Some churches develop programs with tiered curriculum requirements, providing instruction at increasing levels of commitment and difficulty, but gives awards for completing classes and certificates for the completion of a given level of study. While the church should not feel obligated to constantly reward positive behaviors, doing so selectively benefits the individual and the congregation.

Social Cognitive Learning

Social perspectives believe that "people learn from one another, via observation, imitation, and modeling. The theory has often been called a bridge between behaviorist and cognitive learning theories because it encompasses attention, memory, and motivation."[28] It is not like behavioral learning as this theory focuses on the individual's ability to transform their experiences and thoughts into learning. Albert Bandura,

---

[28] Learning Theories Knowledgebase, "Social Learning Theory (Bandura)," Learning-Theories.com. Online: http://www.learning-theories.com/social-learning-theory-bandura.html.

the main architect of social cognitive theory "emphasizes reciprocal influences of behavior, environment, and personal/cognitive factors."[29] Therefore, when students learn, they can cognitively represent or transform their experiences. Bandura created a model to explain observational learning and its four processes: attention, retention, production, and motivation.[30] Within this theory are the cognitive behavior approaches which focus on "changing behavior by getting individuals to monitor, manage, and regulate their own behavior rather than letting it be controlled by external factors" as in behavioral learning.[31] The significance of Bandura's theory for Christian educators is in the understanding that

> People are neither driven by inner forces nor automatically shaped and controlled by external stimuli. Rather, human functioning is explained in terms of a model of triadic reciprocality in which behavior, cognitive and other personal factors, and environmental events all operate as interacting determinants of each other. The nature of persons is defined within this perspective in terms of a number of basic capabilities.[32]

The application to curriculum is that it must reach beyond the classroom to allow for various social, cultural, and environmental forces to establish the standard for behavior. Learning is founded on the standard which is established through culture and environmental forces. Though the individual is able to change his behavior, it is nonetheless established through cultural norms—thus the need for the church to establish the cultural norms and the realization that one community may establish this slightly different from another when doing cross cultural ministry work.

As one comprehends this theory, perhaps the words of Paul come to mind: "Do not be misled: 'Bad company corrupts good character'" (1 Cor 15:33), but the following verse provides even more insight: "Come back to your senses as you ought, and stop sinning; for there

---

[29] Santrock, *Educational Psychology*, 243.

[30] Ibid., 244–45.

[31] Ibid., 249.

[32] Albert Bandura, *Social Foundations of Thought and Action: A Social Cognitive Theory* (Englewood Cliffs, NJ: Prentice-Hall, 1986), 18.

are some who are ignorant of God—I say this to your shame" (1 Cor 15:34). While no one can deny that we learn within a social context, our learning is neither limited to that context, nor is social learning irresistible. The Christian lives in two meta-contexts: the world and the church. Yet Paul asserts, "Do not conform to the pattern of this world, but be transformed by the renewing of your mind" (Rom 12:2a). Scripture would indicate that while learning may occur under the influence of our context, it is not determined solely by contextual learning factors.

While these theories grew out of a reaction to one another, missionary Peter Wagner applies both behavioral theories and social cognitive theory to multicultural training. He notes that classical conditioning, operant conditioning, and imitation learning can each "contribute significantly to understanding others in a multicultural context and thus to effective religious education within that context."[33] There is the potential for a growing understanding of the work of God from other cultural viewpoints when one works within multicultural settings. Iris Cully's reflection on Christian education states, "People can learn through all of their experiences. . . . Materials also should arouse the curiosity of learners by encouraging broad and deeper exploration. . . . Learning occurs when the needs of the learners are being met."[34] Both of these reflections from Christian educators advocate the use of multiple theories for various reasons in the design of the curriculum.

The education ministry's curriculum is most often delivered to groups: youth groups, small groups, and discipleship groups. While individual study is indeed profitable, group studies are typically regarded as being more beneficial for learning. This learning theory emphasizes the influence and importance of learning groups within the church and a curriculum designed to facilitate dialogue between participants that is relevant to the age or life situation of the group. Likewise, groups that are more task-oriented, such as service/ministry groups or cross-cultural missions groups, facilitate learning between individuals.

---

[33] Barbara Wilkerson, *Multicultural Religious Education* (Birmingham, AL: Religious Education Press, 1997), 102.

[34] Cully, *Planning and Selecting Curriculum for Christian Education*, 86–87.

Information-Processing Theory

Cognitivist perspectives view behavior as a measurement of cognitive processes rather than an outcome of learning. The "focus [is] on learning as a mental operation that takes place when information enters through the senses, undergoes mental manipulation, is stored, and is finally used."[35] The focus is on the internal learning not the external behavior. Key theorists are Jerome Bruner, David Ausubel, and the early works of Jean Piaget. Included in this group are theories of information-processing in which the "learner calculates, classifies, coordinates, contemplates, and criticizes information."[36] The term "cognitive psychology" initially explained and examined mental process behavior. Ironically, the cognitive psychologists drew their analogies for memory from the newly invented computer in the late 1940s with the realization that a computer could perform logical operations.[37]

Information-processing is focused on one's ability to transform his or her experiences and thoughts into learning. It is a cognitive approach in which learners watch, manipulate, and strategize their information in the cognitive process of both memorizing and thinking.[38] Several individuals have helped develop this concept of information-processing and various versions of this cognitive theory. Information-processing describes the learner's drive to make meaning of the world through the process of acquiring and organization, sensing problems and finding solutions, and developing a means for conveying answers through concepts and language.[39] This approach is concerned with resources such as capacity and speed of processing and how our brain functions in learning using encoding, automaticity, and strategy construction to grasp knowledge. Three significant models of memory are Baddeley's Working Memory Model, the Atkinson-Shiffrin Model,[40] and Michael

---

[35] Lever-Duffy, McDonald, and Mizell, *Teaching and Learning with Technology*, 15.

[36] Issler and Habermas, *How We Learn*, 51; Cf. Santrock, *Educational Psychology*, 264.

[37] Santrock, *Educational Psychology*, 264.

[38] Ibid., 267.

[39] Bruce Joyce, Marsha Weil, and Beverly Showers, *Models of Teaching*, 4th ed. (Englewood Cliffs, NJ: Prentice Hall, 1992), 71.

[40] Santrock, *Educational Psychology*, 275–76.

Pressley and colleagues' Good Information-Processing Model, which describes three steps for children to become good at cognition.[41]

Shelly Cunningham states,

> In our teaching of the Bible, the goal is to move information that can lead to transformed lives from the sensory register stage of memory into long-term storage. Learning is easier and remembered longer when the material is rehearsed, well orga-nized, related to old information, and perceived as meaningful and significant by the learner.[42]

She echoes the sentiments of Cully who writes, "Repetition and rein-forcement are essential elements in learning. . . . An optimum amount of repetition leads to memorization of words or actions, an increase in skills, and the feeling of assurance that comes from competence."[43] Thus, the memorization of God's Word and rehearsal of various skills for deciphering Scripture are essential to learning.

While on the surface this theory seems ideal to the study of God's Word—ever increasing complexity and deeper understanding, along with an impetus to think more theologically—once again, Scripture was not intended to be solely processed intellectually. Reason must be used to comprehend God's revelation, but there is more to appropriat-ing God's Word into one's life than just the intellectual processing of its contents. Second Timothy 3:14–17 provides a broader concept of process. Paul speaks of the intellectual processing of Scripture, "how from infancy you have *known* the Holy Scriptures, which are able to make you *wise* for salvation through faith in Christ Jesus" (v. 15, empha-sis added). However, he also speaks to the more affective, application aspect of Scripture, a processing of Scripture into life itself, "for teach-ing, rebuking, correcting, and training in righteousness" (v. 16b). He concludes by expressing that Scripture has also "thoroughly equipped [us] for every good work" (v. 17), indicating an active purpose of God's Word. Likewise, James warns his readers, "Do not merely listen to the word, and so deceive yourselves. *Do what it says*" (Jas 1:22, emphasis

---

[41] Ibid., 293.

[42] Shelly Cunningham, "Information processing," in *Evangelical Dictionary of Christian Education*, ed. Michael J. Anthony (Grand Rapids: Baker, 2001), 363.

[43] Cully, *Planning and Selecting Curriculum for Christian Education*, 86–87.

added). Scripture was not meant to be simply read or studied, filling the mind, but also the heart and hands of the believer.

This theory relates to curriculum in the design of teaching strategies or pedagogy. Educators must understand that in order to learn we must not simply hand out information but must also show the learner how it relates or is applicable. The church must transfer the biblical knowledge to the lives of the learner, making connections with what they know, addressing their needs, and making application. Additionally, learners need repetition and rehearsal of their understanding to develop skills and speed. This can only be done when adequate time is given to the content, in order to develop life skills and respond appropriately. Finally, the learner must manipulate or use the information making sense of its meaning and significance. All of this requires an education program and curriculum that leads the believer into a more comprehensive and thorough understanding of Scripture. Congregations must provide tiered programming with the accompanying curriculum that enables believers to be life-long learners. Requiring the curriculum's content to increase in depth and complexity and for the teaching methods to reflect the increasing capabilities of the participants. Thus, the learner is moving from a passive receiver of information, such as listening to a lecture, to an active participant in a group study or even with the use of the library media center in an independent study directed by the congregation.

Constructivist Theory

Constructivist perspectives view knowledge as a constructed element that is the result of learning. Within this understanding, there are two different groups: cognitive constructivist and social constructivist. However, in both groups "knowledge is unique to the individual who constructs it."[44] A key cognitive constructivist is Jean Piaget. Cognitive constructivists view learning as a cognitive effort to construct understanding while social constructivists focus on the social effort to construct understanding from the culture or a group setting.

---

[44] Lever-Duffy, McDonald, and Mizell, *Teaching and Learning with Technology*, 15.

Key social constructivists include Robert Gagné, Lev Vygotsky, and Albert Bandura.

The cognitive constructivist model emphasizes the learner's cognitive construction of knowledge and understanding. Cognitive theorists believe that learning is a reorganization of perceptions. Some of the earliest research by Gestalt psychologist Ernst Mach, Max Wertheimer, and Wolfgang Kohler was conducted in the 1920s.

> It [Gestalt] is a form of psychology that is interested in higher order cognitive processes relative to behaviorism. The aspects of gestalt theory that interest designers are related to gestalt's investigations of visual perception, principally the relationship between the parts and the whole of visual experience. . . . The visual world is so complex that the mind has developed strategies for coping with the confusion. The mind tries to find the simplest solution to a problem. One of the ways it does this is to form groups of items that have certain characteristics in common.[45]

These characteristics are similarity, proximity, closure, and good continuation. Much like other theories, understanding develops through problem solving. For this theory, knowledge is constructed when the learner connects or sees relationships. Learning is recognizing relationships and connections between bodies of knowledge using these suggested characteristics.

Kurt Lewin developed a topological theory similar yet different from the Gestalt in which he emphasizes that learning experiences are determined by an overall pattern of events. He emphasizes personality, social psychology, and motivation, while the Gestaltists focus on perception, learning, and thinking. He contends that learning includes a variety of different phenomena from our complex psychological world.[46]

Gestalt theory was the forerunner laying the foundation for both Jean Piaget's and Jerome Bruner's cognitive theories. Piaget's view has very little consideration for the social or cultural influences but rather

---

[45] James T. Saw, "Gestalt," *Design Notes*, n.p. [cited 31 January 2012]. Online: http://daphne.palomar.edu/design/gestalt.html.

[46] Kurt Lewin, "Field Theory of Learning," *The Psychology of Learning* 41, no. 2 (Chicago: University of Chicago Press, 1942): 219–20, and Zais, *Curriculum: Principles and Foundations*, 283–84.

emphasizes four stages of development: sensorimotor, preoperational, concrete operational, and formal operational. Education is a process of refinement for cognitive skills that emerge on their own. Piaget's role for teachers is that of a facilitator and guide. He is an advocate of the learner's efforts to explore the world and discover knowledge.[47] Many developmentalists, also called neo-Piagetians, offer criticisms of Piaget's theory. Santrock documents five: (1) Estimates of children's competence is often earlier than he proposed. (2) Some cognitive abilities emerge later than he thought. (3) His assumption that the stages are developmental has been proven incorrect. (4) Children can be trained to reason at higher cognitive stages than he believed. (5) Culture and education play a larger role in education.[48] It is well recognized that Piaget has done much with this theory, but there is more to learn. Thus, there is no effort to throw out his research but rather to expand on it with the realization that the focus is on cognitive construction by the learner. However, Bruner asserts that cognitive construction comes about through discovery learning or exploration by the individual. He "found that discovery learning develops better problem-solving skills and greater confidence in the ability to learn."[49]

Christian educators need to develop curriculum that values the process of construction by the learner and acknowledges that such construction is different for each age group. It is a necessary strategy for teaching of any age. The learner needs the opportunity to work at solving age-appropriate problems, a process that will enable their cognitive construction of knowledge. For example, the young child exploring her world requires the Christian educator to guide her into that exploration with a biblical perspective. For the young adult, this is about looking at things with a Christian worldview and finding ways to react and to understand the information.

Social constructivist theorists focus on collaboration with others to produce knowledge and understanding. Lev Vygotsky is a key advocate for this theory, which emphasizes that knowledge is mutually

---

[47] Santrock, *Educational Psychology*, 53.

[48] Ibid., 46–47.

[49] William Yount, "Learning Theory for Christian Teachers," in *Introducing Christian Education Foundations for the Twenty-First Century*, ed. Michael Anthony (Grand Rapids: Baker, 2001), 105.

constructed. Learning takes place in relationship to society. Within this theory, various teaching approaches emphasizing group work have been developed: Situated cognition (context), scaffolding, cognitive apprenticeship, tutoring, cooperative learning, small groups, communities of learners, schools of thought, and collaborative school (parent-teacher cooperative).[50] With all of these approaches, learning becomes part of a community of learners that is actively constructing understanding.

Vygotsky, unlike Piaget, does not see learning in developmental stages but rather developed a theory called Zone of Proximal Development in which the learner is assisted by a peer to take on more responsibility. Education is important in teaching the tools of culture. The teacher is a facilitator and guide, as in cognitive constructivist theory, but is assisted in the role of teacher by the students' peers as well.[51]

Paul reasons, "When I was a child, I talked like a child, I thought like a child, I reasoned like a child. When I became a man, I put the ways of childhood behind me" (1 Cor 13:11). This verse almost lends itself to the constructivist learning theory. One's knowledge is constructed by the individual, and as the individual grows, changes, and develops throughout a lifetime, one's content and conclusions change as well. However, the presuppositions of constructivism are what most Christian educators find objectionable. It is one thing to suggest that as one studies Scripture, that the interpretation and comprehension of the meaning of a text may change over time, becoming more refined, or change in the relative relevance as it addresses different stages of life; but it is entirely another thing to suggest that there is *no* intended meaning in the text, only the meaning you give to it. In Scripture, the notion of truth is less malleable. Jesus prayed, "Sanctify them by the truth; your word is truth" (John 17:17). Paul argued in Romans that "the Jews have been entrusted with the very words of God. What if some were unfaithful? Will their unfaithfulness nullify God's faithfulness? Not at all! *Let God be true, and every human being a liar*" (Rom 3:2–4, emphasis added) and proceeds to quote Ps 51:4. One can readily see the connection between God's Word and the truth. For

---

[50] Santrock, *Educational Psychology*, 337.

[51] Ibid., 53.

the Christian, truth is not a matter of construction. Nevertheless, the general notion of constructivism need not be rejected wholesale, since it does provide insight into how the individual within a given social context facilitates the learning process, and provides methods whereby learners can teach themselves.

Social constructivist learning is easily connected to the churches' tasks of incorporating theory and practice into worship. While not promoting a social constructivist approach to learning, Robert Pazmiño asserts that the church congregation must connect these tasks in order for there to be full understanding, appreciation, and expression of conversion. The tasks "include call and commitment (*kerygma*), community and covenant (*koinonia*), care and concern (*diakonia*), conscience and challenge (*profeteia*), and celebration and creativity (*leitourgia*)"[52] and are part of the educational ministry of the church. This belief is echoed by Maria Harris in her book *Fashion Me a People*.[53] This idea lends itself to the social constructivist model of learning within the context of the church as a learning faith community.

Both Pazmiño and Harris seem to echo social constructivist theory to the development of curriculum, which is dependent on the context of learning within the context of the church community. The church should develop programs in which students can theologize about their lives. This learning theory says it is not enough for a believer to receive theological instructions and become capable of parroting it back. Rather, the individual should be able to build beyond what they have learned, constructing their own understanding and theologically-informed perspective on life, work, and family. As such, the congregation becomes a context in which theologizing occurs. As believers seek to grow in their faith, the curriculum should facilitate a guided approach to thinking theologically. The curriculum needs to be designed to incorporate the community life of the church, for it is within this social context that learning takes place within a learning environment.

---

[52] Robert W. Pazmiño, *Principles and Practices of Christian Education: An Evangelical Perspective* (Grand Rapids: Baker, 1992), 46.

[53] Maria Harris, *Fashion Me a People: Curriculum in the Church* (Louisville: WJK, 1989).

Personal Reflection

As I approached this topic and explored the various theorists and learning theories, I had to sit back to laugh at my work. While we educators continue to grow in our understanding, it is painfully obvious in our labor that our God does wonderful work. Such reflection brings joy as I reflect on the words of the psalmist, "I praise you because I am fearfully and wonderfully made; your works are wonderful, I know that full well" (Ps 139:14).

In an effort to divide and conquer the topic of learning theories, one soon realizes that God is in control. We have been created to learn. We will learn through various means. It is what makes us part of his creation; in some measure it is what separates us from the rest of creation. Yet more importantly, because of the diversity, it is what makes us unique in our individuality and diversity. We have all been given different gifts, and those gifts are good for many things. We all learn differently, and what we learn is used differently. When Christian educators move beyond the simple understanding of learning, we are able to value the uniqueness of each individual, each congregation, and the beauty of the global kingdom of God. When we are able to value God's creation in such a way, we are able to relate to and teach his people in the church.

What Has Learning Theory to Do with the Curriculum of the Church?

Just as topography is essential to understanding the best path to take on a journey, learning theories guide teaching decisions about reaching the purposes, goals, and objectives of a curriculum. Curriculum is a map developed after observing the topography of a learner and understanding the relationship between development and processes. A study of topography leads to determining a path for the curricular journey. We explore the possibilities of a journey with an understanding of learners, knowing how they learn. Existing curricula may currently only consider what the norm is for curriculum in the church, but it will be enhanced when individual needs of learners are considered and addressed. The church is in the business of educating for the kingdom.

The best curriculum for our churches is the one that considers the needs of the learner, the church, and the goals of the kingdom:

1. How has God created individuals to make the learning journey?
2. Has he not created learners with the ability to make accommodations when faced with obstacles, to problem solve and overcome?
3. Is it acceptable to design a path after studying the layout of such features that are natural or constructed?
4. How have individuals adapted, adjusted, or made accommodations to finish the journey?

Once we have observed the topography of the learner, we are a step closer to developing and designing the curriculum; a foundational understanding of the learner, then, affects how we view curriculum. We cannot begin to discuss the nature of curriculum until we understand the learner.

Key Terms and Concepts

| Development | Behavioral | Social |
| Capacity | Cognitive | Constructive |

Reflection Questions

1. How is the metaphor *topography* helpful or unhelpful in understanding the importance of learning theories as they relate to curriculum?
2. What is the relationship of learning theories to curriculum?
3. How is the use of social science research critical to teaching the curriculum of the church?
4. Using information on learning theories, do you plan to change anything about the education ministry of your church?

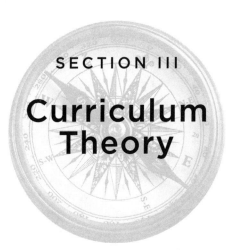

SECTION III

Curriculum Theory

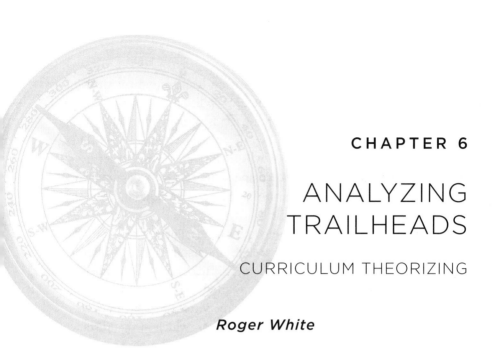

CHAPTER 6

ANALYZING TRAILHEADS

CURRICULUM THEORIZING

Roger White

Behind every decision about curriculum is a theory and behind every theory is a worldview. Before turning to the art of making and using curricula, the many factors influencing how people conceptualize the curriculum design and development process will be considered. Awareness of the theoretical assumptions informing how a curriculum is shaped and how curricula work allows educators to be knowledgeable about their own and others' unique perspectives, preferences, and biases. These starting points or trailheads for curricular journeys determine the paths chosen, destinations sought, and the travel customs followed. This chapter analyzes some of these foundational beliefs shaping curricula and considers where those theoretical and curricular trailheads may lead.

People respond to God and the world in many ways, and some of the ways people respond are remarkably similar. There is a sense in which every individual is like every other, a sense in which they are like some other people, and a sense in which they are entirely unique. Recognizing similarities among people helps us plan and evaluate.

Commonalities reveal patterns and provide background for devising theories, hypothesizing, and constructing "what if" scenarios. These theoretical frames are a way to organize ideas, show how ideas connect together, and highlight the significance of various parts. They assist in predicting how new ideas will fit into an overall structure of understanding. They help us discern and visualize God's ongoing work by showing how God has worked in the past and pointing to how God may work in the future.

As was seen in chapter 2, God communicates, people respond, and teachers partner. When educators seek to understand learners in order to tailor curriculum programs for them, it is necessary to generalize to some extent because it is not possible to know people completely. The same is true when examining curriculum developers and how their various theories apply to curriculum trailheads, which in this instance means the starting point of a path for curriculum planning and subsequent journeys. When considering how these planners approach their task, educators can never understand all the elements of the accompanying thought and practice, but they can discern patterns in the approaches taken that are shared with other curriculum developers. Educators develop their understanding of trends in curriculum practice and gain insights into the accompanying theories by examining these common patterns.

For instance, when Jesus said, "When evening comes, you say, 'It will be fair weather, for the sky is red,' and in the morning, 'Today it will be stormy, for the sky is red and overcast'" (Matt 16:2–3a), he was making reference to weather patterns seen in nature. In another passage, he again alluded to the presence of patterns, this time relating to those observable in people:

> Watch out for false prophets. They come to you in sheep's clothing, but inwardly they are ferocious wolves. By their fruit you will recognize them. Do people pick grapes from thornbushes, or figs from thistles? Likewise every good tree bears good fruit, but a bad tree bears bad fruit. A good tree cannot bear bad fruit, and a bad tree cannot bear good fruit. Every tree that does not bear good fruit is cut down and thrown into the fire. Thus, by their fruit you will recognize them. (Matt 7:15–20)

While familiarity with human response patterns helps educators plan for replicating good patterns, there is also the danger of inflating generally observed patterns to the status of universal rules and absolutes. This leads to mechanistic approaches to curriculum, to insensitive stereotypes, and unrealistic caricatures of individuals uniquely created in the image of God. Purposes and people are uncritically forced into predetermined theoretical boxes, thwarting wisdom and devaluing learners.

Although there are possible abuses, observed patterns when incorporated prudently into the decision making process, provide an important basis for understanding theories and worldviews and discerning the curricular practices that flow out of them. What follows is a consideration of some patterns seen in how individuals view the world (worldviews), how believers view their Christian faith (faith traditions), and how educators have conceptualized curriculum (curriculum theories). This introduction to how theories inform curriculum development gives important background to educator-guides and mapmakers analyzing trailheads.

Worldviews as Trailheads

Everyone has a worldview, a set of beliefs and assumptions about how the world works. These ideas direct all of a person's life activities, including educational practice. Worldviews inform one's philosophy of education and direct an educator's approach to curriculum and instruction. This section defines what a worldview is and considers some examples commonly found in education and curriculum development.

People tend to acquire their worldviews the way they catch colds. Beliefs are caught and adopted from immediate surroundings and important relationships. Parents, family, friends, and teachers influence us. We inherit both explicit foundational beliefs and implicit assumptions from our community's approach to and consensus about life. Traditions and customs practiced in schools, churches, businesses, and governments shape us. Our racial, ethnic, and cultural heritage displayed in literature, music, and the arts and present day expression of that heritage found in society, media, and the Internet affects who we are and what we believe. All these influences fashion and inform a person's worldview.

At the top of every curricular trailhead certain assumptions are in place about the impending journey ahead. Some assumptions are more consistently held or more consciously realized than others. Curriculum developers and guides need to be aware of the presence of these assumptions and the influences leading to these beliefs because curriculum paths involve actively revisiting a constellation of foundational assumptions held about life and how those beliefs work out in everyday living. Curricula and educational journeys inherently convey and challenge worldview assumptions and their implications.

A person's worldview addresses at various levels basic questions of life: Who am I? Where am I? How do I make sense of life? These questions all foundationally relate to what it means to be human. Everyone has formed some operational answers relating to the purpose and problem of being alive. Curriculum developers ask these same questions for themselves and for those with whom they work as they seek to determine what is most worth knowing and experiencing.

Since all these questions are ultimately religious in nature, one of the major themes found in worldview assumptions are considerations relating to God. Views concerning reality and human nature typically flow from this, which in turn leads to perspectives on death, knowledge, ethics, and human history. Since these themes are so crucial to making sense of life, formal disciplines of study have arisen for pursuing in-depth answers related to these areas. Some of these include,

1. Theology	Who is true?
2. Metaphysics	What is true?
3. Epistemology	How is truth known?
4. Ethics	How does truth direct human action?
5. Pedagogy	How is truth taught?

To varying degrees, curriculum theorists consider all these issues in planning out meaningful paths for learners. They do so as fellow travelers, as participants in the ongoing search for meaning, and also on behalf of those with whom they are called to partner. Ideas matter and there are consequences for worldview choices. Everyone has the responsibility to choose well.

While the areas of study listed in the previous paragraph are described in terms of their revolving around God's truth, not everyone in the broader academic community who pursues these studies acknowledges God's centrality. While these individuals may see and discern particular patterns that indeed are helpful and carry explanatory weight for them and others, they do not attribute the accompanying assumptions, related theories, or life applications to divine causes or interests. Worldview explanations reflecting these characteristics are considered naturalistic because they answer the basic life questions based primarily on natural explanations and minimize, ignore, or disregard supernatural accounts and contributions.

The characteristics and influence of naturalistic worldviews sometimes show up in church curriculum approaches. For example, imagine a class considering the fulfillment of Old Testament prophecies in the New Testament period, but disallowing divinely inspired authorship or divine foreknowledge. Or consider a class on the efficacy of prayer when the practice is viewed exclusively as a psychological and emotional benefit for the one praying, but taking no account of God's omnipotence and beneficence. While such an approach is sometimes used as an instructional method to make a point or illustrate an idea, grounding an educational theory and shaping an entire curriculum around it should be approached cautiously and critically because it excludes direct orienting references to God and what we have earlier called "true north." Such connections are made only secondarily by virtue of God's common grace present in the curriculum design, content, and experiences.

Another example of a widely held worldview pattern commonly seen in education and curriculum practice is known as analytic philosophy and relates to the study of knowledge. This approach maintains that difficulties of meaning and understanding in life arise from careless and misleading use of language, not necessarily from the complexities inherent in reality, truth, or value. Therefore, from this perspective, carefully defining terms and ideas is the preferred activity of philosophical and educational endeavors. Finding the common sense meaning of everyday ordinary language is the goal. Analytic philosophy is not considered a traditional systematized philosophy since in practice it tends neither to engage nor address basic philosophical and worldview questions apart from its emphasis on linguistic analysis. While a focus on semantics and clarification of language may keep advocates of this approach from prematurely forcing ideas into predetermined worldviews, continual lack of attention to worldview questions carries its own attending worldview assumptions and implications. Clearing up potential misunderstandings in terminology and ambiguities of language becomes an end in itself.

These characteristics common to analytic philosophy are sometimes seen in Bible studies when excessive attention is given to hermeneutical concerns without considering relevant application. Clarifying the original language, grammatical constructs, historical contexts, and textual variations are all crucial, valuable, and essential aspects of responsible Bible study. However, when these are pursued as ends in themselves and to the exclusion of seeking to know and experience God and forming an appropriate response to truth claims, it can produce the impression that extensive familiarity with the meaning of the Scripture text equates with intimacy with the author or that an accumulation of knowledge is equivalent to the possession of wisdom. While the ministry of the Holy Spirit utilizes fuller understandings of the text's language in those encountering it, educators must intentionally integrate instructional outcomes with the broader goals of the curriculum oriented around God's ultimate purposes.

It is beyond the scope of this book to consider the many curriculum trailheads arising out of worldview assumptions we see patterned in others and ourselves. However, there are a number of helpful resources available that provide a catalogue type listing of worldviews and describe and analyze assumptions accompanying various patterns in how people view the world (e.g., pragmatism, secularism, relativism, nationalism, pluralism, individualism, psychologism, materialism).[1] While these resources are not necessarily geared specifically toward making connections to curriculum, they do provide a starting point for mapmakers who are aware that people's response patterns to basic life questions inform the paths they choose and the maps they make.

In the next section, common patterns observed in how believers have experienced and expressed the Christian faith are considered.

---

[1] See James W. Sire, *The Universe Next Door: A Basic Worldview Catalog*, 3rd ed. (Downer's Grove: InterVarsity, 1997); Steve Wilkens and Mark L. Sanford, *Hidden Worldviews: Eight Cultural Stories that Shape Our Lives* (Downers Grove: InterVarsity, 2009); R. C. Sproul, *Lifeviews: Understanding the Ideas that Shape Our Society Today* (Old Tappan, NJ: Revell, 1986).

These are presented as a way of conceptualizing trailheads that are historically and explicitly Christian and that convey the richness and diversity of the Christian church.

Faith Traditions as Trailheads

Within the Christian church there are a number of distinctive patterns reflecting how believers have historically approached their faith. Recognizing the shared beliefs and practices evident in these approaches helps to identify the common characteristics of various faith traditions (trailheads) and their implications for life paths and journeys. Different approaches to how faith is expressed carry important assumptions that inform educational theory and subsequent curriculum development.

In his book *Streams of Living Water*, Richard J. Foster provides a helpful summary of six major faith traditions, what he calls streams of the Christian faith.[2] Each tradition has certain strengths to commend itself, yet each also has challenges. No tradition is complete, yet each can provide important insights to the nature of faith that are sometimes less visible in the other traditions. Foster's treatment of each tradition's characteristics are used here as a basis for applying those assumptions to curriculum theory and trailheads. The six traditions are:

1. The Contemplative Tradition
2. The Holiness Tradition
3. The Charismatic Tradition
4. The Social Justice Tradition
5. The Evangelical Tradition
6. The Incarnational Tradition

The contemplative tradition is characterized by an emphasis on prayer. All of life is viewed as a sustained meditation to experience more fully the presence of God. This constant contemplative attitude of focused attention on the divine provides a sense of peace for believers and strength for the journey of life. This tradition is closely associated with the monastic lifestyle and believers such as Julian of Norwich,

---

[2] Richard J. Foster, *Streams of Living Water: Celebrating the Great Traditions of Christian Faith* (San Francisco: Harper, 1998).

Catherine of Siena, Brother Lawrence, Thérèse of Lisieux, Thomas Merton, and Henri Nouwen. Curriculum trailheads beginning in this tradition focus on developing the life of prayer, solitude, and intimacy with God. The educational paths of this tradition frequently include the spiritual disciplines, especially prayer and solitude, and sometimes encourage scheduled times of devotion as a means to help develop contemplation as a way of life.

The holiness tradition focuses on virtuous living arising from intimate encounter with God. A renewed heart brings forth holy actions for appropriate living in the midst of a broken and dysfunctional world. Daily reflection on one's relationship with God is accompanied by careful attention to suitable outward expressions of that faith before God and others. Those associated with this tradition include Thomas à Kempis, Ignatius of Loyola, Teresa of Avila, Richard Baxter, John Wesley, Phoebe Palmer, and Dietrich Bonhoeffer. In the case of John Wesley, his approach to holiness gave rise to the Methodist movement named for the methodical curricular emphasis of its members as they intentionally sought holy living and habits. While character transformation is ultimately a work of God's grace, advocates of the Holiness Tradition emphasize in their curricular approaches the importance of personal piety realized through the work of the Holy Spirit in the midst of a supporting community.

The charismatic tradition is known for its Spirit-led living that allows believers to know, love, worship, and serve God. Attention is focused on the supernatural work of the Holy Spirit and the spiritual gifts present in the lives of believers. These benefits come from God and are bestowed as an endowment of grace; they are not earned. Even so, the believer is urged to seek the empowerment of the Spirit earnestly within the expressions of grace received. Faithfully living this way becomes an important witness for God to the world and provides an enriched emotional life in believers as they experience abundant and Spirit-filled living. This tradition is associated particularly with Pentecostalism and is seen in people like Hildegard of Bingen, Francis of Assisi, George Fox, Charles Wesley, and John Wimber. With the emphasis of this tradition being on the Spirit's initiative, curricular plans tend not to be as prescribed and journeys not charted out as intentionally. Greater attention is given to the individual spiritual gifts of educators and ongoing modeling of sensitivity to the internal promptings of the Spirit who guides believers along the twists and turns of life journeys and curricular paths.

The social justice tradition gives attention to helping those in need through compassionate living. Seeking the welfare of others and supporting them particularly when they suffer injustices is a major theme of this tradition. Loving one's neighbor in this way brings God's justice to bear on the world and manifests God's righteousness. In this way the church puts into practice what it believes about social ethics and represents Christ to the world. Examples from church history of people who have powerfully interceded on behalf of the suffering and oppressed include Robert Raikes, William Wilberforce, Florence Nightingale, Mother Teresa, Martin Luther King Jr., and Desmond Tutu. Curriculum paths in this tradition typically travel precisely through areas where hurting and abused people are found. This experience of providing help and seeking to improve their circumstances through direct involvement allows travelers to do the work of God in their ministry and represent Christ to a hurting world.

The evangelical tradition emphasizes the proclamation of the good news and its scriptural witness. This Word-centered approach features the living and written Word of God and the communication of its central message, the gospel. Attention is given to reading, loving, interpreting, knowing, understanding, and applying the Scriptures to all of life and sharing its message with others. Through it, believers are able to experience the knowledge of God and bear witness of God's truth. Those associated with this tradition include Augustine, Thomas Aquinas, John Wycliffe, Martin Luther, John Calvin, Charles Haddon Spurgeon, D. L. Moody, and Billy Graham. Much attention is given in this tradition to basic Bible literacy, hermeneutics, memorization, Bible teaching, and theology. Since these are central, they take a prominent role in curriculum. Learning the message of the Bible and sharing it with others through personal life witness, preaching, teaching, evangelism and discipleship, characterizes educational journeys originating in the trailhead of this tradition.

The incarnational tradition is a call to living life as a sacrament, a holy practice of making the invisible things of the Spirit visible in the world. Since God is manifest around us every day, special attention is given to recognizing and experiencing God in all of life. Those in this tradition have a unique interest in and ability to bring the things of God to light and to assist others in seeing that significance, beauty, and glory in the ordinary experiences and common elements of work and life. Their way of life, approach to vocation, and creative expression are a witness to others of God being present in the world in a variety of ways. Examples of those whose lives exhibited characteristics of the incarnational tradition include Dante Alighieri, Michelangelo, Rembrandt, John Milton, Susanna Wesley, Johann Sebastian Bach, George Frideric Handel, Dorothy Sayers, and C. S. Lewis. Curricular paths flowing out of this tradition are characterized by attention to, appreciation for, and participation in creative expressions like the visual arts, music, theatre, literature, and dance since these can all echo aspects of God's self-disclosure and relational presence in the world. Interaction with these creative arts, the natural world in general, and heightened attention to the divine present in everyday tasks provide curricular orientation for sensing and experiencing God more fully.

Foster's six streams and traditions do not align exactly with Christian denominations. Some denominations may be characterized by a single tradition; others will exhibit a blend of two or more. Regardless of what is typical for a particular denomination, individual congregations can display an affinity for entirely different traditions or combination of them. Elements of all the traditions are found spread across the denominational spectrum.

Christian educator and university professor, Robert W. Pazmiño, drawing on ideas from his former professor Philip Phenix, gives a helpful summary of four major divisions of the Christian church.[3] He identifies some of their major tendencies (patterns) and several ways these starting points (trailheads) result in a particular focus. These areas of focus convey the emphases one would expect to find in curricular paths originating from these trailheads:

1. Roman Catholicism has tended to stress the institutional and organizational dimensions of faith within various struc-

---

[3] Robert W. Pazmiño, *By What Authority Do We Teach?* (Grand Rapids: Baker, 1994), 129.

tures and systems. This results in a focus on the political and broad social dimensions of life.

2. Orthodoxy has tended to stress the rites, rituals, and sacraments of faith embodied in symbols and images. This results in a focus on the aesthetic and affective dimensions of life that hold a potential for integration.

3. Protestantism has tended to stress the creeds and beliefs of faith embodied in doctrines and theological statements. This results in a focus on the intellectual and conceptual dimensions of life.

4. Pentecostalism has tended to stress the spiritual and mystical experiences of faith that restore a sense of joy and fulfillment. This results in a focus on the relational and communal dimensions of life that include the presence and ministry of the Holy Spirit.

In a related fashion, Gary Thomas, popular author and writer in residence at Second Baptist Church in Houston, Texas proposes a list of patterns he sees in how individuals relate best with God. Since people with similar interests sometimes gravitate toward one another in congregational settings, denominations, or faith traditions, Thomas's list of individual patterns aids in conceptualizing how church curriculum may be approached. In his book *Sacred Pathways,* he lists the following types of people and their accompanying inclinations:[4]

1. Naturalists: Loving God out of Doors
2. Sensates: Loving God with the Senses
3. Traditionalists: Loving God Through Ritual and Symbol
4. Ascetics: Loving God in Solitude and Simplicity
5. Activists: Loving God Through Confrontation
6. Caregivers: Loving God by Loving Others
7. Enthusiasts: Loving God with Mystery and Celebration
8. Contemplatives: Loving God Through Adoration
9. Intellectuals: Loving God with the Mind

---

[4] Gary L. Thomas, *Sacred Pathways: Discover Your Soul's Path to God* (Grand Rapids: Zondervan, 1996).

The predominant way people love and relate to God indicates the type of curriculum approaches and paths best suited for them.

These summaries provided by Foster, Pazmiño, and Thomas about faith tradition characteristics seen across the Church are only a few examples illustrating how prevailing inclinations have curricular implications.[5] Common patterns bring about similar expectations. These faith tradition formulations may help educators conceptualize a curricular theory (trailhead) or analyze a preexisting one. In the next section consideration is given to additional patterns seen in the social sciences among curriculum theorists.

Trailheads from the Social Sciences

In the *Handbook of Research on Curriculum*, a project sponsored by the American Educational Research Association, Elliot Eisner describes six prominent positions representing "beliefs about what schools should teach, for what ends, and for what reasons."[6] While Eisner is looking at schools in general, the curricular positions he identifies are also found in other educational contexts.

Eisner calls these positions curriculum ideologies and acknowledges they all emerge from "religious-like views of the world"[7] even though they do not all arise from formal religious settings. These patterns and worldview assumptions inform how various educators approach curriculum development and design. They represent the major theoretical trailheads for educational journeys and curricular paths. Eisner lists these as (1) religious orthodoxy, (2) rational humanism, (3) progressivism, (4) critical theory, (5) reconceptualism, and (6) cognitive pluralism.[8]

---

[5] For an example of patterns seen in the church's posture toward culture, see H. Richard Niebuhr's *Christ and Culture* (New York: HarperCollins, 2001).

[6] Elliot W. Eisner, "Curriculum Ideologies," in *Handbook of Research on Curriculum: A Project of the American Educational Research Association*, ed. Philip W. Jackson (New York: Macmillan, 1996), 302. Also in Elliot W. Eisner, *Educational Imagination: On the Design and Evaluation of School Programs*, 3rd ed. (Upper Saddle River, NJ: Merrill Prentice Hall), 47.

[7] Eisner, "Curriculum Ideologies," 303 (also in Eisner, *Educational Imagination*, 48).

[8] Ibid., 306 (also in Eisner, *Educational Imagination*, 56).

Each of these perspectives provides a frame for orienting curriculum journeys.

Religious orthodoxy views the purpose, goals, and objectives of education as derived from God's communication with the world. Divine revelation to humanity establishes what is important, and educators seek to apply it responsibly to educational practice.

Rational humanism focuses on reason and a person's ability to gain insight through reflection. This optimistic view of rationality advocates learning through student interaction with the best examples of human knowledge evidenced especially through the classic artistic, literary, and philosophical works of a culture.

Progressivism maintains that learners grow through adapting to their surroundings so instruction should focus on problem solving. Growth is viewed as increased competence in using available resources to process life problems at both personal and social levels.

Critical theory seeks to expose the hidden curriculum present in all schools by revealing the political assumptions and values inherent in the educational process. The ideal is to have teachers and students aware of these influences and able to identify aims for themselves separate from those imposed on them through institutional bias.

Reconceptualism conceives educational aims and school procedures in ways that center in the personal life of learners. In contrast to a mechanical view of schooling and an emphasis on set procedures, this view celebrates imagination and creatively connecting to the unique life experiences of each learner.

Cognitive pluralism affirms the human ability to develop and use multiple forms of symbol systems, not just language in a narrow sense. Since we know and manage things in different ways, curricular attention is given to recovering meaning from varied experiences and developing multiple intelligences in students.

Each of these approaches and accompanying worldviews espouses implicit beliefs about education and a rationale regarding curriculum direction.[9] The foundational nature of these values reveals why all

---

[9] According to Eisner, all schools have at least an operational ideology. He explains, "If an ideology is defined as a *public* statement of a value position regarding curriculum, then the absence of such a statement would disqualify it as an

educators must attend to basic life questions and why Eisner refers to the ideologies as religious-like. While adherents to the different perspectives may appreciate and even include in their curriculum work selected aspects of the various approaches, each will tend to orient curricula based primarily on one approach. Religious Orthodoxy is Eisner's category that aligns with the Christian educator's primary view toward curriculum; the other approaches reflect helpful but secondary aspects of conceptualizing curriculum.

Mapmakers need to be able to draw from the insights found in various social scientific approaches, but also be able to recognize the inherent challenges of them. Pre-existing curricula and trailheads must be analyzed for the assumptions they carry regarding the nature and intent of the educational process. Not every worldview orientation or path trajectory informed by social science is compatible with conceptualizing curriculum in a distinctively Christian way.

Conclusion

When analyzing trailheads (worldviews, faith traditions, or social science paradigms), Christian educators will want to ask questions about the purpose of education, the nature of curricular content, the roles of the learner and teacher, and the teaching-learning process in order to reveal the underlying assumptions and to determine whether they align with Christian understandings.

Educators have a variety of factors influencing how they approach curriculum, and they experience these influences in their lives in different ways. Any exposure or commitment to them will vary depending on the educator's background. Given the pre-theoretical nature of

---

ideology. If, however, an ideology also refers to a shared way of life that teaches a certain worldview or set of values through action, then schools everywhere employ and convey an ideology because they all possess, in practice, a shared way of life or what may be called an operational ideology" (Eisner, "Curriculum Ideologies," 306). Also Richard Osmer states, "Whether it articulates it explicitly or not, every educational theory projects a social ideal and concomitant understanding of human maturity that undergirds its determination of the sorts of attitudes, values, skills, and capacities it deems worthwhile and worthy of inclusion in the educational process" (Richard Robert Osmer, *A Teachable Spirit: Recovering the Teaching Office in the Church* [Louisville: WJK, 1990], 213).

worldviews and ideologies, formal explanations and explicit statements about them do not always accompany their spread and transmission among educators. Educational customs and conventions may be passed on without the underlying assumptions being made evident because the foundational beliefs are so naturally embedded in a community's pre-existing learning context. Periodically, for these reasons, communities and educators need to critically analyze curricular programs and recall their educational memory in order to rediscover their unique identity and once again regain a distinctive curricular direction in line with their values.

Analyzing trailheads, the starting points of curricular journeys and paths, begins by acknowledging and recognizing worldview assumptions. These beliefs shape theories about conceptualizing curricula. They inform the entire curriculum design, development, and delivery process. Allegiances to different worldviews and life philosophies naturally lead to different destinations. Social science research seeks to identify where worldview assumptions lead when applied to human societal concerns like education. Attention to these common patterns evident in responses to basic life and worldview questions allows educators to consider where a path leads and a curricular journey is headed, not all of which are compatible with a Christian way of life. Faith traditions within the church exhibit how Christians have wrestled with these same issues and sought to respond faithfully to life claims and demands through their particular perspectives on Scripture, reason, experience, and tradition.

Regardless of one's foundational beliefs about curriculum, looking over another educator's shoulder during the process of recovering educational distinctiveness can shed light on one's own educational starting point. The nature of life-long learning is to be continually open to new understandings. As James Sire, author of *The Universe Next Door*, writes, "For any of us to be fully conscious intellectually we should not only be able to detect the worldviews of others but be aware of our own—why it is ours and why in light of so many options we think it is true."[10] The reflective educator and mapmaker, regardless of worldview orientation, faith tradition, or social science ideology, asks similar

---

[10] Sire, *The Universe Next Door*, [1].

questions: "What's most worth knowing?" "Have the most important elements of life been considered?" "Have I chosen well?" These questions about selection and prioritization precede and accompany considerations about curriculum development and design.

Key Terms and Concepts

Theory	Analytic Philosophy
Worldview	Faith Traditions
Trailheads	Social Science
Naturalism	

Reflection Questions

1. It has been said, "The Greeks learned in order to comprehend, the modern person learns in order to use, but the Hebrews learned in order to revere."[11] What worldview and life assumptions are present in these tendencies?
2. What implications for curriculum can be drawn from Jesus' question, "What good is it for someone to gain the whole world, yet forfeit their soul?" (Mark 8:36; cf. Matt 16:26).
3. How might wisdom from faith traditions and the social sciences be integrated when developing trailheads for curriculum?
4. Of the faith traditions surveyed by Richard Foster, to which one do you adhere? Why? To which other one(s) are you drawn? Why?

---

[11] Abraham J. Heschel as paraphrased by Robert J. Pazmiño in *Foundational Issues in Christian Education: An Introduction in Evangelical Tradition* (Grand Rapids: Baker, 1997), 50.

CHAPTER 7

SURVEYING THE LOCAL TERRAIN

CURRICULUM DEVELOPMENT

Karen Lynn Estep

Using the metaphor "Surveying the Local Terrain," this chapter addresses the background preparation required for planning a curriculum, what we are calling curriculum development. Similar to a preliminary survey map with carefully measured boundaries and elevations, this chapter provides educators with what they need to know to map out a curricular route for use in the church. The first section will look at the historical roots of curriculum development in an effort to define the boundaries of the terrain. Our plot map will include a review of theological foundations for curriculum development, a conceptual model of curriculum development, contextual reflections that influence curriculum development, as well as particular elements of developing curriculum—i.e., purpose, goals, objectives and outcomes, scope, teaching and learning, structures of organization, and evaluation. The chapter will look at each of these pieces with the intention of forming a general understanding and broad perspective of curriculum development for Christian educators and mapmakers.

Historical Roots of Modern Curriculum Development

What we believe about curriculum and how to develop it has progressed over time. While the purpose and organization have both been handed down to us, it is important to understand that context will impact if not determine both. By context, we mean the societal and cultural life of the learner, though later we will include the individual needs of learners from a psychological perspective and the learning environment, which includes facility, materials, teachers, and resources. A curriculum development plan is influenced and organized by context. While the church has made use of curriculum development models, it has never developed a model wholly unique to itself; rather, it has chosen to adapt existing models for Christian education's own use.

Pamela Mitchell traces the development through various periods of history through the nineteenth century (see fig. 7.1 on pp. 136–37).[1]

In the mid-1900s, educators began to plan for education with the development of a system to guide it. Between 1945 and 1950, both Ralph Tyler and Hilda Taba developed similar sequential steps for the development of curriculum, suggesting them as a guide to curriculum development. Their intention was not to mandate steps but rather to suggest guiding ones. The following list and order was generally accepted for a "curriculum plan" and is still used today:

Step 1: Diagnosis of needs   *Biblical illiteracy*

Step 2: Formulation of objectives   *KNOW BE DO*

Step 3: Selection of content   *Bible*

Step 4: Organization of content

Step 5: Selection of learning experiences

Step 6: Organization of learning experiences

Step 7: Determination of what to evaluate and of the ways and means of doing it.[2]

---

[1] Based on information gleaned from Pamela Mitchell, "What Is Curriculum?: Alternatives in Western Historical Perspective," *Religious Education* 83, no. 3 (Summer 1988): 351–52, 354, 356–57, 361.

[2] Hilda Taba, *Curriculum Development: Theory and Practice* (New York: Harcourt, Brace & World, 1962), 12.

Making an impact on both religious and nonreligious educators in developing a plan for curriculum, Tyler's syllabus, "Basic Principles of Curriculum and Instruction,"[3] was selected by the leadership group, Professors of Curriculum, as one of two publications which has had the most influence for the field of curriculum,[4] with his emphasis on society, learner, and subject matter as sources of curricular data.[5] Curriculum development models for Christian Education have gained much from nonreligious influences,[6] incorporating many insights from varied sources.

Mary Osterman's research, which has covered two hundred years of curriculum theory for religious educators, finds Protestants unable to define curriculum. She reports that Christian educators have struggled over the scope or nature of the content, grouping by uniformity or grading, the focus or aim of education, and teaching-learning models that define the nature of teaching and learning for religious education.[7] In the same way that Osterman advocates that Christian educators need to formulate a definition of curriculum development and describe the boundaries for Christian educators, this chapter intends to explore the topic. Having reviewed the historical roots of curriculum development, a general definition of curriculum development is as follows: "A deliberated value-laden process that identifies sources of information from society, students' experiences, and subject matter. This process organizes the curriculum based on contextual norms using a plethora of patterns, including steps, subject grouping, causes, cyclical, and various other divisors." This process of curriculum development applies to both Christian and non-Christian curriculum designs. Curriculum

---

[3] Cf. Ralph W. Tyler, *Basic Principles of Curriculum and Instructions* (Chicago: University of Chicago Press, 1950).

[4] Harold G. Shane, "Significant Writings That Have Influenced the Curriculum: 1906-81," *Phi Delta Kappan*, 62, no. 5 (January 1981): 311–14.

[5] M. Francis Klein, "Alternative Curriculum Conceptions and Designs," *Curriculum Planning: A New Approach*, 6th ed., ed. Glen Hass and Forest Parkay (Boston, MA: Allyn and Bacon, 1993), 312.

[6] Edward W. Uthe, "Developing Curriculum Design for Christian Education," *Religious Education*, 61, no. 3 (1966): 163.

[7] M. J. Osterman, "The Two Hundred Year Struggle for Protestant Religious Education Curriculum Theory," *Religious Education*, 75, no. 5 (September-October 1980): 528–29.

Context	Purpose	Organization
Primitive Cultures	Transmit wisdom of culture to next generation as a means of survival	Life experiences
Greek Colonization of 8th and 6th Centuries BC	Train specialist: scribes, priests, and accountants to expedite governmental, economic, and cultural affairs	Bodies of knowledge and content
Roman Empire 4th Century AD	Plan for living	Steps for daily living of home life with textbooks: content, organization, sequence, and what to do with it guide
Pre-exilic Judaism	Race Experience Knowing the story of your people Meaning of everyday life Maintain group identity and survival	Participation in rituals and daily life
Judaism after Exile	Maintain identity while being dispersed Diverse contexts as culture shifts for each group	Content focused on the study of the law (Torah) for everyone

Judeo-Christian of 5th Century AD	Purpose varies based on cultural norms:	Organization of knowledge into a sequenced plan for instruction of content
Middle Ages	Need for lay ministers to understand Scripture and basic tools of reading and writing	
Charlemagne	Developed a literate clergy to teach everyone	
Renaissance	Broad and rounded background of knowledge, manners and social graces for ruling class with loyalty to basic Christian principles	
1500s	Teaching the ignorant	Systematized with Luther's Catechisms
Reformation	Teaching the congregations	Development of methodologies
Comenius	Individualized daily goals for all	Standard: Daily goals and systematized plan
Enlightenment (Locke & Rousseau)	Learner actualizes his full potential	Focused on selected, guided, ordered, and controlled experiences
1800s	Scientific Production of lessons • Sunday Schools in America • International Lesson System	Standardized and Systematized Lessons

Figure 7.1: History of Western Curriculum Development until 1900

development within the congregation is indeed a Spirit-led process of engaging Scripture, theology, Christian heritage, and the lives and settings of our congregants.

Defining Curriculum Development Boundaries

Since by everyone's definition curriculum development is a process, the concern for defining its boundaries is about describing the guiding principles that have thus far escaped many but not all curriculum designers. The process is an intentionally transforming process with aspiration or goals, which naturally result in desired outcomes. Christian educators such as Randolph Miller and Edward Uthe have followed the ideas of the period, realizing the value of planning as a guide as well as the unique values of Christianity that are for several reasons different.[8] To maintain that uniqueness, Christians must ground curricular foundations in biblical, theological, and historical sources. The question then turns to the role of other elements, such as the needs of learners and community, or contextual influences, which significantly change the character and direction of the curriculum. This is where boundaries need to be determined for curriculum development to be effective.

Although we must still pay attention to the societal influences and cultural context in our efforts to develop the curriculum, both societal and cultural influences are not philosophically identical for all Christians. "Curriculum development is a value-laden process in which leaders choose from many possibilities. A prerequisite to leadership in curriculum is identification and development of a philosophy of education, that is, a clear set of assumptions that will guide decision making."[9] Our Christian convictions guide this process (see Section 1). However, the societal force is an area of weakness for Christian educators, as is commonly noted by missionaries. Too often Christians have ignored it in their efforts to transform society, giving the foundational stage of development precedent and complete authority in determining the curriculum. Christian education should not only teach Scripture,

---

[8] Uthe, "Developing Curriculum Design for Christian Education," 163.

[9] Jon W. Wiles and Joseph C. Bondi, *Curriculum Development: A Guide to Practice*, 8th ed. (Boston: Pearson, 2011), 70.

theology, and our Christian heritage, but also offer curriculum on art, literature, politics, and cross-cultural interests. The curriculum should not omit matters that are not directly regarded as "Christian," but are nevertheless essential for Christians to mature and transform culture.

Both Christian and non-Christian educators firmly agree that societal forces should play a significant role in curriculum development, though that is not what has happened in the past within the church. Often we just transfer the curriculum from one culture to another, assuming it is *wholly* transcultural.[10] Exploring societal forces and cultural needs is well within the boundaries of curriculum development; thus, planning cannot be stagnant. It must be fluid to match the evolving perspectives of societal forces. "Curriculum building is not a process based on precise rules, but involves artistic design as well as critical analysis, human judgments, and empirical testing."[11] It is essential to understand curriculum planning as an ever-changing process influenced by an understating of the process of learning, the needs of the learner individually and culturally, and the political and social agendas of those teaching. Thus, curriculum development is a value-laden process influenced by the context of our congregations and the society in which we minister.

Curriculum Deliberation

Gail McCutcheon identifies the process needed to deal with societal issues as one of *deliberation*. She espouses the necessity of deliberation for both individuals as well as groups within the curriculum development plan and process. Deliberation is a central process to decision-making in curriculum planning, as curriculum development cannot take place in a social vacuum. Individuals must examine the nature of teacher thinking, teachers' practical theories of action and their

---

[10] Yau-Man Siew, "A Curriculum Model for the Evaluation of Existing Programs of Theological Education in Asia," *Asia Journal of Theology* 9, no. 1 (1995): 146.

[11] Ralph W. Tyler, "Specific Approaches to Curriculum Development," in *Strategies for Curriculum Development*, ed. Jon Schaffarzick and David H. Hampson (Berkeley: McCutchan, 1975), 25. Cf. Wiles and Bondi, *Curriculum Development*, 70.

planning, while group deliberation examines issues concerning the social construction of reality, conflict, competing interests, and the roles teachers' practical theories of action play in the process.[12] In essence, the societal factors of curriculum planning must be given a voice in the deliberation. William Rogers relates this to map making: "The integrity of your ministry dictates that you move from the posture and function of a shopper to a farmer, from a spectator to a critic, and from a map-tracer to a cartographer."[13] If not, the plan could fail for the lack of attention to the needs of culture, society, and learners. Similarly, congregations could consider the needs of their ministry context (their town, suburb, or niche population), the needs of the congregation itself, as well as the personal needs of the individuals comprising the congregation. The Christian education team should dedicate time and resources to the periodic review of these needs to assess the relevance of the curriculum to these three sets of needs.

The curriculum developer must create the plan and set it into motion. They must also allow the process to take place, where individuals take part in the process through deliberation. "The serious decisions that go into curriculum design, materials, and procedures constitute an awesome task that should not be shouldered by any one person."[14] This is often the case of those doing cross-cultural ministry. To relate this to our metaphor, "You are not tracing maps on tracing paper, meticulously copying existing and authoritatively produced maps which have been given to you; you are helping others create their maps for their journey acting out of a combination of authoritative and experiential maps."[15] In order to succeed, we must survey the local terrain as it may be representative of goals and objectives not considered and which will prove valuable to the purpose of education.

---

[12] Gail McCutcheon, *Developing the Curriculum: Solo and Group Deliberation* (White Plains: Longman, 1995), xviii–xix.

[13] William B. Rogers Jr., "Curriculum Alternatives for Christian Education," *Review and Expositor* 90, no. 4 (Fall 1993): 475.

[14] A. Elwood Sanner and A. F. Harper, eds., *Exploring Christian Education* (Grand Rapids, MI: Baker Book House, 1978), 178.

[15] Rogers, "Curriculum Alternatives for Christian Education," 475.

Church as Context for Curriculum Development

Within Christian education, the society and culture form the basis for a biblically based, socially relevant, and unique education within the global church. Rooted in the research of Jack L. Seymour,[16] William Rogers points to four dominate examples of how different approaches to Christian education within the church result in different developments of curriculum.[17] From these observations, the four forms of Christian education call for a distinct curricular focus, accompanied by programs designed to facilitate the curriculum.

1. Religious instruction asserts curriculum is decisively Eurocentric with its commitment to repetitive drills, memory work, and recitation that focus almost exclusively on Scripture. The Christian education program would resemble that of a school, consisting of classes, study groups, and large-scale study sessions such as Wednesday or Sunday night gatherings.

2. Faith community formalizes the process of socialization as the focus of its curriculum. The congregation's education program would be more participatory. Rather than being a separate program of Christian education, involvement in the church would be the congregation's curriculum.

3. Spiritual development leans heavily on developmental insights to the process of becoming a whole person in Christ, which is reflected in the experiential elements in the curriculum. Christian education would be far less formal in terms of its structure; facilitating the curriculum would come through mentoring and discipleship. Programically, it would resemble retreats and monastic experiences, with very limited use of classes in the traditional sense.

4. Liberation is more common within third world countries, advocating a curriculum of social change with emphasis on

---

[16] Cf. Jack L. Seymour, *Contemporary Approaches to Christian Education* (Nashville: Abingdon Press, 1982) and *Mapping Christian Education: Approaches to Congregational Learning* (Nashville: Abingdon Press, 1997).

[17] Rogers, "Curriculum Alternatives for Christian Education," 475–81.

the possibilities of the future. The education ministry would appear to be more like a benevolence and community-care ministry, providing for the poor and needy, while encouraging active participation in matters of social justice, such as marches and protests against unjust causes.

Ministry that considers the cultural norms, concerns, needs, and political history will better understand the purpose for their own unique needs.[18] Christian educators seem to agree on multiple purposes for church education: individual understanding, life in the community, individual development, and to liberate or serve.[19] One question with which Christian curriculum developers must wrestle is how to balance the internal norms, values, beliefs, and principles of the Christian community with the societal expectations, values, and norms in which the church exists. Finding this balance is the key to being faithful to God, the Word, the church, *and* the world. By staying in the boundaries, the church is able to fulfill the theological function of its curriculum with a plan to develop, maintain, and enhance understandings, attitudes, and skills that will serve the church in worship, witness and service.[20]

Conceptualizing Curriculum Development

We need to conceptualize curriculum development to guide us in doing a good job.[21] While we can adapt various models to suit the needs of the church, most models will be missing the foundations of Christian

---

[18] Siew, "A Curriculum Model for the Evaluation of Existing Programs of Theological Education in Asia," 149–50; cf. David C. Hester, "Christian Education in a Theological Curriculum," *Religious Education* 87, no. 3 (Summer 1992): 338–39; Sanner and Harper, *Exploring Christian Education*, 162.

[19] Cf. Orville W. Nyblade, "Curriculum Development in Theological Education," *Africa Theological Journal*, 20, no. 1 (1991): 42–43; Vincent M. Novak, "An Approach to Forming a Religion Curriculum," *Religious Education* 61, no. 3 (1966): 196. Many of the ideas contained in this article were first presented by the author in a paper delivered at the Theology Institute of the 1963 Liturgical Week, Philadelphia, August 19.

[20] D. Campbell Wyckoff, "The Curriculum Enterprise in Perspective," *Princeton Seminary Bulletin* (1980): 28.

[21] Taba, *Curriculum Development*, 13–14.

education; namely, the biblical, theological, and historical elements of our faith covered in the first chapters of this book. Having reviewed various models that allow for this unique aspect of Christian education, Yau-Man Siew demonstrates in his curriculum grid model that these elements are in fact the central focus for curriculum planning, listing them as a biblical view of persons, gospel, ecclesiology, mission, and the task and purpose of theological education.[22]

Linear Models

It is only logical that a model is linear or sequential having started somewhere and ending with a plan. Thus, Tyler produced a process model with a linear approach for curriculum development that follows a set of four questions that must be answered in developing a curriculum: (1) What is the educational purpose? (2) What experiences are required? (3) How do you organize the curriculum? (4) How do you determine if the purposes are attained?[23]

Nonlinear Models

A nonlinear model allows educators to enter the processes at any point, skip components or reverse their order as well as work on two or more of the components at the same time.[24] Wheeler suggests a cyclical process to promote a continual cycle of planning. Educators could enter at any point; there is no required first step or order to planning the curriculum.[25] According to Kerr, if you consider the four factors as outlined by Tyler, you could not consider one independently without reference to the others,[26] suggesting review and refinement in addition to a break from earlier progressive linear versions.

---

[22] Siew, "A Curriculum Model for the Evaluation of Existing Programs of Theological Education in Asia," 150.

[23] David Naylor, "Curriculum Development," in *New Movements in Religious Education* (London: Temple Smith, 1975), 121.

[24] Peter F. Oliva, *Developing the Curriculum*, 2nd ed. (Glenview, IL: Scott, Foresman, 1988), 161. See similarities in Galen Saylor, William M. Alexander, and Arthur J. Lewis, *Curriculum Planning for Better Teaching and Learning*, 4th ed. (Chicago: University of Chicago, 1981).

[25] Naylor, "Curriculum Development," 122.

[26] Ibid., 121–22.

Review and Refinement

Review and refinement, also called evaluation, are essential to the process of curriculum development, having been added for the purpose of maintenance. Hooper suggests an iterative process that continually uses questions to assess or verify the process of planning.[27] This echoes Eisner, "One need not begin or end with the factors or aspects as they appear here. Because for the purposes of writing some ordering is necessary, the sequence that follows seems to be reasonable, but one may proceed in curriculum development with a very different order."[28]

So, why do we need curriculum development for the church? Does it serve an additional purpose unlike secular curriculum? Wyckoff offers this:

> If it is the function of the curriculum to provide a plan for developing, maintaining, and enhancing those understandings, attitudes, and skills that serve the church's purposes in worship, witness, and work, the points of the critics have been taken very seriously indeed, but within the context of an organizing principle—the church's developing experience—that no one of them, from their limited standpoints, had been able to see. . . . Instead of "no plan at all," the curriculum anticipates the unexpected in the events of the church and the world. "Self-realization" may find a social context of meaning in the life of the community of faith and its response to the issues that church and person face in the world.[29]

Ultimately, curriculum designers see the need for a curriculum development model for those who plan curriculum with a set of desired outcomes, such as those suggested above—which, for the church, is a distinctly religious purpose.

Tyler bases his model on the content and process of curriculum.[30] Either would be sufficient. However, the content is key to determining the curriculum itself. He lists three data sources (society, students, and

---

[27] Ibid., 122.

[28] Elliot W. Eisner, *The Educational Imagination: On the Design and Evaluation of School Programs* (New York: Macmillan, 1979), 115.

[29] Wyckoff, "The Curriculum Enterprise in Perspective," 30.

[30] Cf. Ralph W. Tyler, *Basic Principles of Curriculum and Instruction* (Chicago: University of Chicago Press, 1949).

subject matter) that are used in development of various designs of curriculum. Often missed by developers is one of Tyler's key beliefs "that the use of one of the data sources alone is inadequate in developing curriculum. A comprehensive curriculum must use all three."[31] Thus, a model should include the use of all three for the sake of balance. Applying this to the church, often Christians see the Bible as the sole data source for the curriculum. The Bible may provide the subject matter, but to have the balance described by Tyler, Christian educators should also see the congregation and the student's Christian experience as legitimate sources for the curriculum. This will insure not only a balanced curriculum, but also a comprehensive and relevant one. In summary, there are four accepted procedures in curriculum development for designers to consider:[32]

1. Understanding curriculum development as a perpetual cycle or a system
2. Regular review of foundational areas of concern, e.g., theology, biblical scholarship, social forces including the social issues for the twenty-first century, knowledge, human development and learning[33]
3. Basing curricular decision making on relevant data
4. Involvement of significant others in the curriculum planning process[34]

These procedures include a system of transition for development with an understanding of the context of learning, with an understanding of the influence of diverse or changing factors. They include the use of evaluation and assessment in driving decision-making, and they value the inclusion of various voices in the deliberation process, which

---

[31] Klein, "Alternative Curriculum Conceptions and Designs," 312.

[32] Cf. Wiles and Bondi, *Curriculum Development*, 2–3.

[33] Cf. Michael J. Anthony and Warren S. Benson, *Exploring the History and Philosophy of Christian Education: Principles for the 21st Century* (Grand Rapids: Kregel, 2003), 411–20.

[34] Mark A. Maddix, "The Rise of Evangelical Christian Education (1951–2000)," in *C. E.: The Heritage of Christian Education*, ed. James R. Estep Jr., Jonathan H. Kim, Alvin W. Kuest, and Mark A. Maddix (Joplin, MO: College Press, 2003), 15: 1–29.

serve to clarify and unite those involved as to the purpose, goals, and objectives.

Contextual Reflection in Church Curriculum Development

There must be a concern for the context of the education program when developing the curriculum. Context is concerned with the needs of the learner, society, and subject.[35] It is necessary to consider the needs of all three in developing curricular objectives that are individualized. After selecting objectives, they must be screened through the congregation's philosophy and psychological understanding of learning, not just one or the other.[36] "It is the function of curriculum to provide a plan for developing, maintaining, and enhancing those understanding, attitudes, and skills that serve the church's purposes in worship, witness, and work."[37] However, this is not the case when there is a breakdown or failure for the education programs of the church.

The many failed attempts at cross-cultural missions and the development of materials for use in other countries serve as examples of such failures. The success of organizations such as Pioneer Bible Translators rests on the understanding that there is a need for translators of the Bible to understand the psychological, societal, and cultural norms of the people for whom they translate. Joe Marlow notes that curriculum developers should be aware of two contextual items: (1) Your cultural context and (2) your church context.[38] As an example, Christian education is too often only directed at those in the church and needs to focus on the "'hidden youth' . . . those not a part of the church."[39] Focusing

---

[35] Taba, *Curriculum Development*, 7; Siew, "A Curriculum Model for the Evaluation of Existing Programs of Theological Education in Asia," 151.

[36] Samuel Joseph, "Curriculum Philosophy of Education and the Jewish Religious School," *Religious Education* 78, no. 2 (1983): 196.

[37] Wyckoff, "The Curriculum Enterprise in Perspective," 28.

[38] Joe D. Marlow, "Curriculum Maps for the Spiritual Journey," *Christian Education Journal* 14, no. 2 (Winter 1994): 69.

[39] Leslie J. Francis and Adrian Thatcher, *Christian Perspectives for Education: A Reader in the Theology of Education* (Leominster, England: Gracewing Fowler Wright, 1990), 294.

on those within the context of your ministry is essential to curriculum development. John Gilbert suggests,

> Both the biblical and the theological foundations of proactive planning suggest a nature of personhood that is developing in the area of secular psychology. That is, the biblical and theological foundations of proactive planning view the person as a shaper of one's future, not a passive participant. . . . And in the new concepts of psychology, especially social psychology, the person is being viewed from the standpoint of developmentalism as both an efficient and a final cause. . . . Proactive planning prescribes little in terms of curriculum resources media, format, method, setting and so on. But it does provide the basic philosophy, namely the intentional creation of the future through the preparation of persons to respond theologically to many situations, on which consumer research in terms of media, format and so on could be conducted.[40]

"Curriculum must minister to the individual in the light of his past experience, his present need and interest, his maturity and aptitude, and his physical and social environment. Planners must realize that intersecting with the experience of the learning is more essential than mere logical continuity of subject matter."[41]

Purpose, Goals, Objectives, and Outcomes in Curriculum Development

Where do we start and where do we end with plotting the course of our map? Curriculum development begins with determining the *purpose*. The *goals* and *objectives* provide the guide or direction for the course. *Outcomes* are where we will end up; when we have reached them, the educational program is complete.

These terms provide a general understanding of our journey. The purpose will give us our sense of direction from a community perspective;[42] thus, there is a need for deliberation to refine this for

---

[40] William A. Gilbert, "Curriculum planning in the proactive mode," *Religious Education* 71, no. 5 (September-October 1976): 542–43.

[41] Sanner and Harper, *Exploring Christian Education*, 166.

[42] Eisner, *The Educational Imagination*, 116.

the community. For Christian education this will not only be based on biblical and theological foundations but also on psychological ones,[43] the latter not taking precedence over the previous two.

The purpose can be different based on the context of the program. David Hester writes, "What Christian education is and what purpose it serves depends on whom you ask and in what context since it is a matter of practical interest to a wide range of Christians crossing all sorts of doctrinal borders and educational approaches."[44] Sanner and Harper note,

> Curriculum is the directing and implementing program of Christian education-including all content and experiences through which God is revealed, and the grace of God's presence is encountered. . . . Curriculum should provide for persons just entering the community of believers as well as for those who are longtime members of that community. An inclusive curriculum should also provide for and relate to every agency of the church that has an educational task to perform. It should provide means and materials for nurture in every aspect of living, which can be fostered in the Christian faith.[45]

Goals sequentially follow the purpose of education. They are in themselves still general. Nevertheless, they are a bit more specific and able to provide a greater focus on objectives as is expected in a planning process that is not only step-by-step but also processes from the general to the specific.[46] Although not all curricula develop using this method, the majority do.

Objectives are the natural step toward plotting the terrain. They come before the outcomes, which are used to evaluate the teaching process. "Meaningful evaluation must begin with objectives that provide a basis for objective comparisons. Some objectives lend themselves readily to statistical comparisons (attendance, offerings, baptisms)."[47]

---

[43] Gilbert, "Curriculum planning in the proactive mode," 538–43.

[44] David C. Hester, "Christian education in a theological curriculum," *Religious Education* 87, no. 3 (Summer 1992): 337.

[45] Sanner and Harper, *Exploring Christian Education*, 164.

[46] Eisner, *The Educational Imagination*, 116–17.

[47] John W. Wade, "Evaluating the Effectiveness of Christian Education," in *Foundations of Christian Education*, ed. Eleanor Daniel and John Wade (Joplin, MO: College Press, 1999), 346.

Harold Burgess identifies four major approaches to Christian education in the twentieth century, each with their own distinct emphases on curricular objectives:

1. *Traditional*—the communication of the divine message
2. *Social Cultural*—the initiation of the young into creative personal and social experiences
3. *Contemporary*—personal growth and development, intellectual growth, understanding of the Bible, and education and training of persons within the church to be the church.
4. *Social Science*—the enablement of Christian living[48]

Religious curriculum should write objectives from all domains not just the cognitive and, in this way, plan for a holistic approach to educating the individual.

Objectives provide the precursor to outcomes, as they "are typically specific statements of what students are to be able to do after having experienced a curriculum or a portion of one. Objectives of the instructional variety are supposed to state with little ambiguity what particular forms of behavior the student will be able to display."[49]

Some educators have moved from an exhaustive list of objectives, activities, and procedures in the curriculum development process to the creation of "measurable objectives,"[50] thus allowing educators the flexibility to design their own activities and procedures on an individual or small group level. However, the issue remains that "it does very little good to list an objective unless activities for achieving it and procedures for evaluating progress are also considered."[51] So if measurable objectives were not the norm, then a list of expected outcomes would be needed to evaluate progress.

---

[48] Harold W. Burgess, *Invitation to Religious Education* (Birmingham: Religious Education Press, 1975), 30, 68, 100–101, 132. Cf. also D. Campbell Wyckoff, "The Sunday School Curriculum," *The Reformed Review* 34, no. 1 (Autumn 1980): 38.

[49] Eisner, *The Educational Imagination*, 117.

[50] R. Heinich, M. Molenda, J. Russell, and S. Smaldino, *Instructional Media and Technologies for Learning*, 7th ed. (Englewood Cliffs: Prentice Hall, 2002).

[51] James R. Gress and David E. Purpel, *Curriculum: An Introduction to the Field* (Berkley: McClutchan, 1978), 337.

While we may talk about objectives from the perspective of learning domains (cognitive, affective, and volitional), Klaus Issler and Ronald Habermas have urged Christian educators to consider the overall outcomes or measurements of our objectives when we develop the curriculum. In particular, they have urged that our outcomes consider capability and performance for a more holistic learning as indicated in Scripture. They write, "Capability refers to what we ask students to do in class, indicating their learning . . . but we are also interested in their life style changes. That's what performance represents; what students normally do in life, right or wrong."[52] They have thus divided the affective domain into two parts, labeling the second *dispositional*. The capability for the affective level in the classroom would indicate certain attitudes and motivations, and the capability for dispositional would be certain values and tendencies. Affective levels of performance would include Christian attitudes and feelings, but dispositional levels of performance would be Christian dispositions with life-style habits.

Organization of Curriculum

Taba notes that the patterns for curriculum organization used to organize pieces of the curriculum will organize the entire curriculum. These include scope, sequence, continuity, and integration.[53] Eisner suggests that there are two unique designs for organizing the curriculum. The first is that of a staircase, with one level of knowledge building on the other until the learner exits at the top of the platform. The second one is a spider web from which the learner is able to select and explore areas of interest. Learning is not controlled but engaging in its creation.[54] Traditionally, the scope of a curriculum has been charted and looks at each of the activities, aligning them to the objectives, creating a vertical and horizontal graphic organizer. However, often the scope of a formal church curriculum is haphazard rather than critically designed.[55] If the church's curriculum is not intentional, then the outcomes will be uncertain and will fall short of desired results.

---

[52] Klaus Issler and Ronald Habermas, *How We Learn: A Christian Teacher's Guide to Educational Psychology* (Grand Rapids: Baker, 1994), 285.

[53] Taba, *Curriculum Development*, 382.

[54] Eisner, *The Educational Imagination*, 122–23.

[55] Francis and Thatcher, *Christian Perspectives for Education*, 293.

According to McKinney, the development of a plan would be guided by three key factors: (1) determining the scope, needs, purpose, and objectives; (2) balancing the priorities with the resources you have; and (3) determining the sequence in which the curriculum would be taught.[56] Problems arise when educators have not considered the extent of the learning in their planning. Outcomes should also be two-dimensional in that they not only look at the content but also the mental processes—that they look at the sequence of learning and determine how broad or deep learning will be.[57] Such a design will yield a desired outcome through intentional planning, as it would look at the continuity, the sequence, and the integration of it all.

Teaching and Learning

Teaching and learning in the church likewise are thought of differently. While some draw from secular approaches, many feel it should be distinct from this. Rather, it should "enable pupils to ask the right questions about the spiritual and moral dimensions of human experience in order that a more tolerant society may be created."[58] Thus, it takes on another design: "Instructional dialogue between believers: sharing of faith insights; continued evangelization of believers; gradual initiation into the faith tradition; religious socialization and enculturation; celebration of faith in liturgy; broad range of faith-engaging experiences."[59]

Robert Pazmiño uses three metaphors to describe the teaching/learning process and its relationship to curriculum in a linear pattern: production, travel and growth, while seeing clearly that there are different types of instruction with each. Curriculum, which is teacher-directed, is considered production, but the extreme is that of growth which is student-directed. In the middle is mutually directed or travel. The extreme views of teaching on this continuum are seen as a science or an art.[60] This is one way of viewing the teaching and learning process.

---

[56] Siew, "A Curriculum Model for the Evaluation of Existing Programs of Theological Education in Asia," 155.

[57] Taba, *Curriculum Development*, 428–29.

[58] Francis and Thatcher, *Christian Perspectives for Education*, 285.

[59] Ibid., 293.

[60] Robert W. Pazmiño, "Curriculum Foundations," *Christian Education Journal* 8, no. 1 (Autumn 1987): 33.

Ted Ward's model seems to combine them all with an understanding of the learning process that would achieve the best of them all. He explains teaching and learning using a concept map that looks like a picket fence. The fence shows an approach to teaching and learning that incorporates study, practice, and sharing, which is a combination of teacher-directed, mutually directed, and student-directed teaching and learning.[61] This model incorporates dialogue in the process of sharing.

Evaluation

Evaluation is about maintenance and integrity. All things related to teaching and learning should be evaluated. In fact, evaluation pervades curriculum development.[62] It is not done as an afterthought but continually and throughout to make decisions. If something is not going as planned, adjustment is necessary. This can only come from routine evaluation and change as a result of assessment. When evaluation is built in to the education system, there is integrity. For no matter how efficiently you begin, the system will ultimately change for the better through this process.

When we answer the questions "who," "what," and "why," we are evaluating the learner. These questions will ultimately go deeper in evaluating the teaching as well as the curriculum and resources as the answers lend themselves to the formation of educational integrity.[63]

Another important element is the evaluation of the curriculum and resources, accomplished by looking at much of the same information suggested above regarding the learner and comparing it to the content sources and the intended goals and outcomes.[64] The curriculum is not just the written resources; it is also the teacher and the methods of teaching.

Plans need to be made for evaluation for the purpose of quality assurance. Such evaluation would ask the following questions: How do

---

[61] See Siew, "A Curriculum Model for the Evaluation of Existing Programs of Theological Education in Asia," 157.

[62] Cf. Eisner, *The Educational Imagination*, 130; Naylor, "Curriculum Development," 131.

[63] Sanner and Harper, *Exploring Christian Education*, 165.

[64] Ibid., 181.

you evaluate the quality of learning? How do you check to see that the ends of education are being achieved? How does one make sure that there is consistency between the aims and objectives? What is actually achieved by students? Does the curriculum organization provide experiences that offer optimum opportunities for all varieties of learners to attain independent goals?[65]

For curriculum development in the church, we must ask if we need a new model, a combination of models, or simply clarification of what the curriculum development process is for the church. A new model is in order but one that is value-laden with a biblical, theological, and historical foundation, one that is attune to today's societal forces, and one that is guided by what we know about the learner and of learning, combining the best of understandings. This model should be simply defined and yet flexible for multiple church ministries. This curriculum development model for the church will have procedures, an understanding of the curriculum components, identified participants in the development process, and a list of essential activities.

Such a process should consider the necessary procedures and components needed. There are four accepted procedures: (1) it can be a cyclical system, (2) it can involve a routine review of foundational areas of concern (as well as recent ones such as the use of technology or globalization), (3) it can use data in decision-making, and (4) it can involve multiple individuals in the planning process.[66] The three components of curriculum development are curriculum as content or procedure, the organization or design of the curriculum, and the sequence for teaching.

Our proposed model is unique as it accepts a dual definition of curriculum. It is important to understand that curriculum is content and process, a dual definition, which demands equal treatment in our curriculum development. Models of curriculum development relate to and are dependent on the definition we give to curriculum. There are two distinct definitions, one defining curriculum as a process and the other defining it as content. To design a model for curriculum development we must

---

[65] Taba, *Curriculum Development*, 13.

[66] Cf. Wiles and Bondi, *Curriculum Development*, 2–3; Anthony and Benson, *Exploring the History and Philosophy of Christian Education*, 411–20.

understand the perspectives of both definitions and their relationship. It is this author's view that curriculum can be defined as both process and content; thus curriculum development is dependent on both definitions of curriculum, though that has not been the historical precedent.

Organization or design of curriculum is considered in various ways, and educators should pick from them according to their aims and purpose allowing them to guide their curriculum development plan. While there are any number of measured curriculum designs, the most commonly discussed are subject-centered, societal-centered, and individual-centered.[67]

Tasks for Curriculum Development

What are the tasks for curriculum development, where does it begin, how is it managed, and where does it end? There are multiple elements to be arranged and obviously many suggestions.[68] It would be beneficial to learn from history and the previous insight of others who have gone before. We should first approach curriculum development in a linear manner with each stage preparing for the next. However, as we proceed, we will also need to evaluate and deliberate on each of these stages routinely and in an ongoing manner in an effort to align them and allow for change, so our plan does not become stagnant but rather able to change as the needs may change.

The foundational step is the first stage. While it is possible your church has already established this, it is important to proceed here for the sake of clarification and refinement. It would be important to review the biblical, theological, and historical foundations of your ministry; and, if they are not determined, take the time to establish

---

⁶⁷ Klein, "Alternative Curriculum Conceptions and Designs," 312.

⁶⁸ Cf. Wiles and Bondi, *Curriculum Development*, 71; Henry Kelly, "Technology and the Transformation of American Education," in *Curriculum Planning: A New Approach*, 6th ed., ed. Glen Hass and Forest Parkay (Boston: Allyn and Bacon, 1993), 83; Merril M. Oaks, Jeff Worthy, and Anne Remaley, "Confronting Our Nation's At-Risk and Dropout Dilemma," in *Curriculum Planning: A New Approach*, 6th ed., ed. Glen Hass and Forest Parkay (Boston: Allyn and Bacon, 1993), 94–127; Glen Hass and Forest Parkay, eds., *Curriculum Planning: A New Approach*, 6th ed. (Boston: Allyn and Bacon, 1993), 287.

and clarify your mission and purpose. This is not a task that should be undertaken by individuals outside the ministry, as that would only confuse the purpose. Neither should it be done without regard to the context in assessing the need for ministry.

The second stage is the preliminary stage designed to assess the context or needs of the community of learners and to decide how these needs can be aligned with the purpose already determined. This preliminary stage will give voice to the societal, cultural, and psychological needs routinely reviewed in order to make ongoing changes and improvements. In its initial development, this stage takes on a linear process, which becomes cyclical or sporadic as determined by the educators for the purpose of advancement. Finally, it is important that this step does not overpower or omit the foundational purpose for ministry. This might cause a disconnection and not allow the ministry to reach the needs of the people. Two examples of changing needs are in the area of learning resources or facilities. As learners mature and develop, needs change; therefore, the curriculum should also change to match the new needs. Likewise, as the size or age of the learning community changes, the limits of a facility or learning resources may actually hinder teaching. The plan must always evaluate the contextual needs and align them with the purpose of the ministry.

The third stage of this plan is the development stage. This stage deals separately with the components of content and learning experiences. Often this is seen incorrectly as the only stage in the curriculum development plan. Within this stage there are a variety of options that must be determined by your ministry team related to who will be involved in the planning and how the curriculum will be determined, aligned, and delivered. The way a church does this is dependent on the context of the ministry and the alignment to the preceding stages. There are different roles in this stage that are uniquely determined by the qualification and authority given to different players, all of which is unique to the specific church ministry.

The evaluation stage is the last process in this curriculum development model. It is in the phase of development that evaluation mechanisms are established for the curriculum resources, the teacher, and the learner. This phase does not evaluate the mission and purpose except to determine whether the desired outcomes were met.

The key to each stage is the process of deliberation. Those involved limit deliberation at each stage by design. However, it broadens our perspective and understanding of the key factors that influence curriculum allowing for multiple voices to be heard in the deliberation. While it clarifies and validates the process at each stage, it does so by reflecting on the work preceding it. Moving in a linear or even cyclical manner to the next step does not weaken the development of curriculum. Rather it is strengthened by the development of the relationship between the stages as they deliberate and align them in the process.

The final stage is the perennial stage. This stage is recurring and enduring. It allows for the discontinuing of a curriculum as a natural process if it has served its purpose. It also allows for changes such as an increase of a specific class's age grouping as its members grow older and desire to remain intact as a group. This perennial stage will also routinely evaluate the purpose and context of ministry along with the development and assessment of the other stages. The proposed model has been developed using the best insight from those who have gone before us (see fig. 7.2 on pp. 157–58).

Key Terms and Concepts

Deliberation	Evaluation
Outcomes	Context

Reflective Questions

1. What key knowledge is gained through understanding the historical roots of curriculum development?
2. What is the value of deliberation in the curriculum development process?
3. How is evaluation tied to curriculum development?

Stage	Players in the Deliberation of This Stage	Component(s) Involved	Task(s)	Responsibility
Foundation	Ministry Team Christian Educators	Mission	• Review Foundations • Deliberate and Clarify Mission and Purpose	Determine Ministry's Mission and Purpose for Christian Education
Development	Ministry Team Christian Educators Community Parents Learners	Context	• Develop a Psychological Understanding • Survey/Research Demographics on Societal and Cultural Factors • Survey/Review Needs and Interests of Learners • Survey/Review the Needs and Interests of Teachers • Determine Available Materials and Resources	• Determine Characteristics, Needs and Interests of Learners • Determine Characteristics, Needs and Interests of Teachers

	Roles	Component	Tasks	Outputs
Development	Ministry Team Christian Educators Parents (optional) Learners (optional)	Content	• Review Possible Sources of Content • Review Possible Conceptions of Curriculum • Review Organizing Principles • Review Possible Organization of Content	• Conceptualize Curriculum • Determine Elements and Organization of Content • Establish Conceptualized Framework for Curriculum
	Ministry Team (optional) Christian Educators	Experiences	• Select • Develop • Organize	• Design the Curriculum
Evaluation	Ministry Team Christian Educators	Evaluation	• Plan Evaluations • Design Evaluations	• Design Evaluation System for the Assessment of Teachers, Curriculum, and Learners
Perennial	Ministry Team Christian Educators Parents (optional) Learners (optional)	Advancement	• Plan Monitoring System for Review of Assessments • Plan Professional Development/Trainings • Plan process for implementation of Change	• Continual Cycle of Evaluation • Sporadic Evaluation

Figure 7.2 : Curriculum Development Model for the Church

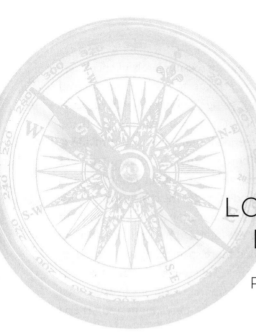

CHAPTER 8

IDENTIFYING LOCATIONS AND DESTINATIONS

PURPOSES, GOALS, AND OBJECTIVES

Roger White

dentifying key locations and destinations on the educational journey is an important consideration for mapmakers (educators who develop curriculum). Designing and implementing the ideal curriculum map begins by discerning God's ultimate desires for creation and humankind and identifying God's directives for humanity. Identification of map locations and curricular destinations arise out of this discernment. For those seeking to orient to true north, locations and destinations are rooted in God's desires and directives for humanity. These desires and directives form the basis for the purpose, goals, and objectives[1] of the educational or curricular plan. These locations and destinations become the foundation for decisions about what is taught and how the curriculum is delivered.

---

[1] Objectives are also referred to as learning outcomes.

Purposes, goals, and objectives reflect increasing levels of specificity related to an educational plan. Purposes relate to the big picture and address the question, "Where are we going?" Goals provide a sense of direction and inform decisions about the best way to get there. Objectives are related to specific intended outcomes and provide a means for determining whether and how progress is being made. For example, a congregation's mission and vision statement communicates the overarching identity of the church and provides the basis (purpose) for its educational programs. The goals of the educational program flow out of this purpose statement and describe the intended result of the learning experience. When these goals are applied more specifically to instruction, they yield objectives and learning outcomes. Together all these expressions of intent provide educational norms and standards for an instructional endeavor. They give direction for designing the curriculum and criteria for assessing the educational plan and the progress of the learner.

Because formal statements and accompanying educational plans are always incomplete due to our finiteness and the limitations of condensing life into short propositions, educational aims such as purposes, goals, and objectives require ongoing review and revision. New trends and approaches to education usually arise in response to situations where one or more foundational education values fail to receive enough attention. Aligning and balancing the curriculum with appropriate purposes, goals, and objectives is an ongoing task of educators—even for those who may not use formal statements in the process of describing what they plan to do.

Some curriculum trends are welcomed correctives aimed at addressing the complexity of life and balancing the curriculum, but when isolated as singular educational themes they may become reductionistic and too narrowly focused. Educators must be selective and concentrate on particular purposes, goals, or objectives for a time, but any attempt to view certain ones too exclusively will eventually distort them by ignoring the broader experiential context and removing connection to other important purposes, goals, or objectives. This is the reason why mapmakers in the church need to be wise when evaluating and responding to current educational trends.

Educators (mapmakers) are influenced in their planning by their internal convictions, their immediate community, and their educational heritage and associated traditions. Educators experience these influences in different ways depending on their background. Given the pre-theoretical nature of some educational assumptions, formal explanations and explicit statements about educational beliefs do not always accompany the transmission of educational aims between generations of educators. Periodically, educators need to rediscover their distinctive direction in order to prioritize the steps in their path.

C. S. Lewis speaks of a universal principle relating to what he calls first and second things. He says, "You can't get second things by putting them first; you can get second things only by putting first things first."[2] It is a profoundly simple life principle. When we try to put second things first we fail to experience the second things completely and end up missing the fullness of first things. But when we put first things first then not only do we gain the first things but also the second things.[3] In the process of educational planning and determining purposes, goals, and objectives, educators attempt to discover what is first and what is second.[4] In doing so they interpret what is important in life and clarify the primary and subordinate ends of education.

The Christian faith asserts that God is the ultimate first thing and that any and all second things proceed from God. Human purposes need to be oriented or reoriented to God's purposes (God's desires for creation and directives to humanity) in order to form the basis for curricular maps and educational plans. All other competing influences on educational purposes, goals, and objectives while important, are secondary. For Christians, the recovery of educational distinctiveness depends on this orientation to true north (see chap. 2). Knowing God and God's intentions for creation and humanity is the starting point for Christian educators.

---

[2] C. S. Lewis, "First and Second Things," in *God in the Dock: Essays on Theology and Ethics* (Grand Rapids: Eerdmans, 1970), 280. Lewis also states, "Every preference of a small good to a great, or a partial good to a total good, involves the loss of the small or partial good for which the sacrifice was made" (280).

[3] Lewis writes, "Aim at heaven and you get earth thrown in. Aim at earth and you will get neither" (C. S. Lewis, *Christian Behavior* [New York: Macmillan, 1945], 55).

[4] As Lewis goes on to explain, ". . . the question, What things are first? is of concern not only to philosophers but to everyone" (Lewis, "First Things," 280).

An important avenue for discerning God's desires and directives is through the Scriptures. This chapter will begin with an overview of key passages and narratives of Scripture that illuminate God's desires and directives related to creation and humanity, followed by a thematic summary of these passages and narratives. The chapter will conclude with a proposal for an educational taxonomy that is predicated on this foundational understanding.

Discerning God's Desires

The desires of God and his purposes for creation and humanity are not all revealed collectively in a single place in the Bible. What we do find throughout the narratives of Scripture are numerous references to God's will, including God's decrees, purposes, counsels, and commands. From these life directives and pronouncements of divine resolve and volitional activity, God's desires are discerned. Through knowing and seeking God and honoring his desires, educators contextualize teaching responsibilities and educational endeavors so that they align with God's ultimate intentions. Investigating God's desires—especially his purpose and will—yields several key life directives and themes. These themes provide a foundational framework from which educational purposes, goals, and objectives may be derived.

God's Hidden vs. Revealed Will

The will of God and his accompanying desires can be understood in different ways. When theologians talk about God's desires, they will sometimes distinguish between God's *hidden* will and God's *revealed* will.[5] The hidden will involves God's unseen comprehensive plan for the world whereby he ordains what happens,[6] as seen in Eph 1:11 where we read that God "works out everything in conformity with the purpose of his will." In contrast, God's revealed will is characterized by

---

[5] Wayne Grudem, *Systematic Theology: An Introduction to Biblical Doctrine* (Grand Rapids: Zondervan, 1994), 213; Thomas C. Oden, *Systematic Theology, Volume One: The Living God* (San Francisco: HarperCollins, 1992), 95. Cf. Deut 29:29.

[6] Question number seven of the Westminster Shorter Catechism defines the decree of God as "his eternal purpose, according to the counsel of his will, whereby, for his own glory, he hath foreordained whatsoever comes to pass."

the giving of precepts addressing creaturely duty and moral obligation. These conditions and stipulations express God's nature and direct us as to what we ought to do. Hundreds of such instructions and principles are given in the Bible (for example, the Ten Commandments).

Educators use the revealed aspect of God's will for identifying curricular purposes. Through consideration of God's revealed moral will—particularly as evidenced through the precepts and stories of Scripture—educational goals are formed, and from these, objectives are identified. This process is like the general Christian practice of discerning how God's intentions apply to life, but it goes further and relates them to the aims of *teaching* Christianly. In both cases believers and educators are pursuing an appropriate response to God's revelation—all of life rightly lived in light of all we know of God's desires.

God's Desires in the Narratives of Scripture

God is purposeful. Passages such as Ps 33:11: "The plans of the LORD stand firm forever, the purposes of his heart through all generations," reveal this truth. God's eternal purpose is ultimately accomplished in Jesus Christ (Eph 3:11) and those who love God and are called according to God's purposes are assured that God is working good for them in all things (Rom 8:28).

God's desires and purposes for humanity are not realized simply through abstract declaration; they are evident in the way God relates personally to people across history. God's relational nature is expressed in the Incarnation. God became human in Jesus and lived among us, modeling this relational way of living and communicating. The Holy Spirit is provided as a counselor to guide us in life and the discovery of God's purposes. Through God's people—the church—the community of believers is built up and equipped. God is made known in many ways and God's desires can be gleaned from this divine and multifaceted self-disclosure. A primary means of God's personal revelation to all humanity flows through the narratives of Scripture.

In Mic 6:8 we read, "He has showed you, O man, what is good. And what does the LORD require of you? To act justly and to love mercy and to walk humbly with your God."[7] Although directed to a particular

---

[7] Cf. Hos 6:6.

people at a given point in history, the message is timeless. In the Gospel of John (6:28–29) we see a similar inquiry. Someone asks Jesus, "What must we do to do the works God requires?" Jesus replies, "The work of God is this: to believe in the one he has sent." These passages and the narratives in which they are embedded illustrate a human interest in knowing God's desires, and they provide examples of God's will revealed and expressed through specific life directives: act justly, love mercy, walk humbly with God, and believe in the One he has sent.

The Scriptures include examples of people who sought to put God's revealed will into practice. The apostle Paul's daily living, ministry practice, and language all reflect how personal goals grow out of an understanding of God's purposes. For example, he tells the Philippians, "One thing I do: Forgetting what is behind and straining toward what is ahead, I press on toward the goal to win the prize for which God has called me heavenward in Christ Jesus" (Phil 3:13b–14). The calling, an expression of God's will and purpose, is Paul's focus; he aligns his life accordingly.

To Timothy he writes, "The goal of our instruction is love from a pure heart and a good conscience and a sincere faith" (1 Tim 1:5 NASB). To the Colossians he asserts, "We proclaim him, counseling and teaching everyone with all wisdom, so that we may present everyone perfect in Christ. To this end I labor, struggling with all his energy, which so powerfully works in me" (Col 1:28–29). He makes direct reference to the aims of his ministry and incorporates education-related language in the process.

Later in Colossians, Paul explains the direction of his ministry further, "My purpose is that they [those to whom he is referring in the letter] may be encouraged in heart and united in love, so that they may have the full riches of complete understanding, in order that they may know the mystery of God, namely, Christ, in whom are hidden all the treasures of wisdom and knowledge" (Col 2:2–3). This explanation aligns with the anticipated outcomes Paul specifies for those exercising the spiritual gift of teaching, who are "to prepare God's people for works of service, so that the body of Christ may be built up until we all reach unity in the faith and in the knowledge of the Son of God and become mature, attaining to the whole measure of the fullness of Christ" (Eph 4:12–13). In both of these ministry outcome descriptions

Paul highlights the goals of knowing Christ and the unity of believers, both important aspects of God's will.

In a number of cases it is easy to draw a connection between life directives given by Paul to statements he makes about God's purposes. For example, he directs the Galatians, "as we have opportunity, let us do good to all people" (Gal 6:10).[8] Why are his followers to do good? An explanation can be seen in his letter to the Ephesians, "We are God's workmanship, created in Christ Jesus to do good works, which God prepared in advance for us to do" (Eph 2:10). God's desires explicitly include people being empowered to do good works. Such a view of the Creator's purpose provides a basis for Paul's ministry-related mandate to "do good."

We see in 2 Corinthians another example where God's purposes provide a basis for one of Paul's life directives. In a discussion about the future, Paul explains that God has prepared a place in heaven for believers. The reader is told, God "made us for this very purpose" (2 Cor 5:5). As Paul wrestles through the issue of remaining mortal in his "earthly tent" or becoming clothed with the heavenly dwelling provided by God, he makes his ambition abundantly clear, "we make it our goal to please him, whether we are at home in the body or away from it" (2 Cor 5:9). Paul wants to please God because he knows that while he was made for something greater, he will be judged nonetheless for his earthly response to God and held accountable for his life lived in the body (2 Cor 5:10).[9]

Pleasing God, doing good works, knowing Christ, and being complete in him are just a few of the themes present in Paul's life goals and ministry aims. They find their origin in Paul's relationship with God and sensitivity to God's desires and directives. God's purposes inform the life directives that Paul follows and that he envisions for others. While Paul does not rank or order the themes, their collective priority is evident from the goal-related language he uses. It sets them apart from the many other general directives found throughout his writings.

---

[8] Cf. Titus 3:8a, "This is a trustworthy saying. And I want you to stress these things, so that those who have trusted in God may be careful to devote themselves to doing what is good." Cf. Col 1:9–10.

[9] Cf. Rom 12:1; Eph 5:10; 1 Thess 4:1a; see also Rom 14:17–18. For a reference to God's will and pleasing God in the book of Hebrews, see Heb 13:21.

These themes represent some of the primary aims of Paul's ministry and reflect what he considered the educational goals worth attaining.

Discerning God's Directives

In addition to addressing God's desires for creation and humanity, Scripture also contains directives that educators may utilize to inform goals. The directives summarized below address human responsibility and moral obligation in ways that transcend one's cultural background, developmental stage, life circumstances, or specific vocation.

Steward the Earth: The Cultural Mandate

The first life directive recorded in Scripture is found in its opening pages:

> So God created man in his own image, in the image of God he created him; male and female he created them. God blessed them and said to them, "Be fruitful and increase in number; fill the earth and subdue it. Rule over the fish of the sea and the birds of the air and over every living creature that moves on the ground." (Gen 1:27–28)

In the very beginning, humans were given a responsibility related to creation.[10] They were told to multiply, fill the earth, and subdue it. This by necessity includes interacting with the physical world and having a degree of knowledge and understanding about the nature of things. Men and women were to steward creation and govern the earth on God's behalf. Concerning this charge the psalmist acknowledges to God, "You have given them dominion over the works of your hands" (Ps 8:6a NRSV).[11]

---

[10] Whether the statement is merely a proclamation of what God intends to do or a direct instruction for humans to follow, its meaning related to purpose and educational goals remains unchanged, for it is an expression of God's desire. Educators will want to align their educational endeavors with God's original intent for humanity.

[11] See context of Ps 8:5–8; see also Heb 2:5–9 where the writer applies the passage to Christ. Note themes from Gen 1:27–28 present in Ps 115:14–16.

This first directive is commonly referred to as the *cultural mandate*.[12] The responsibility it corporately assigns to humanity continues throughout the Bible. Beginning in the creation account Adam is assigned a specific expression of the stewarding role, the task of cultivating the ground, "The LORD God took the man and put him in the Garden of Eden to work it and take care of it" (2:15). Neither Adam's disobedience (referred to as the fall) nor the subsequent disobedience of future generations negated this directive. Noah receives a renewal of the part of the command that might have been in doubt following the widespread destruction of humanity: "As for you, be fruitful and increase in number; multiply on the earth and increase upon it" (Gen 9:7). Stewarding creation remained an ongoing part of the mandate that carries significant eschatological implications.[13] The cultural mandate calls for inhabiting and caretaking the earth in a way that honors God's intentions.

Fear and Know God: The Wisdom Literature

The pursuit of wisdom is addressed throughout the Old Testament, particularly in the wisdom literature. Proverbs states, "wisdom is supreme; therefore get wisdom" (4:7). Attaining and knowing wisdom is one of the purposes given for the book of Proverbs (1:2) and the first nine chapters is an extended exhortation to acquire it. The Old Testament wisdom literature of Job and Ecclesiastes similarly emphasizes the application of wisdom to all of life. The foundational essence of wisdom is described in Proverbs with the statement, "The fear of the LORD is the beginning of wisdom, and knowledge of the Holy One is understanding" (9:10). The first portion of this passage affirms that fear of the Lord—having a reverence for God—is the beginning of wisdom. The second phrase states that knowledge of God, the Holy One, is understanding. Reverencing God and knowing God reflect wisdom and understanding respectively.

The importance of this directive—to fear and know God—is underscored throughout the wisdom literature. The book of Ecclesiastes

---

[12] James W. Sire, *Discipleship of the Mind: Learning to Love God in the Ways We Think* (Downers Grove, IL: InterVarsity, 1990); Arthur F. Holmes, *The Idea of a Christian College* (Grand Rapids: Eerdmans, 1975).

[13] Cf. Rev 5:10.

concludes its reflection on the meaning of life with the instruction to fear God. The final paragraph begins, "The conclusion, when all has been heard, *is*: fear God and keep His commandments, because this *applies* to every person" (12:13 NASB). Fearing (reverencing) God was also one of the main responses expected from the Israelites after they heard the teaching of God's commands through Moses:

> These are the commands, decrees and laws the LORD your God directed me to teach you to observe in the land that you are crossing the Jordan to possess, so that you, your children and their children after them may fear the LORD your God as long as you live by keeping all his decrees and commands that I give you, and so that you may enjoy long life. (Deut 6:1–2)

Likewise, the "knowing God" theme is also referenced elsewhere. In Jeremiah, God declares, "Let him who boasts boast about this: that he understands and *knows* me" (9:24a, emphasis added) and in the New Testament, Jesus defines eternal life as *knowing* God and the one he sent (John 17:3).[14] The commands to fear and know God provide a foundation for living wisely.

Seek First His Kingdom and His Righteousness

In the opening pages of the New Testament, Matthew records the start of Jesus' ministry by emphasizing the place of the kingdom of heaven in Jesus' preaching. Jesus proclaims the kingdom of heaven is near and preaches its message of good news (Matt 4:17,23).[15] It is in this context that we find another key life directive. In the Sermon on the Mount, Jesus explains kingdom living and says of the heavenly Father, "Seek first his kingdom and his righteousness" (Matt 6:33). The primacy urged in this command emphasizes God's sovereign rule over all and the rightness of God's ways (i.e., righteousness). These parallel concerns are to be sought and pursued as basic life commitments. Development of this kingdom mentality and outlook

---

[14] Cf. "This is good, and pleases God our Savior, who wants all men to be saved and to come to a knowledge of the truth" (1 Tim 2:3b–4).

[15] Jesus distinguishes the kingdom of heaven from a kingdom built on the standards of the world when he says, "My kingdom is not of this world" (John 18:36).

is given supreme importance in Jesus' teaching. The prayer that Jesus taught the disciples includes the surrender and affirmation to God: "Your kingdom come, your will be done on earth as it is in heaven" (Matt 6:10).

The idea of a righteous kingdom began in the Old Testament with God's intent to be in a special relationship with a particular group of people. God tells Moses concerning the Israelites, "Although the whole earth is mine, you will be for me a kingdom of priests and a holy nation" (Exod 19:5b–6a). The idea of a unique people under God's rule continues throughout redemptive history, and we find it referenced again at the close of the New Testament. In the book of Revelation the saints before the throne sing to the Lamb about the redeemed, "you have made them to be a kingdom and priests to serve our God" (Rev 5:10).[16] Acknowledgement of the reality of God's kingdom is to characterize our living.

Love God and Neighbor: The Greatest Commandment

When a tutor of the law asked Jesus which of the commandments was most important, Jesus responded that the commandments are all summed up in the directive to love God and neighbor (Matt 22:34–40; Mark 12:28–31). The greatest commandment is recognized as central to living Christianly. At the time, those in Jesus' hearing asked for further clarification as to his meaning (Luke 10:25–29). One listener asked, "Who is my neighbor?" to which Jesus answered with the parable of the Good Samaritan (Luke 10:30–37). The parable suggests that a neighbor is anyone in need (even if an enemy); therefore, caring for the needs of others is part of fulfilling this command.

What about loving God? First John 5:3 reads, "This is love for God: to obey his commands," and in John 14:15, "If you love me, you will obey what I command." In order to follow the greatest commandment to love God one must not ignore the other commandments but acknowledge the full scope of God's directives and how they communicate his purposes for humanity. John goes on to explain, "his commands are not burdensome" (1 John 5:3b), and it is clear from Paul's writings that acceptance before God does not rest solely on our obedience to

---

[16] Cf. Rev 1:5–6.

the commands (Rom 3:20),[17] but is an important evidence of faithful Christian living.

When Jesus answered the question concerning which command was most important, he quoted several Old Testament passages (Deut 6:5; Lev 19:18). Statements in Deuteronomy immediately following the command to love God (6:5) help illustrate its practical application. Verse six explains that attention to the commands is foundationally a heart issue and verse seven directs parents to "impress them on your children" (6:7). The believing community's everyday experience of loving God was evidenced by acknowledging with one's whole being God's words and ways and communicating the commandments to children (cf. 6:6–9), all clear examples of connecting God's purposes with educational goals.

Scripture records two occasions where Jesus summed up the Law and the Prophets. Once, as we have just seen, where he was asked about the most important command, but also near the end of the Sermon on the Mount where he concludes, "In everything, do to others what you would have them do to you" explaining, "this sums up the Law and the Prophets" (Matt 7:12). This second summary is known popularly as the "Golden Rule," the goal of valuing others the way you want to be valued and desiring for them your own preferences.[18] Both of these important summaries are examples of God's desires.[19] God's followers are to love God and their neighbors.

Make Disciples: The Great Commission

The last words Jesus spoke to his followers before ascending into heaven include the directive that has heavily influenced evangelistic expressions of Christianity. Known as *The Great Commission* or *The Missionary Mandate*, it concludes Matthew's account of Jesus' ministry:

> Then Jesus came to them and said, "All authority in heaven and on earth has been given to me. Therefore go and make disciples of all nations, baptizing them in the name of the Father and

---

[17] Cf. the assurance of Rom 8:28 and the connection between loving God and being called according to his purposes.

[18] See also Gal 6:2.

[19] Cf. Rom 13:8–10.

of the Son and of the Holy Spirit, and teaching them to obey everything I have commanded you. And surely I will be with you always, to the very end of the age." (Matt 28:18–20)[20]

Believers are commanded to go and make disciples, communicating to others the full message of Christ. Particular importance has been placed on this directive since it is one of Jesus' last commands and because it includes a specific preface regarding its authoritative nature. As we saw above in considering the directive to love God, a connection is made to a broader range of commandments. Preaching the gospel and baptizing converts should be accompanied by teaching obedience to all of Jesus' commands. Attention to such a wide scope of commands was not something new for the people of God. In Leviticus, God commanded Aaron, "You must teach the Israelites all the decrees the LORD has given them through Moses" (Lev 10:11). All of God's directives are important to consider in the journey of living and making disciples.

All of God's desires and directives as revealed in the Scriptures are the foundation and basis for identifying locations and destinations on curricular maps and determining the purposes, goals, and objectives of educational plans. Every day in the midst of changing circumstances, new dynamics, applications, and outcomes of God's will are realized. There are many applications and outcomes of God's desire that are uniquely realized in one's specific calling and setting, but the process begins by discovering and embracing God's most fundamental intentions.

A Thematic Summary of God's Desires and Directives

God's desires and directives discussed in the previous sections of this chapter explicate God's foundational intentions with regard to creation and humanity, which form the basis for educational maps and curricular plans. God's intentions translate into curricular purposes and goals that may be applied to specific objectives and outcomes appropriate to particular learners and learning contexts.

---

[20] Cf. Mark 16:15; Acts 1:8.

While there are many ways to synthesize God's desires and directives, they may be summarized for curriculum development in a framework of three themes:

1. Relationship with God and self
2. Relationship with others
3. Relationship with creation

These themes are intentionally stated in relational terms. This context respects the relational nature of God (the Trinity), the centrality of relationship between God and humanity from the beginning (Adam and Eve), and God's expressed intention for the way humanity was to relate to creation (fill and care for the earth). This relational context is an important corrective to tendencies educators may have to focus only on cognitive or behavioral evidence of Christian growth.

The Scriptures are full of references to the importance of the heart or inner life as the source of outward relational expressions of faith.[21] In both the Old Testament and the New, those seeking to live a faithful life are encouraged, exhorted, and commanded to attend to both inner and outer realities. Being in right relationship with God is the foundation for an accurate view of self and is the source of love for others.[22] Being in right relationship with God also provides the crucial reference point for what humanity is to be about while on earth.

These themes do not refer to discreet domains of relational activity; they are interactive, reciprocating, and mutually influencing, as illustrated in figure 8.1 (opposite). When in right relationship with God, we experience being God's beloved. This received love can then be extended to others and expressed through care for what God has made. Also, the experience of loving and serving others and being loved by them may deepen one's appreciation for God's love. Additionally, understanding and caring for God's creation may enhance the awe and wonder we have for God in view of the complexity and majesty evident in all God has made.

---

[21] Rom 10:10; Jas 2:24.
[22] Cf. 1 John.

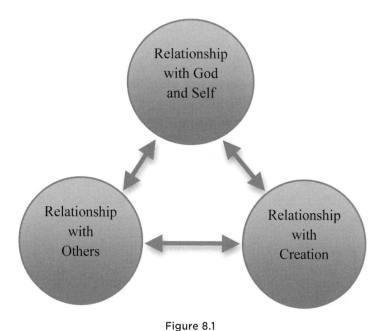

Figure 8.1

All of God's desires and directives contained in the Scriptures can be referenced within this framework. What follows is an expanded, though not exhaustive, list of related purposes and goals:

- Relationship with God and self—*Being in a right relationship with God*
  - Fear (Revere) God
  - Love God
  - Have appropriate self-regard
  - Be aware of heart motives/attitudes
  - Experience being the beloved of God
  - Be perfect and holy
  - Know God
  - Glorify God
  - Obey God
  - Please God
  - Seek God

- Relationship with others—*Reflecting God's image*
  - Love neighbor as self (the greatest commandment)
  - Make disciples (the Great Commission)
  - Do good works
  - Love enemies

- ■ Proclaim God's truth
- ■ Evangelize the lost
- ■ Care for widows, orphans, and the downtrodden

- • Relationship with creation—*Stewarding the creation*
  - ■ Be fruitful
  - ■ Fill the earth
  - ■ Rule over creation
  - ■ Protect and care for the earth (the creation mandate)
  - ■ Further God's kingdom and righteousness
  - ■ Advance the welfare of the world

For organizational and illustrative purposes, these examples have been located in specific thematic areas. In reality and practice, however, there is reciprocal influence. Many scriptural directives overlap in underscoring these themes, highlighting the inextricable link between them. Micah's exhortation to act justly, to love mercy, and walk humbly with God is an example of this (Mic 6:8). Acting in accordance with God's justice, loving mercy, and walking humbly with God reflects all three of these themes. Central passages in the Old Testament (the creation mandate, the Ten Commandments) and the New Testament (the greatest commandment; the Sermon on the Mount) all contain directives from God that may be understood in light of these themes.

These three themes address at the most fundamental level who we are meant to be and what we are meant to do. Educators partner with learners in becoming all they were created to be as they discover and attain their unique created purpose in God's overall plan. With this thematic framework in mind, reflecting God's purposes and goals for creation and humanity, educators are able to develop age-appropriate, context-specific educational objectives and curricular maps that learners may use in their journey to grow in relationship with God and self, relationship with others, and relationship with creation.

Selecting Educational Objectives that Reflect God's Desires and Directives

With God's purposes (desires and directives) clearly in mind and with a holistic framework of foundational goals (being in right relationship with God and self, others, and creation) in hand, the Christian educator undertakes the task of identifying specific objectives related to these aims. In the chapters that follow, more attention is given to how this process translates to specific learners and contexts, but in this final section educators are provided with general guidelines for selecting objectives and choosing curricular paths.

The purposes, goals, and objectives a local church congregation chooses to pursue are determined at several different levels of leadership. Regional or denominational leaders and their publishing departments provide various degrees of specificity regarding educational purposes and goals from which, at the local level, increasingly specific curricular and instructional objectives are determined. In these contexts and in independent churches, selections are usually made by the senior pastor or designee (such as a minister of education, pastor of spiritual formation, Sunday school superintendent, or youth minister) or by a leadership team within the church (see chap. 11). Sometimes these decision-makers in the church will defer the selection to individual teachers or specialists outside the local church such as authors of popular Christian books or publishers of non-denominational pre-packaged curriculum materials. Regardless of circumstances and the level at which objectives are formulated, the following guidelines may be kept in mind.

First, objectives should align with and be more specific than purposes and goals. This increased explicitness and clear connection to foundational curricular aims helps educators be more precise in curricular and instructional planning. The selection of objectives in a curriculum plan will reflect all the relevant aspects of an educational program's purposes and goals. This resulting balance and comprehensiveness helps assure that a church's intentions are fully addressed.

Second, objectives should clearly communicate what is envisioned for the learner. Some insist that objectives be formulated in such a way that any learning resulting from the curriculum and instruction be easily observable, measured, and assessed.[23] Others find that simply

---

[23] Robert F. Mager, *Preparing Instructional Objectives* (Belmont, CA: Fearon, 1962).

adding clarity and specificity in terms of the learner is sufficient for finding one's instructional way and that objectives need not be overly reductionistic or prescriptive.[24]

Third, in order to help learners respond fully to curricular purposes and goals, the objectives need to be holistically applied and address multiple aspects of the learner's makeup and experience. The social sciences characterize the human condition in many ways, but one classification system, or taxonomy, advanced by Benjamin Bloom,[25] and later expanded and revised by his colleagues[26] and other collaborators,[27] has found widespread use among educators for generating instructional objectives. This approach includes three domains of learning: cognitive (knowledge: mental skills), affective (attitudes: emotional skills), and psychomotor (behavior: physical skills). Learning objectives are established for each domain in a manner consistent with learner and contextual variables (e.g., age, developmental ability, nature of lesson material). All three domains are equally important, as together they reflect a holistic approach to learning. Each domain also includes successive levels of complexity and mastery, from the most basic to the most advanced.

Objectives within the cognitive domain relate to developing knowledge comprehension and critical-thinking skills. Objectives in the affective domain relate to developing emotional skills such as healthy attitudes and the capacity to feel and respond to the joy and pain of others. Objectives in the psychomotor domain relate to behavior and physical skills. Figure 8.2, a Thematic Curricular Taxonomy, takes these three domains of learning and reformulates and presents them in relation to the thematic framework earlier presented (see pp. 178–79).

---

[24] Elliot W. Eisner, *The Educational Imagination: On the Design and Evaluation of School Programs* (New York: MacMillan, 1979).

[25] Benjamin S. Bloom, ed., *Taxonomy of Educational Objectives: The Classification of Educational Goals. Handbook I: Cognitive Domain* (New York: McKay, 1956).

[26] David R. Krathwohl, ed., *Taxonomy of Educational Objectives: The Classification of Educational Goals. Handbook II: Affective Domain* (New York: McKay, 1964).

[27] Anita J. Harrow, *A Taxonomy of the Psychomotor Domain* (New York: McKay, 1972); Elizabeth Simpson, *The Classification of Educational Objectives: Psychomotor Domain* (Urbana, IL: University of Illinois Press, 1972).

In developing curricular maps, Christian educators can utilize existing taxonomies in a way that helps form learners according to God's desires and directives. These existing taxonomies, and the levels and types of learning they represent, can be combined with the three themes presented above that summarize God's purposes for humanity. Curricular journey locations and destinations are identified through discernment of God's desires and directives and through selection of related goals and objectives. Jesus' command to follow him[28] can be realized for learners through such curricular endeavors. Travelers can better find their way and grow in the process[29] with the help of educator guides who have intentionally identified the key locations and destinations for the journey.

Key Terms and Concepts

Purpose	God's Desires and Directives
Goals	Taxonomy
Objectives	

Reflection Questions

1. What aspects of God's desires for humanity are evident in the directives of the following passage?

> And now, O Israel, what does the LORD your God ask of you but to fear the LORD your God, to walk in all his ways, to love him, to serve the LORD your God with all your heart and with all your soul, and to observe the LORD commands and decrees that I am giving you today for your own good? (Deut 10:12–13)

---

[28] The idea of following, modeling, and imitation may be seen in the following passages: 1 Cor 4:16; Heb 6:12; 13:7; 3 John 1:11; 1 Thess 1:7; 2 Thess 3:7,9; 1 Cor 11:1; cf. Matt 9:14.

[29] Cf. 1 Thess 4:1; Eph 4:11–16; Deut 10:12–13,20–21; 2 Peter 1:5–7; Matt 7:24; Jas 1:25.

LEARNING DOMAINS

		Cognitive [31] (Knowledge: Mental Skills)	Affective [32] (Attitudes: Emotional Skills)	Psychomotor [33] (Behavior: Physical Skills)
GOD'S DESIRES AND DIRECTIVES	**Relationship with God and Self**	• Fear (Revere) God • Love God • Have Appropriate Self-Regard • Be Aware of Heart Motives/Attitudes • Experience being the Beloved of God • Be Perfect and Holy • Know God • Glorify God • Obey God • Please God • Seek God	Example: Learners will be able to remember, understand, apply, analyze, evaluate, and creatively arrange information about God and self . . .	Example: Learners will be able to receive, respond to, commit to, prioritize, and integrate attitudes and values in relationship with God and self . . .	Example: Learners will be able to imitate, practice, refine, coordinate, and initiate physical actions in relationship with God and self . . .
				. . .consistent with God's desires and directives.
	Relationship with Others	• Love Neighbor as Self • Make Disciples • Do Good Works • Love Enemies • Proclaim God's Truth • Evangelize the Lost • Care for Widows and Orphans, and the Downtrodden	Example: Learners will be able to remember, understand, apply, analyze, evaluate, and creatively arrange information in relationship with others	Example: Learners will be able to receive, respond to, commit to, prioritize, and integrate attitudes and values in relationship with others . . .	Example: Learners will be able to imitate, practice, refine, coordinate, and initiate physical actions in relationship with others . . . .
				. . . consistent with God's desires and directives.

Relationship with Creation	Example: Learners will be able to remember, understand, apply, analyze, evaluate, and creatively arrange information about the created world . . .	Example: Learners will be able to receive, respond to, commit to, prioritize, and integrate attitudes and values in relationship with the created world . . .	Example: Learners will be able to imitate, practice, refine, coordinate, and initiate physical actions in relationship with the created world . . .
• Be Fruitful • Fill the Earth • Rule over Creation • Protect and Care for the Earth • Further God's Kingdom and Righteousness • Advance the Welfare of the World			

. . . consistent with God's desires and directives.

Figure 8.2: Thematic Curricular Taxonomy

---

[31] Based on a revised taxonomy of Benjamin Bloom found in Lorin W. Anderson and David R. Krathwohl, eds., *A Taxonomy for Learning, Teaching, and Assessing* (New York: Longman, 2001).

[32] Based on a taxonomy of David Krathwohl as found in David Krathwohl, ed., *Taxonomy of Educational Objectives: The Classification of Educational Goals. Handbook II: Affective Domain* (New York: David McKay, 1964).

[33] Based on a taxonomy of R. H. Dave as found in R. H. Dave, "Psychomotor Level," in *Developing and Writing Educational Objectives*, ed. R. J. Armstrong (Tucson, AZ: Educational Innovators Press, 1970), 33–34.

2. What do we know today that Thomas did not know when he asked Jesus, "LORD, we don't know where you are going, so how can we know the way?" (John 14:5).

3. American educational philosopher John Dewey once said, "The educational process has no end beyond itself; it is its own end."[31] Do you agree with him? Why or why not?

4. How might your congregation determine purposes and goals for its education ministry?

[31] John Dewey, *Democracy and Education: An Introduction to the Philosophy of Education* (New York: Macmillan, 1938), 59.

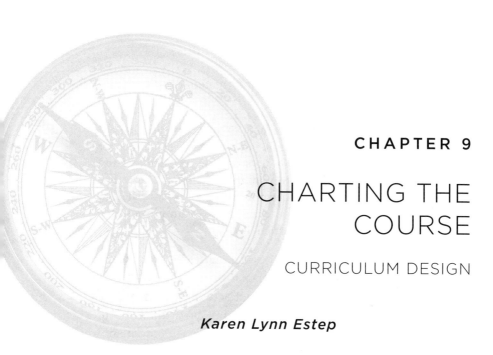

CHAPTER 9

CHARTING THE COURSE

CURRICULUM DESIGN

Karen Lynn Estep

So, do we get to Lexington by passing through Louisville or Cincinnati, I-64 or I-75?" Anyone on a long trip has taken the time to review atlases or visit mapping websites. Another crucial step in trip-planning is determining how the legs of a journey link together. These are the details of the itinerary that answer a traveling group's questions about the trip prior to starting out on the journey: how long will it be, where will it take us, and in what order will we do these things? This metaphor relates to curriculum design. Like the itinerary of a trip, curriculum design outlines the details and arranges the various components.

What Is Curriculum Design?

Defining curriculum design is just as frustrating as putting together the details of your travel plan unless you have experience and a well-founded understanding of what to do. It is confusing for a novice because there have been many designs over the years, some with great detail and others providing very little information prior to the journey. Leroy Ford defines it this way:

> A curriculum design is a statement of and elaboration of the institutional purpose, institutional goals and objectives for learners, scope, contexts, methodology, and instructional and administrative models involved in an educational effort. The design is organized in such a way as to ensure appropriate and balanced emphasis upon each element. A design provides the basis for "blueprinting" a curriculum plan.[1]

James E. Plueddemann simplifies the matter by defining curriculum design with only three components: the teaching/learning context, expected outcomes, and the educational activities. He notes that the context is oftentimes overlooked in designing curriculum.[2] Context is essential to the identity and uniqueness of Christian education, which seeks to reach the world with its purpose. When missing, it affects the success of the education ministry. When congregations fail to connect to their community, their ministry becomes ineffective and unrecognized. The same is true for curriculum. When it does not prepare Christians to live in the real world, the curriculum is irrelevant, and is likewise ineffective for preparing individuals to live a genuine Christian life.

Sanner and Harper, who include context in their model, pattern their work after Wyckoff, identifying and emphasizing the need for interdependent and interactive components:

> The *objective* is synonymous with the aim or purpose of the total design. *Scope* implies the total area that should be explored. *Context* is the setting in which Christian education is attempted. The *learning tasks* are the activities consciously pursued by the learner in order to acquire what he wants to know. The *organizing principle* describes the way the various components of the design are related to one another.[3]

---

[1] Leroy Ford, *A Curriculum Design Manual for Theological Education* (Nashville: Broadman, 1991), 34.

[2] James E. Plueddemann, "Curriculum Improvement through Evaluation," *Christian Education Journal* 8, no. 1 (Autumn 1987): 56–57.

[3] A. Elwood Sanner and A. F. Harper, *Exploring Christian Education* (Grand Rapids: Baker, 1978), 163.

The variation of terminology is not the only confusing part about curriculum design. Educators even have difficulty describing the relationship between the terms they use. This chapter seeks to make a new model that incorporates the best of their designs for the ministry of the church, emphasizing both the context and the interconnectedness of the components. As Wyckoff has noted,

> The context of Christian education is seen as the worshiping, witnessing, working community of persons in Christ. The scope of Christian education is the whole field of relationships in the light of the gospel. The purpose of Christian education is awareness of revelation and the gospel, and response in faith and love. The process of Christian education is participation in the life and work of the community of persons in Christ. The design of Christian education consists of sequences of activities and experiences by which the learning tasks may be effectively undertaken by individuals and groups.[4]

We need a new understanding of curriculum design components as our understanding for Christian education is broadening with growing understanding and becoming more global though the realities of mobility and technology. This understanding for the church is comprised of five components: ministry mission, context, content, learning experiences, and evaluation (see fig. 9.1 on p. 184).

These components are defined in such a way as to encompass the diverse ministries of Christian education in the church. This list does not propose to define the ministry of the church beyond echoing broadly that the purpose is twofold: (1) to establish an awareness of revelation (knowledge) which includes the gospel (salvation) and (2) to guide the learner's response (decision) in faith and love (living the life of a Christian). Having said this, the mission must be uniquely defined for individual organizations, paying particular attention to their unique context. To ensure this is achieved, the Christian education ministry leadership should review these components annually, and based on the evaluation stage of the process, re-align the curriculum. Without this practice, the curriculum could drift into irrelevancy.

---

[4] D. Campbell Wyckoff, *Theory and Design of Christian Education Curriculum* (Philadelphia: Westminster, 1961), 83–84.

Figure 9.1: Curriculum Design Components

Ministry Mission and Curriculum Design

Curriculum design starts with the ministry's mission: "All curricula, no matter what their particular design, are composed of certain elements. A curriculum usually contains a statement of aims and of specific objectives."[5] Using our metaphor of planning the itinerary, we need to determine where we are going. The ministry must determine the purpose (aims), goals, and objectives for ministry. Various individuals have defined these terms differently, though ultimately they are synonymous with outcomes. The mission and goals ultimately link to the objectives, which will in turn link to outcomes, simply because the mission of a ministry is to reach the desired outcomes (see chap. 8). Consider learn-

---

[5] Hilda Taba, *Curriculum Development Theory and Practice* (New York: Harcourt, Brace & World, 1962), 10.

ing outcomes of the curriculum to be the exegesis of the congregation's mission statement. The outcomes represent how the mission will be lived out in the lives of the congregation.

Technically, we break these terms down to define them and then place them in a sequence in order to design a path to achieve the outcomes. This process develops into a piece of our curriculum plan. While the ministry's mission will focus on God's plan, it will still require deliberation and acceptance by all those involved (as discussed in chap. 7). It is thus necessary to

> review the fundamental objectives in religious education. Without this refinement of aims there is the risk of talking and planning at cross-purposes. In the teaching of religion it should be clear to all that we are not concerned to impart knowledge for the sake of knowledge. Our aim extends beyond the academic situation of the classroom. We aim to prepare our students for the fullness of Christian living. To be more theologically accurate, we aim to dispose them for God's grace to inspire and motivate them toward their cooperation with grace in the living of a vital faith. The teacher of religion can be described as a bridge-builder; he helps to construct the bridge upon which students meet their Lord and pledge to him their personal faith-commitment.[6]

A distinctive feature of our curriculum design is the element of "deliberation," which will be seen in our model.

Context and Curriculum Design

The context of curriculum is an essential component and a necessity for educators to include in their design. The elements worthy of consideration are (1) psychological understanding, (2) societal and cultural factors, and (3) the learning environment, which includes facility, materials, teachers, and resources.

1. *Psychological Understandings.* Psychology is concerned with how people learn. Psychology provides a basis for understanding the

---

[6] Vincent M. Novak, "An Approach to Forming Religion Curriculum," *Religious Education* 61, no. 3 (May-June 1966): 189–90. Many of the ideas contained in this article were first presented in a paper delivered at the Theology Institute of the 1963 Liturgical Week, Philadelphia, August 19, by the author.

interrelation between teaching and learning process. It provides the theoretical understanding for the principles that influence teacher-students behavior and is an essential component to understanding the characteristics, needs, and interests of the teacher and learner, and how they affect and influence education. Chapter 5 has been devoted to understanding many of these psychological pieces with the overview of learning development in relation to learning theories.

2. *Societal and Cultural Factors.* The church is a global kingdom of God's people with diverse social and cultural needs. Mission work has often failed as Christian educators have transferred their conceptions of knowledge from one region to another without understanding the unique context for individual ministries. Therefore, it is important to change this pattern through the review of the historical, political, economic, population demographics, culture norms and social life at a minimum, developing an understanding of the context of the learner and raising the possibility of learning opportunities through the realization of multiple sources of data. While Christian education carries with it unifying sources of data from God's revelation, both the application of meaning and the focus of needs will all vary as a direct result of the societal and cultural factors. As Sowell observes, "Society usually dictates purposes of education."[7] Thus, when educators design curriculum without considering these factors, there is a strong possibility that the curriculum will not meet the needs of the learner in this context and will fail to carry out the purposes of the ministry. When was the last time your congregation did a community survey? Congregations that connect to their community are more often able to reach people and minister within it. Beyond the accessing of demographic information about the congregation's community context, surveying neighborhoods or even having a focus group from the community to ascertain insight about their needs and the church's reputation within the congregation may provide valuable insights for changes to its curriculum and ministry.

3. *Learning Environment.* A final consideration for the context of teaching is the learning environment. Context does not refer to the psy-

---

[7] Evelyn J. Sowell, *Curriculum: An Integrative Introduction* (Columbus, OH: Merrill, 1996), 85.

chological and social-cultural factors alone but to the facility, materials, teachers, and resources available to the learners and teachers involved in the process. This is an area often overlooked in curriculum design yet critical to its success. The facilities are important to an understanding of context and have a positive or a negative influence on the design of the curriculum. For example, does the furniture match the developmental needs of the learner? Do the furniture and space allow the appropriate learning activities to support the learning objectives? Is the facility capable of providing for the size of the group it serves? These are among the key questions curriculum designers should ask about the learning environment. The learning environment also includes materials. This is not limited to published materials. While a publisher may provide a curriculum plan, curriculum materials, or even a textbook of sorts, the materials can come from a variety of places and serve multiple purposes, including equipment and access.

Teachers are also important to the learning environment, as they are responsible for ensuring that curriculum (the sum total of learning) takes place.[8] Their qualifications, abilities, and development are part of the learning environment. Teachers have needs and desires, which directly influence the learning environment and have an impact on the context for teaching.

To meet the objectives of the curriculum, do you have appropriate resources to support learning? Resources refer to these items for both the learner and the teacher. These are usually the tangible items that can be purchased or collected such as manipulatives, educational games, craft materials, paper, pencils, and even a printed curriculum. It can also include the intangible items such as faculty development and new opportunities.

The oversight of these curricular design elements is the responsibility of Christian educators and accompanying support team. These three essential components should be assessed annually, with insights given to the strategic planning process of the congregation in order to insure that the curriculum maintains its vitality and effectiveness. It is easy to overlook something as simple as having the right learning

---

[8] See Howard P. Colson and Raymond M. Rigdon, *Understanding Your Church's Curriculum* (Nashville: Broadman, 1981), 40.

resources such as technology in the classroom that is required by pack-
aged curriculum or desired by the teacher.

Content and Curriculum Design

Curriculum design is concerned with the four aspects of content:
(1) the sources of content, (2) conceptualization of content, (3) organizing principles, and (4) the organization of content.

1. *Sources of Content.* Curriculum conceptions imply a purpose of
education and that the content from one or more sources will enable
learners to reach that purpose.[9] The key to understanding content is
not only understanding the difference between sources but also understanding the value of using multiple sources to reach the purpose of
education.

Following Ralph W. Tyler's work, most curriculum scholars have
long advocated the use of the same sources: subject matter, society
and culture, and learners as the main sources of curriculum content.[10]
However, others have been identified, such as science and eternal
and divine sources. Science is seen as a source because "the scientific
method provides meaning for the curriculum design."[11] Those who
advocate eternal and divine sources are not necessarily indicating a
belief in the God of the Bible, as is the case of Dwayne Huebner who
equates this source with being "in touch with the forces or energies of
life."[12]

Evangelical Christians maintain Scripture as a primary source
of curriculum content, though usually not negating the use of other
sources in our efforts.[13] In practice, though, we have often limited our
curriculum to Scripture only, or perhaps theology and church history,

---

[9] Sowell, *Curriculum*, 60.

[10] Ibid., 37; M. Francis Klein, "Alternative Curriculum Conceptions and
Designs," in *Curriculum Planning: A New Approach*, 6th ed., ed. Glen Hass and
Forest Parkay (Boston: Allyn and Bacon, 1993), 312.

[11] Allan C. Ornstein and Francis P. Hunkins, *Curriculum: Foundations,
Principles and Theory*, 2nd ed. (Boston: Allyn and Bacon, 1993), 234.

[12] Ibid., 235; and Dwayne E. Huebner, "Spirituality and Knowing," in
Learning and Teaching the Ways of Knowing, ed. E. W. Eisner (Chicago: National
Society for the Study of Education, 1985), 163.

[13] Donovan L. Graham, *Teaching Redemptively: Bringing Grace and Truth into
Your Classroom* (Colorado Springs: Purposeful Design, 2003), 223–24.

but rarely anything that could be deemed secular. However, God not only revealed himself through the incarnation of Christ and through his Word but also through creation itself. Some churches shy away from discussing scientific findings, for example, as a means of understanding God's created order. But this limits illustrative material that could be used responsibly in a Bible study. Churches would do well to maintain their unwavering commitment to the primacy of Scripture while exploring extra-biblical material.

> While each objective may make a different use of it, Scripture is nonetheless the central content of a Christian curriculum. The content-centered approach is aimed at making students master the actual content of Scripture and theology and further develop their theological reasoning abilities. A student-centered approach would aim students toward making use of Scripture devotionally or as a source for theological reflection. Even the process-centered approach toward education, designed primarily to equip students with ministry skills, would make use of Scripture to explain the rationale, motive, and "oughtness" of Christian ministry. It would be difficult to assess any curriculum as being "Christian" if it in fact omitted Scripture.[14]

2. Conceptions of Curriculum. Content is important to conceptualizing a design for curriculum, which is a fluid process that involves the consideration of the purpose of Christian education, ideas about appropriate content, and organization. This process will include consideration of the subject matter, the needs of society and culture, and the needs and interests of learners.[15] Chapters 6, 7, and 8 are dedicated to this form of conceptualizing as it applies to curriculum development and the formation of purposes, goals, and objectives for Christian education in the church. Figure 9.2 (see p. 191), based on insights gleaned from Evelyn Sowell,[16] itemizes these curriculum conceptions as they might apply to Christian education.

---

[14] James R. Estep, "Toward a Theologically Informed Approach to Education," in *A Theology for Christian Education*, ed. James R. Estep, Michael J. Anthony, and Gregg R. Allison (Nashville: B&H, 2008), 270–80.

[15] Sowell, *Curriculum*, 40.

[16] Ibid., 82–87.

3. *Organizing Principles.* Curriculum designers have various organizing principles that describe the approach used in designing curriculum.[17] Each approach is guided by the context and purpose for learning. There are four major organizing principles used by curriculum designers; these principles often have a few options within them: subject matter designs, society-culture based designs, learner based designs, and development of cognitive processes designs.

Subject matter designs are very traditional in the U.S. and expected by the culture. There are multiple approaches: single subject (based on one of the academic disciplines or subject areas), multidisciplinary, interdisciplinary or broad-fields. The curriculum is technologically planned prior to instruction, and close attention is given to sequencing.[18] Congregations should give attention to producing a tiered curriculum within the church. What do new believers need to know, experience, and be able to do? What then is the next step? The curriculum should equip the Christian to be a lifelong learner within the congregation. The sequence of subject matter, as well as other desired learning experiences, is crucial for the congregation to determine, providing a path for the believer to follow.

Society-culture based designs are a study of life, society, social life activities, and social problems. The problem-solving process is the focus of this curriculum design as the learner acquires and develops social-human relations skills rather than content knowledge. While there are outcomes, they are not preplanned outcomes with the curriculum but rather an outgrowth of the education process. The curriculum is not planned in a traditional technical way.[19] Congregations can adopt this approach by basing its education ministry on a mentor-discipleship based posture, one characterized by relationally driven ministry programming, rather than the notion of classes and studies.

Learner-based designs organize around the needs and interests of learners. The purpose for learning is determined with input from the students. While the teachers prepare in advance, they do not

---

[17] Klein, "Alternative Curriculum Conceptions and Designs," 312–15.
[18] Sowell, *Curriculum*, 55–56.
[19] Ibid., 57.

Curriculum Conceptions	Purposes of Education	Content Sources	Application to CE
Cumulative tradition of organized knowledge	To cultivate cognitive achievement and the intellect	Academic disciplines, subject matter	*Purpose:* Bible Knowledge *Source:* Bible
Social relevance-reconstruction	To prepare people for living in an unstable, changing world; to reform society	Needs of society and culture	*Purpose:* Life and Work *Source:* Christian Living, Ministry, and Mission work
Self-actualization	To develop individuals to their fullest potentials	Needs and interests of learners	*Purpose:* Spiritual Formation, Determine Gifting and Calling *Source:* Needs and Interest of Individual
Development of cognitive processes	To develop intellectual processes*	Any source, but usually subject matter	*Purpose:* Develop intellectual abilities (Memorization, problem solving, interpreting, and predicting) *Source:* Any
Technology	To make learning systematic and efficient*	Any source, but usually subject matter	*Purpose:* Bible Quiz-bowl, Hebrew, and Greek Languages *Source:* Any

Figure 9.2: Conceptions of Curriculum

*This purpose is a process goal that does not state an educational end.

predetermine the objectives.[20] Two designs have evolved from this larger one: core curriculum and activity curriculum. In the core curriculum, a select part of the curriculum is predetermined, though students may choose the other portion. Students select learning experiences or opportunities provided in the given environment based on their interests.[21] Congregations can reflect this approach by providing not only "required" classes, such as a new member's program, orientation to serving in the congregation, or leadership training, but also by providing a variety of "elective" opportunities—all of which are guided by overarching curricular ideas, but not specified outcomes.

Development of cognitive process designs do not use any particular content source but rather focus on the process used in the development of cognitive processes. They can use a variety of content. There are four main ones: competency approach, process skills, technology, and core. Competency approach design uses behavior objectives to list what knowledge students are to learn. Technology as curriculum design has a developed set of objectives sequenced with learning activities. The design focuses on the organization of knowledge. Core curriculum is organized around two parts. The first benefits everyone, and the second is selected through student interest.[22]

4. *Organization of Content.* Two approaches toward curriculum designs involve the organization of content knowledge for Christian educators—namely, objective and subjective. The objective approach is familiar to most ministries but not necessarily structured the same. This approach can be cyclical and repetitive. The curriculum by design will repeat the teaching of objective content in an effort to ensure total understanding. The objective approach can also have linear divisions. In the linear design, there are points along the way, typically marked by years or units of study, where the content starts up with fresh materials or themes.

A third design for the objective approach is a spiral mode. This design combines the best of the previous two objective designs by

---

[20] Ibid., 57–58.

[21] David G. Armstrong, *Developing and Documenting the Curriculum* (Boston: Allyn and Bacon, 1989), 57–58.

[22] Sowell, *Curriculum*, 58–59.

repeating the content each year and then keeping it fresh by broadening the area of knowledge when repeated. Leroy Ford identifies two additional variations of models that he labels the Anchor Plan and the Wheel Pattern. The Anchor Plan starts with the first unit as an overview to anchor the other units that follow. The Wheel Pattern simultaneously works together each unit of study with the activities happening at the same time and in a repeated fashion. This model focuses on the learner's interpretation and is a subjective model. This approach focuses on one's personal response to the Christian message and call to action.[23] Figure 9.3 (on p. 194) illustrates these five ways of organizing curriculum's content.[24]

Domains of Learning. While we are most familiar with designs that focus on content, there is more to Christian education than content knowledge—in particular, spiritual growth and a call to service. Christian educators need to teach and expect growth in all three learning domains: cognitive, affective, and volitional. If our content is purely focused on the cognitive domain, we become the "Bible thumping" congregation with no practical application and ministry service. We can also sin with our acts of the heart (affective domain) and service (volitional domain), as Paul warns in Romans 1:

> For although they knew God [cognitive domain], they neither glorified him as God nor gave thanks to him [volitional domain], but their thinking became futile and their foolish hearts were darkened [affective domain]. . . . Therefore, God gave them over in the sinful desires of their hearts [affective domain]. . . . They exchanged the truth of God for a lie [cognitive domain]. . . . Since they did not think it worthwhile to retain the knowledge of God, he gave them over to the depraved mind, to do what ought not to be done [volitional domain]. . . . Although they know God's righteous decree [cognitive domain] that those who do such things deserve death, they not only continue to do [volitional domain] these very things but also approve [affective domain] of those who practice them. (vv. 21–32)

---

[23] Novak, "An Approach to Forming a Religion Curriculum," 192–93.

[24] These figures are adapted from the models previously mentioned in this section.

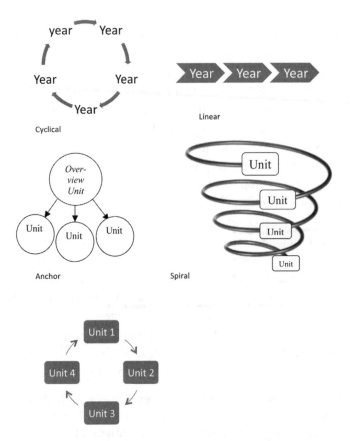

Figure 9.3: Organizing Curriculum's Content

In addition, one cannot serve (volitional) without love (affective). There must be a balance of learning and growth in all three domains. This is explained in 1 Corinthians 13, a chapter that addresses an imbalance:

> If I speak [volitional domain] in the tongues of men and of angels, but have not love [affective domain], I am only a resounding gong or a clanging symbol. If I have the gift of prophecy [volitional domain] and can fathom all mysteries and all knowledge [cognitive domain], and if I have a faith that can move mountains [cognitive domain], but have not love [affective domain], I am nothing. If I give all I possess to the poor [volitional domain] and surrender my body to the flames

[volitional domain], but have not love [affective domain], I gain
nothing. (vv. 1–3)

The emphasis on a balanced approach to curriculum design is
important. It should be one that incorporates the cognitive, knowledge
elements of learning, as well as the equally valid domains of affect and
volition. Our faith is more than our minds but encompasses the whole
of our existence. The curriculum should do the same. Learning outcomes should be expressed in all three learning domains.

Horizontal and Vertical Organizations. Often curriculum planners
organize the subject(s) of curriculum in a horizontal fashion. This provides an understanding of the scope and integration of subjects used
in the curriculum. The scope provides an understanding of the extent
and depth of content coverage including topics and learning experiences, having implications for instructional time.[25] The integration of
subjects is a design that links both knowledge and experiences from two
or more areas within the curriculum to assist the learner in constructing meaning. "Teachers using the cognitive processes conception might
operate more from the information processing models of teaching as
conceptualized by Joyce and Weil, while academic rationalists might
more often employ behavioristic models."[26] The vertical organization of
material communicates the sequence and continuity of the curriculum.
Sequence communicates an ordering of knowledge that tradition and
logic dictate,[27] typically moving from simple to complex knowledge;
thus providing reasons for prerequisites and a chronological order for
some curriculum. Continuity refers to the continual repetition of skill
practice in development.[28] It also seeks a seamless transition from one
point to another. Organizing curriculum to flow from one ending point
will segue into the following beginning point.[29]

---

[25] Armstrong, *Developing and Documenting the Curriculum*, 54–55.

[26] Klein, "Alternative Curriculum Conceptions and Designs," 313; and
B. Joyce and M. Weil, *Models of Teaching* (Englewood Cliffs: Prentice-Hall, 1980).

[27] Armstrong, *Developing and Documenting the Curriculum*, 55.

[28] John Ritz, "Note Taking Guides: Curriculum Design," Old Dominion
University, n.p. [cited 31 May 2011]. Online: http://www.odu.edu/~jritz/oted885/
ntg4.shtml.

[29] Armstrong, *Developing and Documenting the Curriculum*, 57.

Two other dimensions used to organize curriculum would include articulation and balance. Articulation addresses knowledge relationships within the curriculum or lost knowledge not related. Albert Oliver suggests that "articulation refers to a relationship between two or more elements of curriculum that is simultaneous rather than sequential. . . . Articulation reaches out laterally to cross subject-area boundaries in an effort to maximize potential relationships among many kinds of content."[30] Balance communicates the appropriate weight as distributed to each piece of the design.[31] The balance of the domains is essential to good education. Christian education should educate the whole person. While we do not want to water down or skip over the cognitive content, we must also be careful to give equal attention to the other domains of learning, as all are essential to the aims, purposes, goals, and objectives.[32] Articulation and balance may or may not relate to the horizontal and vertical organization of curriculum depending on our design.

Experiences and Curriculum Design

Learning experiences are important because they are the means for achieving the objectives and meeting the desired outcomes. There are three important processes involved in designing the curriculum in this area: the selection of experiences, the development of experience, and the organization of experiences. In regard to the selection, Tyler outlines four types of learning experiences useful in attaining various kinds of objectives: (1) learning experiences to develop skills in thinking, (2) learning experiences to acquire information, (3) learning experiences to develop social attitudes, and (4) learning experiences to develop interests.[33] Both the selection and the development processes follow the development of objectives.[34] A benefit in developing these

---

[30] Albert I. Oliver, *Curriculum Improvement: A Guide to Problems, Principles, and Process*, 2nd ed. (New York: Harper & Row, 1977); and Armstrong, *Developing and Documenting the Curriculum*, 56–57.

[31] Ritz, "Note Taking Guides: Curriculum Design."

[32] Novak, "An Approach to Forming a Religion Curriculum," 196.

[33] Ralph W. Tyler, *Basic Principles of Curriculum and Instruction* (Chicago: University of Chicago Press, 1949), 68–82.

[34] James G. Henderson and Richard D. Hawthorne, *Transformative Curriculum Leadership* (Upper Saddle River, NY: Prentice Hall, 2006), 84.

learning experiences is one of communication to educators on how to implement the curriculum.

Essential to the design of curriculum is the relationship of the learning experiences to three organizational aspects of the content: continuity, sequence, and integration,[35] all of which require the designer to consider these three steps simultaneously. The third process of organization is also determined in relationship to the other two, often at the same time with the understanding that all refer to the means for achieving the objectives of the curriculum.

Evaluation and Curriculum Design

To evaluate the effectiveness of the curriculum, educators need to collect data on teachers, the curriculum, and students alike. The data needs to be linked directly to the objectives. When data is collected initially, it provides a form of feedback that can be used immediately but over a period of time can also be beneficial in other ways that aid in explaining cause and effect.

Teachers. The evaluation of teachers happens at various levels: initial evaluation to determine qualification and placement, and reflection on practice to assess the needs of the program and make changes for improvement. Changes can involve the various materials and resources but should also include the need for professional development and training for teachers. Teacher evaluation can take the form of a simple dialogue with a teacher about their own self-assessment of need to develop or change, or can be done by a team of teachers who work with one another and provide feedback and alternatives for improvement. In time, teacher evaluation is actually welcomed as a means of improvement to their ministry.

Curriculum. This evaluation should not be limited to the content but also should include learning experiences.[36] As with other forms of evaluation, an evaluation of the curriculum should include multiple voices, which would at least include the ministry team, parents, and students. As Sowell argues,

---

[35] Robert S. Zais, *Curriculum: Principles and Foundations* (New York: Ty Crowell, 1976), 366–67.

[36] Ibid., 104.

Curriculum evaluation should be tied to the intended purpose of education, so that studies of subject matter affect curriculum evaluation whenever the purpose of education or the emphases for learning outcomes are altered. . . . Therefore, evaluation of group outcomes against a predetermined criterion is relatively simple. If the purpose of education is not subject matter proficiency, however, evaluation must focus on learners' developmental changes or degrees of societal reform—both of which require different evaluation approaches. . . . Changes in the emphasis for learning outcomes typically require revisions in evaluation processes. Evaluation of thinking skills or problem solving skills, for example, requires changes in methods of data collection and interpretation.[37]

Curriculum evaluation should discern strengths and weaknesses in order to drive program improvement using data analysis. These decisions may include such things as the need for new materials and resources, training, changes in the organization, or delivery of curriculum. One need not rely on surveys to gather information on which to base the evaluation, but could use focus groups of various individuals involved in the teaching ministry, or even students in the education ministry.

Learner(s). The design of evaluation tools used to assess student learning needs to correspond to ministry objectives and desired outcomes. While traditionally we have viewed assessment as seeking an understanding of what students know, we should also use new forms of assessment[38] to discern their developmental progress, skills, and dispositions.

Assessment Analysis for Change. Christian education is about advancement. Assessment serves multiple purposes: to establish both the needs of the learner and the objectives, to determine progress for providing additional enrichment or establishing new objectives, and to determine if the objectives have been met. The focus of assessment is to use the evaluations you have established to advance the cause forward. Possibly that means to review, reorganize, move on, or even change because of the maturity and growth toward Christlikeness. Why do we

---

[37] Sowell, *Curriculum*, 81.

[38] Henderson and Hawthorne, *Transformative Curriculum Leadership*, 88.

assess our forms of evaluation and assessments? We do so to advance the cause of Christian education in the church in order to meet the needs of a growing ministry or to problem solve when our ministry is not growing.

Curriculum Design Model for Christian Education

The curriculum design model for Christian education described in this chapter is organized around Scripture. This is a common practice for Christian education in the church. Even though the organizing principles may vary based on the design employed and their application to various factors (such as culture, developmental needs, geographic location, socio-economic status, families, educational backgrounds, or political preferences), what they all have in common is the guiding role of Scripture.[39]

The heart of figure 9.4 is clarifying your mission via Scripture. The curriculum design model for Christian education must be organized around this one principle. The diagram thus illustrates the relationship to the other components from the center moving outward. This design

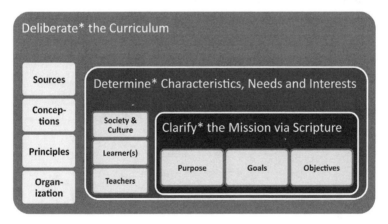

(*) Denotes annual and routine evaluation on the part of the ministry team, including voices of parents, students and educators in an effort to the maintain relationship between each curriculum component of the curriculum

Figure 9.4: Curriculum Design Model for Christian Education

---

[39] Ford, *A Curriculum Design Manual for Theological Education*, 49–50.

model does not limit the organization of the curriculum like previously mentioned models. Rather it shows the relationship of Scripture to addressing the mission; determining the characteristics, needs, and interests; developing the curriculum; and analyzing evaluations.

Key Terms and Concepts

Context	Domains of Learning	Balanced
Content Sources	Learning Activities	Evaluation

Reflective Questions

1. What is the importance of understanding context in curriculum design?
2. Describe how God's revelation is a source of content knowledge.
3. Why is evaluation essential to curriculum design?

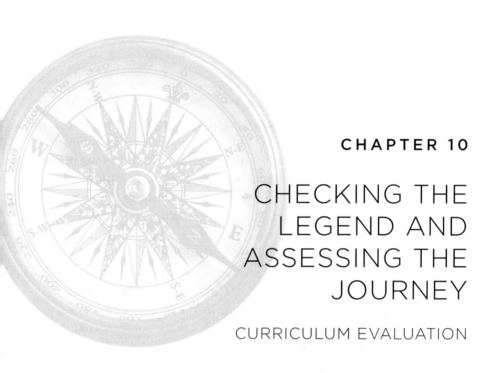

CHAPTER 10

CHECKING THE LEGEND AND ASSESSING THE JOURNEY

CURRICULUM EVALUATION

Karen Lynn Estep and James Riley Estep Jr.

How many more miles?" Kids are amazed when Mom or Dad can tell them "53 miles to our exit!" How? How did Mom or Dad know that? Kids do not usually know that exits are mile markers and every mile has a marker along the roadside. Just do the math, and the kids are amazed. Maps do not arbitrarily represent roads, bridges, exits, natural terrain, or distances. The map is a scaled, precision representation of the reality it depicts. To achieve this, cartographers make use of different types of lines, symbols, benchmarks, and labels for the reader to interpret. How does the reader know what the cartographer meant? You consult the legend, a small box on the map that explains the meaning of symbols, lines, and labels, including the scale to which the map was drawn. That is how we know where we have been, how far we have traveled, and what should be coming up in the next few miles. It is how we track our progress along the journey.

A final step in developing curriculum maps involves setting up criteria to determine the context and needs of the learners as well as to measure and evaluate progress. These generally relate to the purpose, goals, and objectives, but include hearing from the traveler about how useful the map was for their journey. Recognizing that there may be other unanticipated outcomes along the way helps with map refinement as does checking the accuracy of the standards set forth in the map's legend. Assessing both the map and the traveler's experience as well as the navigator's (teacher's) perspective provides useful and meaningful input for revising and updating future educational plans.

This chapter will address the evaluation of curriculum by responding to three questions: (1) Why evaluate? This section will provide a rationale for the evaluation of curriculum in the local congregation. (2) What do we evaluate? This will establish criteria for curriculum evaluation, depicting the key features in either selecting prefabricated curriculum or developing curricula within the congregation. (3) How do we evaluate? This section introduces you to the process involved in conducting curriculum evaluations. Assessing the effectiveness of the curriculum is critical, but if it does not have a specified application or benefit to the education ministry of the congregation, it is of no use. The chapter will introduce you to the overall scope of curriculum evaluation in the church. Whether our congregation's curriculum relies on prefabricated materials purchased from a curriculum house, on studies produced by a publisher, on internally developed curricula independent from anyone else, or is a hybrid that uses both produced and purchased curricular materials (which is most commonly the case), evaluation is needed to ascertain the success of the curriculum.

Why Evaluate?

Evaluation serves the purpose of providing information about individuals and curriculum. We evaluate the Church's education programs to determine where to start, see how we are doing, and to determine how we finished. As Donovan Graham notes, "Evaluation is a judgment of how what was measured stands against some desired norm."[1] The

---

[1] Donovan L. Graham, *Teaching Redemptively: Bringing Grace and Truth into Your Classroom* (Colorado Springs: Purposeful Design, 2003), 252.

evaluation of curriculum in the education ministry will cover the three basic forms of assessment: pre-assessment, formative assessment, and summative assessment. Although we may say it differently, the purpose of evaluating our curriculum is to assess the needs yet to be met, to determine how we are or how we can do Christian education better to meet the purpose, goals, and objectives of the church. We do *not* evaluate because we *have* too, as if it were an ancillary matter or a mere obligation; rather we evaluate because of the need to make better decisions about the education ministry. While Scripture is eternal, our cultural and societal contexts are not. We live in a state of flux, and curriculum needs to adjust as it seeks to apply God's wisdom to the ever increasing complexities of our world.

> Changing times and changing needs will continue to require changing curricula. We must be sure that God's message is put in understandable terms and that our Christian teaching is relevant to man's needs. Only thus can we help men to move even closer to "the measure of the stature of the fullness of Christ" (Eph. 4:13) . . . [and to] accomplish this, the curriculum must be researched and evaluated continually.[2]

Evaluative assessment becomes the catalyst for change or improvement, the means for discovering strengths and areas that need strengthening.[3] For example, Dan Lambert suggests that the purpose of evaluation is to become great teachers in order to win as many as possible to Christ.[4] Without evaluation, one would have no means of ascertaining the effectiveness of a teacher, nor have insight as to how one might improve as a teacher. James E. Plueddemann writes:

> One of the best ways to improve the practice of Christian education in local churches is to do better curriculum evaluation, and do it more often . . . the proper use of curriculum evaluation will not only improve the practice of Christian educations in the local church, but will also help develop leadership and

---

[2] A. Elwood Sanner and A. F. Harper, *Exploring Christian Education* (Grand Rapids: Baker, 1978), 182–83.

[3] Eugene C. Roehlkepartain, *The Teaching Church: Moving Christian Education to Center Stage* (Nashville: Abingdon, 1993), 95.

[4] Dan Lambert, *Teaching That Makes a Difference: How to Teach for Holistic Impact* (Grand Rapids: Zondervan, 2004), 167.

teaching abilities. Careful evaluation will provide a framework for group dialogue and self-reflection among Christian educators in a local church. A good model of curriculum evaluation will encourage educators to be curious about educational processes and results.[5]

Many ministries are uncomfortable with evaluation, as it would mean evaluating volunteers; yet it remains an essential piece in establishing a healthy Christian education ministry. The "Effective Christian Education" study observed that congregations are more likely to evaluate programs than people, even though 50 percent of the Christian educators surveyed have expressed an interest in evaluating their work, and 80 percent of church programs dealing with children, youth, and adults are evaluated at least annually.[6] Evaluation validates the educational integrity of a ministry that must constantly change to serve the needs of the church.

> To achieve educational integrity, curriculum planners must allow flexibility. Provision must be made for formal and informal learning, individual and group learning, central and peripheral learning, first exposure and reinforcement learning. Planners must balance tradition and innovation, boldness and carefulness, the long range and the immediate, the ultimate and the instrumental. Educational integrity must deal with the immortal man in his life as he lives it.[7]

Assessment data provides the feedback we need about the ever-changing needs. Additionally, it provides an understanding of individual needs as the church serves both the mature and immature Christian, regardless of age.

Evaluation requires us to continue our focus on the goals and objectives of the curriculum as opposed to focusing on the programming of events. Which is better: four ministry programs with distinctive curricula that can be proven effective in their achievement, or the proliferation of programs none of which can actually be proven to

---

[5] James E. Plueddemann, "Curriculum Improvement through Evaluation," *Christian Education Journal*, 8, no. 1 (Autumn 1987): 55.

[6] Roehlkepartain, *The Teaching Church*, 95.

[7] Sanner and Harper, *Exploring Christian Education*, 165–66.

achieve its described purpose? Lois E. LeBar observes, "It is easy to feel successful when we have put on a smooth program, but the crucial question is, what is happening to the people? The test of our teaching is the changed lives of the person."[8] Curriculum is the connection between the program and the person. Too often, we look at the events that have been coordinated to evaluate ministry, but in reality, we need to know if the events served the purpose and fulfilled the mission of the ministry. We need to understand the curriculum's effectiveness can only be seen in the life of those it has touched.

What Do We Evaluate?

Curriculum is more than the pouch of lesson plans and materials purchased for use in the Sunday school or the study guide used in a small group. While this is part of it, curriculum also involves almost every aspect of the education ministry; hence, its evaluation is much broader than just what can be purchased at a store, online through a publisher, or developed by a Christian education taskforce. For example, Dan Lambert suggest that congregations evaluate teachers, the learning environment, program and instructional goals, the curriculum itself (meaning lesson plans and materials), and the students.[9] Similarly, Eleanor Daniel suggests several organizational structures to evaluate within a typical congregation starting with the agencies within the education program, facilities, curriculum (goals and objectives), teaching personnel, and the students.[10] Similar lists are available throughout the literature of Christian education. Upon surveying the literature, six dimensions of evaluation must be recognized as forming a cumulatively exhaustive basis for curriculum evaluation (see fig. 10.1 on p. 206).

---

[8] Lois E. LeBar, *Introduction to Biblical Christian Education*, ed. W. C. Graendorf (Chicago: Moody, 1981), 168.

[9] Lambert, *Teaching That Makes a Difference*, 168–69.

[10] See John W. Wade, "Evaluating the Effectiveness of Christian Education," in *Foundations for Christian Education*, ed. Eleanor A. Daniel and John W. Wade (Joplin: College Press, 1999), 350–53.

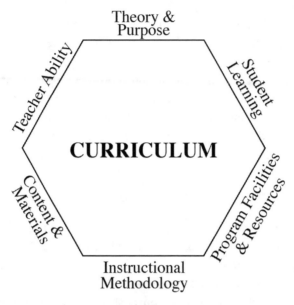

Figure 10.1: Dimensions of Curriculum Evaluation

Theory and Purpose

Curriculum is based on theology, philosophy, learning theories, and even divergent processes of constructing the curriculum itself. A principal question that must be asked of curriculum is what is its theoretical basis, and for that matter its ultimate purpose? The theory and purpose of the curriculum must be assessed to ascertain whether the theoretical assumptions of its design and stated educational purposes is not only achieved through the curriculum but is also consistent with that of the education ministry. This is especially important theologically. What if the curriculum assumes a definition of spirituality that is not consistent with that of your congregation? What if it has the desired outcomes of creating a pluralistic theological perspective rather than a unified one? The curriculum may not be *wrong*, but what if it is not suited for a particular context or purpose of the program? Checking the theoretical basis is as simple as contacting the publisher, or if it is being developed internally, spending time conversing with one another and determining an overarching purpose and design for all curriculum in the congregation. The following list of questions may be used to start this evaluative conversation.

Evaluation Criteria/Questions

- Does the curriculum meet the overall purpose of the education ministry?
- How might you generally describe the curriculum?
- What assumptions seem to be made about the purpose of learning?
- Are the stated goals and objectives consistent with those of our congregation?
- Does the explicit curriculum match the implicit? What about the null curriculum?[11]

Student Learning

Do we really want to give our students a test? Define "test." If curriculum has objectives, we need to evaluate not only the objectives themselves, but also if the students are achieving the intended result of the curriculum design. Nothing is more important than what happens with our students as an end product. The evaluation of student learning will tell us if we have met our objectives. This should not only take place in each lesson plan, but for the curriculum overall and the congregation as God's curriculum. What are people learning in our congregation? The education ministry? Their class or group? Evaluations are looking at not only the quantity of learning (the breadth of knowledge) but are taking into account the quality of learning (the depth of knowledge). Christian educators should determine the consistency between the stated curricular learning objectives and evaluate if the curriculum provides the necessary content and experiences for accomplishing this objective.[12]

---

[11] Robert W. Pazmiño, *Principles and Practices of Christian Education: An Evangelical Perspective* (Grand Rapids: Baker, 1992), 153. Pazmiño's questions emerged from Elizabeth Vallance's description of the hidden curriculum. See Vallance, "Hiding the Hidden Curriculum: An Interpretation of the Language of Justification in Nineteenth-Century Educational Reform," *Curriculum Theory Network* 4 (1973–1974): 5–21.

[12] Hilda Taba, *Curriculum Development Theory and Practice* (New York: Harcourt, Brace & World, 1962), 13.

Does the curriculum produce the student learning objectives promised? The following list of questions may be used to start this evaluative conversation.

Evaluation Criteria/Questions

- Does the curriculum state objectives that are attainable and measurable?
- Do students affirm or demonstrate that the learning objectives are being achieved?
- Do teachers affirm or demonstrate that the learning objectives are being achieved?
- Do parents affirm or demonstrate that the learning objectives are being achieved?
- To what degree are student learning objectives achieved?
- What does the curriculum assume about the student's current abilities, e.g., level of Bible knowledge, student's vocabulary?
- Does the curriculum reflect learning in all three domains of learning (cognitive, affective, and behavioral)?
- Does the curriculum relate to the students' lives? Is it applicable?
- Does the curriculum relate to the students' culture/society? Is it applicable?

Program Facilities and Resources

Learning takes place in a context, and each one places on the teacher and the learner possiblities and boundaries based on its resources. Contexts can be institutional, such as defined as a program; others are physical in terms of the physical classroom and the resources made available to the teacher. As Plueddemann observes, "The first step of curriculum evaluation begins even before the teacher teaches the lesson. Is there a logical relationship between the assumed educational context and the planned educational activities?"[13] For example, if one is using a DVD-based curriculum, it assumes that the congregation has the technology to play the DVD. Similarly, if it is a small group, a television may be used to view the DVD; but if it is a large class, a pro-

---

[13] Plueddemann, "Curriculum Improvement through Evaluation," 57.

jection unit with a large screen may be required. What if the lessons in the curriculum require an hour and a half to teach, but your learning venue only lasts an hour? A lecture based curriculum requires far less space than one calling for active students. One dimension of the evaluation of curriculum must consist of the program, facility, and resources required by the curriculum. The following list of questions may be used to start this evaluative conversation.

Evaluation Criteria/Questions

- Does the curriculum match our program's grouping, e.g., divisions within the education ministry?
- Does the curriculum fit within the program's time constraints?
- Does the congregation have access to facilities required by the curriculum?
- Does the congregation possess the technological capabilities required by the curriculum, i.e., audio, video, computer, Internet?

Instructional Methodology

Lecture? Discussion? Case studies? Games? The list is endless. One dimension of evaluation must take into account the preferred or dominant methodology called for by the curriculum. This is a reflection of the theory behind it, and often times the preferences of the individual writing the curriculum, but does the curriculum provide enough variety in teaching method to keep students attentive and engaged? It is the prescribed instructional method that connects the desired learning objective to the participant. The following list of questions may be used to start this evaluative conversation.

Evaluation Criteria/Questions

- Does the curriculum employ a variety of teaching methods?
- Is the curriculum more lecture/content based or discovery/ activity based?
- Are the learning activities meaningful to the student or more like "busy work"?
- Is the curriculum adaptable, alterable by the teacher?

- Does the curriculum explain instructional methodologies adequately for teachers to use them?
- Do the methods address the depth of learning, not just the breadth?
- Does it provide alternative teaching methods for teachers to consider?

Content and Materials

It is often too simple to think of curriculum as the facts and information, its resources, or saying that Scripture is all we need to take into account. These are common "myths" held about curriculum.[14] The reality of the matter is that the content has to do with what we desire participants to know and how we need them to know it.[15] Additionally, what teaching materials are provided by the curriculum to aid in the teaching process? If one is utilizing the prepackaged curriculums or books designed for use in a small group, what is provided in addition to this for the teacher to use? For example, a Bible study on the Acts of the Apostles is one thing, but if it has maps, charts, diagrams, and student handouts that accompany the lectures, then it becomes more usable to the teacher and potentially beneficial to the student. Evaluating the content and the materials related to the content is essential to ascertaining the effectiveness of the curriculum. The following list of questions may be used to start this evaluative conversation.

Evaluation Criteria/Questions

- Does the curriculum reflect the theological affirmations of the congregation?[16]
- Does the curriculum affirm and appeal to Scriptural authority?
- Is Scripture regarded as *truth*, the ultimate source of the curriculum?

---

[14] Karen B. Tye, *Basics of Christian Education* (St. Louis: Chalice, 2000), 48–52.

[15] Ibid.

[16] Cf. Jeff Astley, "Theology and Curriculum Selection," in *Christian Perspectives for Education: A Reader in the Theology of Education*, ed. Leslie J. Francis and Adrian Thatcher (Leominster, England: Gracewing 1990), 265–72.

- Is the curriculum Christ-centered, pointing the student ultimately toward him?
- Is it sensitive to denominational heritage or tradition?
- Is the curriculum material's appearance appealing to the student and teacher?
- Is the curriculum timely? For example, is it up-to-date, reflective of today, not yesterday?
- Is there anything grossly missing from the curriculum? For example, the null curriculum?
- Are the goals stated or interpreted so that they point teachers and students beyond knowledge to changed attitudes and behaviors?
- Do the materials (visual, audio, technological) support learning activities? That is, they are not ancillary elements of the curriculum.
- Is the preparation time for using the curriculum acceptable?

Teachers

In terms of effectiveness, the teacher is perhaps the most important element of the learning process. The teacher is the curriculum *incarnate* and the living connection between the content and the student. The following list of questions may be used to start this evaluative conversation.

Evaluation Criteria/Questions

- Does the congregation provide teachers with adequate curriculum?
- Does the congregation provide teachers with adequate resources to make effective use of the curriculum?
- Are teachers oriented and trained to use the curriculum effectively?
- Are teachers trained how to make use of visual, audio, or technological resources in teaching?
- Does the teacher relate well with students? Do students respect and befriend the teacher?
- Does the teacher communicate adequately as required by the curriculum?

- Is the teacher flexible in his use of instructional methods?
- Does the teacher's life exemplify Christ and a mature Christian faith?
- Is the teacher exemplifying servant leadership about teaching, e.g., enthusiasm, improving through self examination?

These six sides of curriculum evaluation, as depicted in figure 10.1, provide a comprehensive matrix for evaluation and improvement. As Edward W. Uthe reminds us,

> A sound design will assist the planner as he attempts to evaluate current practices and new proposals on bases other than tradition applies to content areas, teaching method and devices, organizational patterns. A design which includes all elements will help keep the total scope of the curriculum prominent and should help avoid practices which work against one another within the total educational programs. The various elements can be combined in a harmonious pattern rather than being pieced and patched together on the basis of expediency and changes in educational fashion.[17]

While criteria and questions may be added to each, perhaps some that are more tailored to your own ministry setting or reflective of your congregation's curriculum or education ministry, these six sides frame the curriculum and give the Christian educator a starting point for evaluation.

How Do We Evaluate?

Christian educators may embrace the need to evaluate curriculum and even affirm the criteria for evaluating it. But exactly how does a Christian education ministry evaluate the curriculum? Before Christian educators can engage in the process of curricular evaluation, they must understand the basic cycle of evaluation. Figure 10.2 represents this cycle.

---

[17] Edward W. Uthe, "Developing Curriculum Design for Christian Education," in "Symposium: Current Curriculum Theory," ed. Randolph Crump Miller, *Religious Education* 61, no. 3 (May-June 1966): 165.

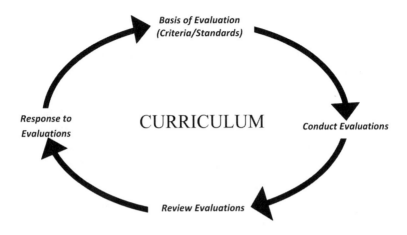

Figure 10.2: Process of Curriculum Evaluation

The process has four components: (1) establishing a basis for evaluation, i.e., criteria; (2) conducting the evaluation, i.e., evaluation methods; (3) reviewing the evaluation data, i.e., interpretation and analysis of the evaluation data; and (4) responding to evaluation, i.e., rendering a decision on how to act in response to the data. This section will explore this process as it aids in the improvement of curriculum in the congregation.

Basic Principles for Curricular Evaluation

How does one really engage in the evaluation of curriculum? One general principle is the *frequency* of evaluations. Some elements of the evaluation may be more frequent than others. Some recommend frequent evaluations, such as quarterly evaluations for new teachers or small group leaders, while other elements of curriculum evaluations need not be as frequent, such as those involving perhaps the annual Sunday school curriculum renewals. The point is simple: establish routine, regularly scheduled periods of evaluation. Christian educators who rely on unprompted or spontaneous evaluations can give the impression that evaluation is relatively unimportant to the ministry, and even worse that it is personally or problem-driven. Whatever evaluation methods one may elect to use, they must be used on a regular basis.

What type of data is needed for evaluation? Another general principle for consideration is distinguishing between quantitative and qualitative information. Methods of evaluation are designed to generate different kinds of information. The two basic categories of evaluation methods are those that yield quantitative data and those producing qualitative data. Quantitative information is numerical, i.e., quantities. An example of quantitative data might be a survey showing that 4.6/5.0 teachers "strongly agree" that the materials accompanying the lesson plans are of benefit to students. Analysis of quantitative information is understood through statistical analysis, e.g., determining the average/mean, median, mode, and standard deviation. In short, quantitative information is numerical data analyzed statistically. Quantitative methods of evaluation are primarily surveys, distributed either as paper-pencil inventories or digitally through a congregation's website or via e-mail, usually employing the familiar Likert scale, rating one's degree of disagreement or agreement along a spectrum of 1 to 5 in response to a given statement. Another form of quantitative information that is useful in some instances would be a statistical analysis of attendance records for given programs. In either case, evaluation is done by the "numbers."

On the other hand, qualitative information is more substantial. This information deals with statements and opinions, and hence data is in the form of words rather than numbers. Rather than statistical analysis, as was used with quantitative data, such analysis requires no numbers. Since qualitative information is verbal, delivered in words, the analysis is somewhat broader. It is the detection of themes, clusters of opinion, common sentiments in the words of those sharing them. For example, if a Christian educator were to ask an open-ended question, such as, "How well does the church's technology support the curriculum?" Teachers and high school students may give positive and negative feedback, make comments about the speed of the Internet connection, or perhaps speak of the frustration of competing for DVD players, televisions, or projectors. This verbal, or qualitative, information is valuable in making determinations about the curriculum's technological requirements and the education ministry in general. Common qualitative methods are one-on-one interviews of various ministry participants, focus group discussions, or perhaps something resembling essay tests given to selected individuals asking about curriculum, all gathering verbal insights into its effectiveness.

Oftentimes a thorough evaluation process will rely on both qualitative and quantitative evaluation methods. The qualitative methods generate the list of possible responses while the quantitative methods can be used to determine the strength of the responses. Oftentimes the qualitative methods will raise most or all the possible options when addressing the content of the curriculum, and then a quantitative inventory can generate the numerical data to determine how strongly respondents feel about the curricular content. For example, after asking a group of teachers and students about the technological capabilities of the education ministry, as described above, researchers give a survey to all teachers and high school students using the insights gleaned from the earlier discussions: "On a scale of 1–5, strongly disagree to strongly agree, rate the following statements [notice, not questions]. . . . The education ministry has adequate technology for teaching our Sunday school class." Figure 10.3 (p. 216) may serve as a resource to this end. In the first column, you may place the criteria deemed suitable for measuring the effectiveness of the curriculum, with a numerical ranking in the second column (quantitative information). The final column invites the evaluator to provide some commentary (qualitative information).

The Christian educator can have both verbal and numerical insights on which to evaluate the effectiveness and efficiency of the curriculum. Plueddemann writes, "The understanding of the relationship between these questions will not only tell us if we are successful, but will give us information as to why the curriculum did or didn't work. It will also give us ideas for improving the curriculum."[18] Good evaluation asks questions with the intent of acting on what has been discovered through the answers.

Continual Evaluation

"But we looked at it once. Isn't that enough?" On any trip, looking at the map, gauging one's progress on the journey, is not merely done once, but throughout the journey until reaching the final destination.

---

[18] Plueddemann, "Curriculum Improvement through Evaluation," 58–59.

Criteria	Evaluation	Comment
	① ② ③ ④ ⑤	
	① ② ③ ④ ⑤	
	① ② ③ ④ ⑤	
	① ② ③ ④ ⑤	
	① ② ③ ④ ⑤	
	① ② ③ ④ ⑤	
	① ② ③ ④ ⑤	
	① ② ③ ④ ⑤	
	① ② ③ ④ ⑤	
	① ② ③ ④ ⑤	
	① ② ③ ④ ⑤	
	① ② ③ ④ ⑤	
	① ② ③ ④ ⑤	
	① ② ③ ④ ⑤	
	① ② ③ ④ ⑤	

Figure 10.3: Curriculum Criteria Selection Form

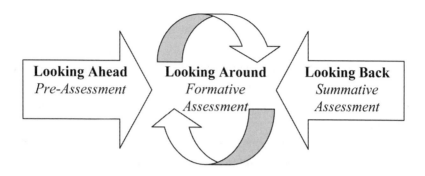

Figure 10.4: Continual Evaluation

Evaluation is the same. The evaluation process has three stages that require cyclical and continual assessment, each one denoting points of the journey (see fig. 10.4).

Looking ahead at the journey before departing, one must determine his current location. It is like hitting the target symbol on a GPS device and watching it zero-in on your present location. This pre-assessment is used to find a starting point. Like the other two stages, it is an essential step in the curriculum planning as well as for curriculum evaluation. Along the journey, while on the journey itself, travelers frequently check the location again on an atlas or using the directions feature on a GPS, evaluating their progress through the trip.

Formative assessment provides ongoing, occasional feedback that informs ongoing changes during the process of curriculum evaluation on the level of the congregation, ministry, program, or even individual. Likewise, it requires the curriculum specialists to stay in the mode of continual evaluation. After a long journey, especially a vacation, families spend time thinking back on how far they traveled, what they experienced during the journey, and then talk about what they might remember or learn from the trip, helping to inform the next one.

Summative assessment provides end-product feedback and is most useful for continuous improvements. It provides the information to tell us if we have met our objectives and provides a measure of their quality and relevance. Ultimately, it prepares us to start the next journey, to re-engage in the pre-assessment that initiates the whole process once again.

Roads change, routes are renumbered, services at exits close and open; one cannot assume that the journey will always be the same. With the realization that our society and culture are changing, evaluation guides necessary decisions about what must change in order to maintain relevance. All three of these stages, when routinely evaluated, produce a cycle of evaluation. They also require the gathering of information on an ongoing basis, which can come in multiple forms of formal and informal observations and survey analysis. It seems a bit strange to have an entire chapter on evaluation until you realize it is an essential key to curriculum planning.

Principles of Effective Evaluation

First, evaluate the congregation as curriculum and the curricular programs comprising the education ministry. Wyckoff suggests evaluating the curriculum of the church within five different representative groups, i.e., congregation members at-large, families within the church, as well as those involved in the children, youth, and adult education ministries.[19] In addition, evaluation should also assess how each of the program's curricula relates to one another, assuring that curriculum is comprehensive through the lifespan of the Christian. Each program's curriculum comprising the congregation's educational ministry, and even the congregation as a whole, could be evaluated. There are layers of curricular evaluation, ranging from the congregation as a curriculum, to the education ministry's curriculum, program curriculums, and curriculum used in individual classes or groups.

Second, curricular evaluation should give representative voice to all those involved in the education ministry. Who is involved in your education ministry? Each of them is involved in some capacity with the curriculum of the ministry. Evaluation should not include only the congregation's pastoral staff. It should also include the teachers and leaders who serve in the classes and groups comprising the education ministry. Likewise, the participants or learners should also be heard regarding their assessment of the curriculum. Regarding children and adolescents, their parents may offer keen insight into the effectiveness

---

[19] D. Campbell Wyckoff, *How to Evaluate Your Christian Education Program* (Philadelphia: Westminster Press, 1962), 35.

(or inadequacy) of the curriculum used with their children. Other ministry participants often overlooked in curriculum matters may also be insightful in this instance, such as those who serve in the church library ministry, or perhaps those who are involved in the Vacation Bible School. The voices of all those involved should be heard.

Third, evaluation of the curriculum must become a natural or symbiotic part of the education ministry. Daryl Eldridge advises that evaluation must (1) grow out of the congregation's educational objectives, (2) be based on commonly agreed upon standards of expectation, (3) be inclusive, not exclusive, of all those who are involved in the education ministry of the congregation, and (4) be comprehensive, covering all aspects of the programs.[20] In short, evaluation cannot be something else we do, another aspect of our ministry; it must be an indispensible part of our ministry, integrated into how we do education in the congregation. Each program in the congregation's education ministry should have an accompanying plan of evaluation to assure its continued improvement and effectiveness.

Conclusion

We check the legend of the map to determine with precision and certainty our location on the map—especially if the journey is into territory unfamiliar to the travelers. This is the expected role of the co-pilot, anyone who is riding shotgun, keeping the travelers on track. Evaluation keeps the education ministry "on track," assuring that it is achieving its purpose and being effective and efficient in the process. What is its purpose? Improvement! Advancing the effectiveness of the curriculum as it equips the church to be the people of God and servants to the congregation and community.

---

[20] Daryl Eldridge, *The Teaching Ministry of the Church: Integrating Biblical Truth with Contemporary Application* (Nashville: B&H, 1995), 30 note.

Key Terms and Concepts

Evaluation   Pre-assessment

Frequency   Formative

Quantitative   Summative

Qualitative

Reflection Questions

1. How do you think evaluation is related to understanding the explicit and the null curriculum of a congregation?
2. Without evaluation, how would you know what you are teaching and what you are not teaching?
3. How does your congregation evaluate curriculum? What questions does it ask? What questions does it fail to ask?
4. What is the value of curriculum evaluation? Practically speaking, why should a congregation evaluate its curriculum?
5. What are the inherent risks associated with *not* evaluating curriculum in the congregation?

CHAPTER 11

SUPERVISING TOUR GROUP ITINERARIES

Administering Curriculum

James Riley Estep Jr.

have never been to Texas before—anyone else?" Not the most confident words spoken by a tour guide, the leader of the class's fieldtrip to Galveston. What is needed to undertake such a trip? An experienced guide, familiar with the travel path as well as what the destination has to offer. Master travel guides in the form of supervisors or superintendents are needed for the educational journey because they have wisdom, trail experience, and familiarity with the overall educational plan of the church; therefore, they are uniquely equipped to assist entire bands of travelers and tour guides. Like a travel agent, this individual helps the church manage the logistics of map distance, tour guide assignment, provision of traveling gear, and scheduling. The church's education pastor needs to be a travel guide, a curriculum specialist.

The Christian educator's role as the congregation's curriculum specialist, as the one responsible for leading the congregation through the process of developing a curriculum and evaluating curriculum for educational improvement, will be examined in this chapter. Additionally, the chapter will examine the role of the curriculum specialist in regard to program development, curriculum deliberation and selection, and the appropriate use of prepackaged, prefabricated curriculum. Curriculum supervision is an indispensible ministry of the congregation in its purpose to "go and make disciples" (Matt 28:19a) so "that we may present everyone perfect in Christ" (Col 1:28b).

Christian Educator as Curriculum Specialist

For Christian educators, curriculum is a means of transformation; educators must engage in transformative curriculum leadership, meaning that change is achieved through the collective process of all involved in the education of the church (e.g., pastors, parents, volunteers, teachers, and students).[1] A single pebble tossed into still water seems as if it would have little effect, but the ring of ripples emanating from its point of impact amplify the event, resulting in a change of the water's texture far beyond the point of impact. Curriculum can indeed have a significant impact not only on the life of the individual Christian, but ultimately on the whole world. With Scripture at its core, curriculum can have a transformative ripple effect throughout the congregation, even into the community and world. As illustrated in figure 11.1, curriculum centered on Scripture transforms the individual, the class or group, the ministry (such as children, adolescent, and adult), the congregation as a whole, and even beyond the community of faith, into the community and world in which it ministers.[2]

As a transformational curriculum leader, the Christian education pastor exhibits leadership through the three general themes of leadership theory.[3] First, the transformational leader exhibits personal traits that indicate his role as a leader. For example, consider the list of leadership qualifications found in Scripture for an elder (1 Tim 3:1–7; Titus 1:6–9; 1 Pet 5:1) or deacon (1 Tim 3:8–13).[4] Leadership is recognized

---

[1] Cf. James G. Henderson and Richard D. Hawthorne, *Transformative Curriculum Leadership*, 2nd ed. (Upper Saddle River, NJ: Prentice Hall, 1995), 181.

[2] Adapted from ibid.

[3] Adapted from Ronald C. Doll, *Curriculum Improvement: Decision Making and Process*, 8th ed. (Upper Saddle River, NJ: Prentice-Hall, 1991), 466.

[4] Cf. Jim Estep, "Biblical Qualities of an Elder," in *Answer: His Call*, ed. Jim Estep, David Roadcup and Gary Johnson (Joplin: College Press, 2009), 47–61.

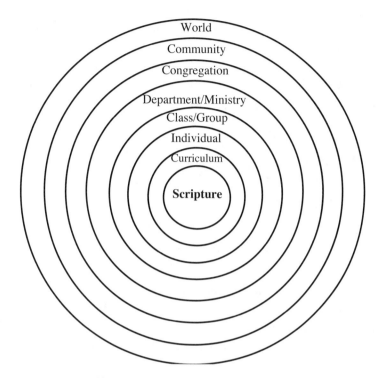

Figure 11.1: Transformative Leadership

and enacted through the exhibition of desired leadership traits. These traits come from Scripture but also from the expectations of the local congregation and/or denomination, as well as from the community beyond the congregation. Transformation starts within the life of the leaders themselves as they transform their own life.

Second, transformational leaders work with and through people in groups. Christian education pastors serve on church staffs, generally have some form of Christian education committee, and have various teams. They are recognized as leaders by their role and contribution within these groups. They invest in people, facilitate proactive teams, and focus their efforts to fulfill a common vision.

Third, transformational leaders are able to adapt their style of leadership to the situation. Leadership is relational. Individuals relate to one another, individuals relate to circumstances in which they serve, and the leader relates to both the individual and the circumstances. They are able to maintain the relationship with people within a given context, and thus leadership is also situational, not enacted the same with each individual, group, or context. Situational leadership is not capricious but simply assesses the situation in terms of the individual's capabilities and the particular task or responsibility ascribed to the group.

Transformational curriculum leaders embrace their leadership through embodying expected admirable character traits, serving with others in various group settings, and focusing on essential tasks through relationships with others.

Actions of Curriculum Leaders

How does one actually lead through the curriculum? Curriculum plays a pivotal role in the life of the congregation. Educational leadership is in effect curricular leadership, since curriculum reflects the congregation's theological convictions, translated into programs and ministries. The curriculum takes it cues from Scripture, theology, history, and educational theory, but manifests these as actions within the church (see fig. 11.2).

The curriculum leader has the responsibility of capturing the congregation's mission and casting an educational vision consistent with it. If the mission of the congregation is to mature individuals toward Christlikeness, then the curricular leader must pose the question,

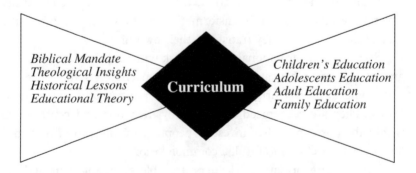

Figure 11.2: Pivotal Role of Curriculum Leadership

"How does the education ministry of the congregation align itself with this mission?" Learning objectives, programs to deliver instruction, and ministries are formed to address specific life needs as a means of living out the congregation's mission through an educational vision. This entails encouraging people to share in the vision, to appropriate it for themselves, and to make it their own for their ministry in the congregation. Naturally, educational vision requires strategic planning, not merely casting a vision, but developing the step-by-step tactic to bring about the desired educational vision while also addressing the inevitable resistance or even conflict that may arise due to implementing change to the congregation.

Curriculum leaders must also build relationships with those who serve with them. These relationships are pastoral at their core, but leaders also assume the co-laborer posture within the educational ministry of the congregation. The curriculum leader must commit himself to inspiring the confidence of team members by developing their competence through equipping and training them. As ministry participants, teachers, or program directors begin to exemplify resourcefulness and their abilities increase, they may be recognized as being capable of assuming a leadership role in the congregation's educational ministry.

Resources are never limitless; hence, an important responsibility of a curriculum leader is to manage the educational ministry's resources. The appropriate allocation of resources should be based on insight from the continual evaluation of programs, personnel, and the resources in support of the curriculum. The development of relevant policies and procedures is an indispensible part of the administration of curriculum, especially in regard to the determination of curriculum selection and program development.

Curriculum and the Education Ministry

Curriculum and administration are not separate elements of the education ministry. They complement one another. Does curriculum comply with administrative structure, or does structure comply with curriculum? The character of the curriculum, the manner in which it determines its contents and the degree of changes to the curriculum's content and methodologies aligns with administrative practices, which reinforces the curriculum.

Ronald Doll provides three metaphors to describe the curriculum: fireworks, refrigerator, and construction. Based on Doll's metaphors, one can extrapolate the administrative posture required to provide supervision and leadership. Curriculum can be fireworks, spur of the moment decisions, almost fad-driven, with a reactionary administration providing the impulsive selection and decision-making. It can also be described as a refrigerator, with a curriculum frozen in tradition, unchanging content and methodology, with a rigid administration to preserve the status quo. Finally, Doll describes curriculum as a construction site, rebuilding and demolishing, where the curriculum is in a continual state of revision and where a progressive administration provides supervision to the process.[5] Each curriculum type described by Doll requires an appropriate, accompanying form of administration.

The more fluid the curriculum, the more fluid the administration required to support it. In such an instance, the administration is somewhat reactionary and change is the norm of operation. Since the curriculum is in a constant state of flux, the supervision of it must also be readily adaptable to the needs of the new curriculum, calling for short-range planning. The curriculum selection process is indeed almost fad-driven, based on the perceived interests and desires of the congregation. For example, a new book becomes the latest Christian "fad," or a popular movie challenges Christian belief, and the congregation jumps onto the proverbial "bandwagon" and adjusts their curriculum accordingly, awaiting the next fad or hot-topic.

The more fixed the curriculum, the more fixed the administration. Aiming at the preservation of status quo, the administration is more bureaucratic, emphasizing policy and procedure, so as to maintain a stable curriculum. This administration does not react to the forces from within or to the leadings of the external influences of the congregation or society. For example, the Bible always being relevant to the Christian life, the curriculum is a series of biblical and theological studies that are rooted in the historical tradition of the church, relatively unchanging to the times or ministry context.

---

[5] Doll, *Curriculum Improvement*, 17.

The progressive curriculum, which determines the need for curriculum change through the continual process of reassessing curriculum in accordance to changing needs of the congregation and society, needs a proactive administration. It must anticipate the needs of the congregation and the community in which it ministers and make proactive adjustments to the curriculum. For example, the curriculum leader perceives the need for Christians to hone their cross-cultural relationship skills due to a demographic shift in the community's ethnicity. Consequently, to better reach out to the community, the leader suggests the church begin teaching Spanish and study Hispanic culture with an emphasis on their religious and moral beliefs.

Curriculum Structuring the Educational Ministry

The ministry of Christian education is not homogenous. It is not any one single program, age group, or venue for providing instruction within the church. It is the variety of educational venues, each with its own curricular purpose and emphasis that makes for the diverse spectrum of programs comprising the education ministry.[6] Likewise, programs do impact curriculum, both in terms of imposing restrictions and raising possibilities. One aspect of a Christian education may be instructional systems, such as frequently occurring educational venues like Sunday school, or routine but infrequent venues like seasonal seminars and lectureships with special speakers. Other aspects may include educational venues that are off site, away from the congregation, such as small groups or field experiences. This removes the congregation's curriculum from the confines of its building and classrooms, placing it in the home or such locations as a museum or college campus. Similarly, self-directed study, with the aid of the congregation's library and guides to online studies, not to mention reading groups, provide a level of non-directed, lifelong learning within the congregation's education ministry. But, what is the connection between the administrative structures and curricular supervision? This is the matter referred to as *grading* or *alignment*.

---

[6] Cf. Leroy Ford, *A Curriculum Design Manual for Theological Education: A Learning Outcomes Focus* (Nashville: Broadman, 1991), 201–10.

There are kinds of alignment in the education ministry of a congregation between the curriculum and programs.[7] One of the most common forms of alignment is *uniform* in which a uniform theme is consistent throughout the whole education ministry; for example, Sunday school classes study the book of Romans regardless of age or life situation. This approach provides for the greatest degree of alignment that curriculum and program administration can offer. Another is described as *unified* alignment, which is similar to uniform in that the theme is consistent, but it utilizes different materials based on age group or life situation; for example, a small group may want to focus on relationships, but use different materials depending on the age or life situation of the participants. *Program alignment* is frequently used in larger congregations in which the curriculum is diversified into departments or perhaps ministries; for example, perhaps the adults in the Sunday school are studying one curriculum, small groups are studying another, and youth groups yet another. This does provide for a diversity of curricular approaches and offers individuals some level of flexibility and choice of subject matter. A fourth means of alignment is described as *closed*. This is almost a level of non-alignment, providing the least degree of cohesion between curriculum and programming. It breaks the alignment into minute themes or general content directions; for example, if a congregation uses an elective system in their education ministry, then naturally one would expect there to be a loose alignment at best within the curriculum and program.

Levels of Curriculum Supervision

The guidance and direction given to the process of supervising curriculum, its development, design, and even selection of specific resources and materials, occurs at multiple levels. Many Christian educators underestimate the level of influences in their curriculum deliberations and selections. Perhaps the metanarrative that informs their decisions is the entirety of the Christian tradition. That we are Christian educators does indeed impose certain confirmations and denounce-

---

[7] Cf. Elmer L. Towns, *How to Grow an Effective Sunday School* (Lynchburg: Church Growth Institute, 1987), 100–102.

ments. Perhaps more evident is the impact of denominational identity and heritage, with many denominations having their own curriculum and publishing houses providing books and prepackaged curricula for congregations within that denomination (e.g., Lifeway in the Southern Baptist Convention). In some denominations, curricular decisions are influenced by regional or district authorities, guided by an association of pastors within a given geographical location. All of these levels of curricular supervision are beyond the walls of the church building; they are beyond the local congregation's decision-making paradigm. However, they do influence curriculum deliberations from a distance.

The leadership of the local congregation can be influential on the establishment of curriculum guides, determining what purpose and objectives should be achieved by the education ministry. This would be true for satellite congregations established by a parent congregation, perhaps augmenting curricular designs slightly based on the distinction of the satellite from the parent campus. Within the congregation, each ministry and department with a ministry may prescribe program specific curricular initiatives, ones that reflect their uniqueness and distinction within the congregation. For example, while adult and adolescent curricula may be similar, we would not expect it to be identical but reflect the lifespan differences and relevance of content to the different age groups. Usually, the only individuals aware of these deliberations and decisions are involved in the education ministry itself, the superintendents, directors, teachers, and facilitators of specific educational venues.

Most individuals involved in the education ministry of the congregation as a teacher or participant see curriculum only as it relates to their particular class or small group. Their curricular view is limited to their own involvement in the congregation's education ministry. The teacher of the class or facilitator of a small group has some voice in determining the curriculum utilized in their education venue. At this level, even the participants within the class are aware of the curriculum. "What are you studying in Sunday school?" Nevertheless, curriculum supervision is not an automatic process, nor is it made by an inanimate object. It is a very human activity, one that comes down to the individual. As Wyckoff observes,

> The individual himself has the ultimate responsibility for curriculum-building. The curriculum is his, or all the rest of the

building is in vain. The curriculum is made or broken on the goals that the individuals sets for himself and works toward in company with others or alone. . . . The curriculum may help, but the responsibility is his, as God gives him grace to accept that responsibility.[8]

Curriculum Deliberation

Although it is not the only question, the inescapable question in all curriculum supervision and deliberation is, Who controls the curriculum? Given all the levels of curriculum supervision just discussed, this is not an answer that is immediately discernable. Curriculum is symbiotic. It may be directed from the leadership of the congregation, such as the board, pastoral staff, or Christian education pastor; but it must be made in response to the perceived and real needs of the individual and the participants within a program, class, or group. In terms of the church-as-curriculum aspect, the denomination and leadership of the local congregation are perhaps the most significant voice in the deliberation. In terms of a specific ministry or program within the congregation, curricular deliberations rest with the pastoral staff, pastor, and perhaps even the leaders within that ministry, such as its teachers or sponsors. However, on a fundamental level, curriculum plays out in the individual educational venue, such as the classroom and small group settings. Curriculum permeates the congregation on every level of its existence, from its mission statement, to the purposes, goals, and objectives of programs comprising the education ministry, even to the packet of materials purchased for the teacher of a children's Sunday school class.

The education ministry of the congregation is the most obvious place where the curriculum receives continual attention, evaluation, and change. Consistent with the congregation's mission and vision for ministry, the education ministry establishes its purpose, goals, and objectives for those participating within its ministry. These are typically determined by the congregation's leadership and the pastoral staff with input from other individuals who have a significant investment

---

[8] D. Campbell Wyckoff, *Theory and Design of the Christian Education Curriculum* (Philadelphia: Westminster, 1961), 204.

in the education ministry, such as experienced teachers or directors of programs. From these deliberations, a general direction is determined for the education ministry and individual programs.

When it comes to the particulars of what is taught in the individual classroom, or within the small group Bible study, or youth group, a process for selecting, determining, and approving the curriculum is needed. Although this process may appear linear, step-by-step, it is usually anything but linear. Rather, it is interactive and culminates in a forward progression, moving an agenda; but it is not clear, nor linear.

Is the curriculum dictated by the leadership or by members of the pastoral staff, or is it the prerogative of the teacher or even the students to select what is taught? In the symbiotic relationship within the education ministry, perhaps the best model calls for dialogue between the teacher and pastor responsible for education, with the pastor of education serving as a resource person for the class, as a coordinator of the available options. Whether the idea originated from the learner or teacher, the Christian education pastor can encourage them to choose from recommended alternatives. Thus, the teacher is empowered to make curricular decisions but has the benefit of gaining approval and support from the pastoral staff. It is not a matter of trust, as if teachers cannot be trusted to make decisions beneficial for their classes, but one of coordination, resourcing, publicity, and intentionally aligning it with the purpose, goals, and objectives of the education ministry. In this instance, the teacher has to be primarily concerned with the curriculum in his classroom or group; the pastor is responsible for the education ministry of the church and has to assess not only this, but the broader impact of the curriculum on the whole congregation and how it relates to what may be occurring in other classes and programs. This process of curriculum deliberation creates an atmosphere of cooperation between the participants, teachers/leaders, and the pastoral staff in regard to what is being adopted as curriculum in the congregation's classrooms and groups.

Curriculum Deliberation Considerations

The deliberation between the Christian education pastor and those teaching in the classroom or group is crucial to arriving at a sound decision about curriculum. First, consider as many curricular alternatives as reasonably possible. Do not make decisions with tunnel vision, considering only what is in your immediate purview; instead, explore what may be available from multiple sources. For example, if a small group facilitator wants a study on James, examine several possible curricular resources from various acceptable publishers or authors that he may use with the group.

Second, give consideration to the purpose and objective of the study. Each resource considered will have a different set of assumed reasons for engaging the study, each with its own stated learning objectives. These need to be assessed not only in reference to the desired objectives of the class or group, but also in regard to their alignment with the stated purpose and goals of the program. For example, what if one of the stated objectives of one of the studies on James is theologically incompatible with the congregation? That should be taken into consideration when selecting the resource.

Third, determine if the congregation has the resources that are required by the curricula being considered. Such incidental details as time period, required technology, or even what it expects of the teacher in terms of preparation time and prior knowledge must be assessed. If one study on James lasts an hour, requires a DVD player, and needs a teacher who knows Greek, then your small group, which only studies for 30 minutes and has a DVD player and a teacher who does not know Greek, needs a different curriculum. Make sure the curriculum is a match for the given setting in which it will be used. Failure to do so makes its use a frustration to both the teacher and the participants.

Yet another consideration to make is the spiritual dimension of the curriculum. What does the curriculum say about the believer's relationship with God? Is the application prescribed by the curriculum for the individual and the congregation acceptable for all those involved? When considering curriculum, the spiritual aspect of how it aids our relationship with God must be ascertained. For example, consider the book of James. What if the curriculum's author comes from a background of liberation theology, applying James' concern for the poor and call for equality within the Christian community to mean the radical political and even violent overthrow of civil authorities? Or, perhaps the application calls Christians to be more aware of the poor and social injustices, to identify ways they can be more generous and attentive toward the marginalized in society, and to work constructively to address these situations through both Christian benevolence and political action. Once again, this is a matter that must be considered in selecting curriculum.

Cocurricular Considerations

Curriculum supervision overlaps the administration of the congregation's educational ministry in two more evident ways: the development of teachers and instructional resources. Curriculum places different requirements on the teachers using it in terms of flexibility in instructional methodology, assumed biblical/theological knowledge on the part of the teacher, level of expertise in using instructional methodologies, and technological abilities of the instructor. The more sophisticated the curriculum, the more expectations are made on the teacher's abilities to fulfill its requirements. The curriculum specialist is in part responsible for the orienting and training of teachers to be the most effective teachers they can be, making the maximum use of the curriculum in their classrooms or groups. A comprehensive teacher development initiative provides the teacher with four developmental venues. (1) Group study—a classroom setting in which teachers are oriented to the role of a teacher, the nuts-and-bolts of the congregation's education ministry, and the use of technological resources. Most importantly teachers could be shown the appropriate use of curriculum, demonstrating how to make the most effective use of it and even how to augment purchased curriculum materials. (2) Mentoring—beginning teachers should be assigned a more experienced teacher or even spiritual director to be a personal mentor to them during their first few years as a teacher. Biweekly one-on-one mentoring meetings could be done to pray for one another, confess life struggles, and aid in developing the teacher's spiritual life. (3) Supervised experience—what cannot be taught in the classroom can be taught by experience. Beginning teachers can teach alongside a more experienced teacher, one who knows their students and is an exemplary teacher, but only if a more experienced teacher can provide feedback to the beginning teacher as they begin their teaching ministry. Finally, (4) independent study—education ministries should resource their teachers, providing books, magazine or journal subscriptions, websites that have proven their worth to the teacher, and even DVD Bible study resources; anything that would prove a useful resource for independent study. The combination of these four approaches ensures the best results in terms of developing new teachers into experienced, capable teachers able to make the most effective use of the curriculum.

Similarly, curriculum has an assumed level of technological sophistication for the congregation's education ministry. In the past, a curriculum would assume chalkboards, Bible maps, flannel graphs, and perhaps an overhead projector. Today it is quite different. It is more common to assume the presence of computers with projection capabilities, on which a DVD can be used, and Internet access at the church building for streaming video or even a video-contact to invite guest speakers, such as missionaries, into the classroom from any distance. In addition to this, the general resources needed for the different age groups and programs within the education ministry, such as copier access, crayons/markers, paper, pencils, *ad infinitum* are equally necessary for effective teaching. Curricula assume a level of resourcing. In fact, many lesson plans begin with a list of required resources with alternatives that should be available. One administrative aspect of the curriculum specialists is to advance the education ministry's instructional resources, to ensure they are not only well stocked and accessible, but also current with the technological demands of the curriculum.

The Value of Prepackaged Curriculum

Most education provided within congregations utilizes pre-packaged curriculum. Sunday school teachers are provided a pouch of lesson plans, essential resources, and on occasion even a website from which they can download additional materials if so desired. Prepared curriculum oftentimes aims for the lowest common denominator in terms of student expectations and provides overly simplified theological content to avoid theological controversy. It is also described as being "off the rack" as opposed to a tailored curriculum for a class or group. Likewise, it is not unique to one's own congregation. However, all these criticisms have a flawed assumption. They all assume that the curriculum was intended to be the end of teachers' preparations; just hand them the packet and they are ready to teach. It assumes the pre-packaged curriculum is the final word, not the launching point from which a teacher starts.

Prepackaged curriculum does provide some definite benefits for the teacher. Most congregations do not have the personnel or insight to develop a comprehensive curriculum for its entire educational ministry, and are therefore dependent on the availability of pre-packaged curriculum for use in ʻclassrooms and groups. The purchased curriculum can be used to supplement a study, utilizing its overview and resources to introduce a much deeper and broader study. As such, the prepackaged curriculum serves as the basis or resource for a more tailored curriculum prepared by the teacher. Material and questions relevant to the class or group, or even congregation, can be added to the purchased curriculum to make it tailored without burdening the teacher to prepare the entire curriculum. Also, even if it is considered too basic and generic for more advanced participants, it may fulfill the purpose of introducing individuals to a newfound faith, or even a non-believer to what the Bible teaches. Prepackaged curriculum is not one-size-fits-all but can place useful materials in the hands of a knowledgeable teacher for use in a classroom or group study.

Finishing the Journey

The journey of the Christian faith is not a solo passage; it happens in the community of other travelers. Fortunately, others who have traversed before us, or are more experienced travelers, are able to provide the resources necessary for the pilgrimage ahead. They have left roadmaps, directions, navigational clues, and the means to make sense of them. These tools guide us on our journey into the Christian faith.

Curriculum is not solely an academic matter, nor is it ancillary to the ministry of the congregation. It translates the beliefs, heritage, mission, vision, and values of a congregation into a tangible expression by which these convictions can be instilled and adopted by a new generation of Christians. The curriculum reflects the soul of the institution. It is the roadmap for discipleship and growth toward Christlikeness.

Key Terms and Concepts

Transformational Leadership   Cocurricular

Curriculum Supervision   Curriculum Deliberation

Curriculum Specialist

Reflection Exercise

1. In your congregation, who makes curricular decisions—teacher, pastoral staff, congregational leadership, learners, or a combination?
2. What bases are considered in administering curriculum decisions?
3. What kind of prescribed procedure does your church have for determining curriculum selections?
4. Is there a "final approval" stage concerning which curriculum your church uses? How is the decision ultimately made? Confirmed?

SECTION IV

Curriculum Practice

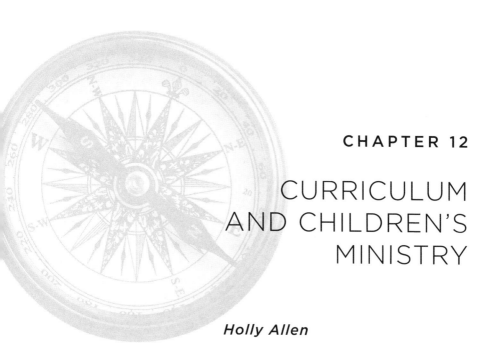

CHAPTER 12

CURRICULUM AND CHILDREN'S MINISTRY

Holly Allen

Recently I was asked to assist the parents and children's ministry leaders of a church to re-vision their ministry to children and to offer guidelines for a curriculum that would align with this new vision—a curriculum that would foster spiritual development in their children. After meeting, greeting, and praying together, I opened the conversation with an important question: What do you want for the children in this community of believers? That is, What do you want them to know? How do you want them to live? Who do you hope they will become? After a few moments of concentration, they slowly began to construct their list; momentum picked up and they quickly completed their list (see fig. 12.1 on p. 240).

When this group of loving parents and hopeful ministry leaders completed their list, I asked, "Do you think we can create a children's ministry in this church that can do all of this?" Dozens of doubtful faces turned to me in dismay. Really, can any children's ministry do all of this?

Fortunately, children's ministries need not bear the full weight for the spiritual nurture of the children they serve. Most Christians

What we hope for our children	
That they will . . .	*And that they will begin to acquire an understanding of . . .*
know God	
believe that God is	their place in the kingdom
love God	the role of Holy Spirit
receive Christ	the Trinity
love their "neighbor"—serve the poor, the hurting, the broken	the central importance of Scripture
pray	the power of sin
know the "Master Story"	the crucial role of the church as an essential community of Christ-followers
desire to worship God	
share Jesus with others	
be growing in compassion, humility, love, mercy	the need for Christ to save them
have their identity in Christ	

Figure 12.1: Children's Learning Goals

recognize that parents are the primary spiritual guides for their children. Typically, parents themselves agree that they have the principal responsibility for the moral and spiritual development of their children.[1] Scripture indicates that parents are key agents as spiritual leaders for their children, and theologians throughout the ages have tended to agree. For example, Martin Luther said, "Most certainly father and mother are apostles, bishops, and priests to their children, for it is they who make them acquainted with the gospel."[2]

We agree with the basic tenet that parents are their children's primary spiritual guides. It is not the job of children's ministry to take the place of parents; nevertheless, children's ministries do play an impor-

---

[1] C. J. Boyatzis, D. C. Dollahite, and L. D. Marks, "The Family as Context for Religious and Spiritual Development," in *The Handbook of Spiritual Development in Childhood and Adolescence*, ed. E. C. Roehlkepartain, P. E. King, L. Wagner, and P. L. Benson (Thousand Oaks, CA: Sage, 2006), 297–309.

[2] Helmut T. Lehmann and Walther Immanuel Brandt, *Luther's Works: The Christian in Society II, Volume 45* (Philadelphia: Fortress, 1962), 46.

tant role as they join parents in the mutual goal of nurturing children on their journeys of faith.

Which Approach?

Once spiritual goals have been identified, these parents and ministry leaders asked what types of ministry models or approaches might be utilized to meet their goals. In order to discern which approaches to consider, I asked several questions regarding venue: Will the primary children's ministry venue take place largely during the hour before (or after) the main worship hour? Will it be during the main worship hour? Will there be an additional setting—perhaps a Wednesday evening venue or an intergenerational venue? Will the children be separated closely by age or will several age groups be together? And of course, the number of children affects which approach might be considered— what is possible to do with 25 children may be less so with 200 or 300. In general, once these basic questions are answered, then the idea of approaches can be considered.

The first chapter in a recent book by a group of educators describes five metaphors or models for ministry with children: the school model, the gold star/win a prize model, the carnival model, the pilgrim's journey model, and the dance-with-God model.[3] Michael Anthony frames four approaches to children's ministry somewhat differently: the contemplative-reflective model, the instructional-analytic model, the pragmatic-participatory model, and the media-driven active-engagement model.[4]

---

[3] See Scottie May, Beth Posterski, Catherine Stonehouse, and Linda Cannell, *Children Matter: Celebrating Their Place in the Church, Family, and Community* (Grand Rapids: Eerdmans, 2005).

[4] See Michael J. Anthony, "Children's Ministry Models, Learning Theory, and Spiritual Development," in *Nurturing Children's Spirituality: Christian Perspectives and Best Practices*, ed. Holly Catterton Allen (Eugene, OR: Cascade Books, 2008); id., "Introduction," in *Perspectives on Children's Spiritual Formation: Four Views*, ed. Gregory C. Carlson and Michael J. Anthony (Nashville: B&H, 2006). Anthony constructs these four models by integrating Urban Holmes's phenomenology of prayer (*A History of Spirituality* [New York: Seabury Press, 1980]) and David Kolb's Model of Learning (*Experiential Learning: Experience as the Source of Learning and Development* [New York: Prentice-Hall, 1984]).

For the purposes of this chapter, I will group the various approaches into four types: school models, large group/small group approaches, contemplative models, and intergenerational approaches. Along the way, I will make connections to the models of Anthony as well as May, et al.

School Models

Sunday schools were the most common approach to children's ministry in the twentieth century. Though Sunday school attendance has been waning in recent years, millions of children (and adults) still participate regularly in small, age-graded Sunday school classes. Excellent material is available in print and online—much more holistic, less school-like than previous renditions, with more opportunity for active participation, for drama, for creative output, for service, and for fun! Sunday school is still a strong, viable option for thousands of churches.

Another school model is Awana, which May, et al., describe as the gold star/win a prize model. Anthony places Awana-type programs in his instructional-analytic model, where Sunday school would also fit.

Churches that highly value a systematic approach to Bible learning should recognize that a Sunday school approach may best fit their most cherished goals. Choosing or writing excellent curriculum is the key, curriculum that aligns with the desires and hopes for the children of this community of believers. Also, as with all approaches, this model has some weaknesses and should be supplemented with a more relational model, perhaps a contemplative or intergenerational approach.

Large Group/Small Group Approaches

Large group/small group approaches are common currently, with both Group and Cook offering good biblically-based materials that are built around this format. Also, various programs available for purchase online such as 252 Basics follow this model.[5] Large group/small group designs provide one way to manage large groups of children; in addition, these approaches may utilize fewer actual teachers—though the number of volunteers altogether may be substantial since many are needed to lead small groups.

---

[5] See online: http://whatisorange.org/252basics.

Some large group/small group curricula include elaborate stage designs for monthly themes and a variety of media-led options, as well as other options for live story-telling, drama, and worship that call for near-professional level emcees. After the large group story-telling time and usually a skit and some singing, the large group of 50-300 children is divided into small groups made up of 6-20 children with two leaders (a married couple, senior adults, college students, or perhaps teens). These small group facilitators are asked to commit to a several-month stint to provide ongoing relational opportunities for the children. In the small groups, the leaders and children process the key biblical insights discerning together real-life applications; the small group leaders pray with and for the children; the children sometimes make a craft or play a game that connects to the Bible story.

Anthony's last two models—the pragmatic-participatory model and the media-driven active-engagement—tend to be large group/small group approaches, while May's "carnival" models typically employ large and small group settings. Churches with large children's ministry budgets tend to utilize these materials. Mid-size churches sometimes adapt the materials to fit their needs. Small churches may find these materials difficult to scale down for their settings, perhaps too expensive and sometimes overwhelming. Though an exciting, energetic large group/small group venue can draw children into its orbit and offer biblically sound content, this approach also should be supplemented with a more contemplative or an intergenerational model.

Contemplative Approach

Anthony's material identifies this approach as the contemplative-reflective model; he writes,

> This quadrant is characterized by periods of quiet reflection, introspective prayer, and storytelling. Its goal is twofold. The first goal is to empty the mind of self-absorbed thoughts to enable one to come before God as a clean vessel. Confession and honest self-assessment are essential to this process. The second goal is to find a place of solitude for quiet meditation. One can meditate on Scripture, reflect on a quiet song playing in the background, or gaze at a piece of artistic expression of spirituality (e.g., a sculpture, painting, etc.). Individuals in this

quadrant can usually recall moments when God was "real" to them in a time of turmoil, doubt, or transition.[6]

In the typology of May, et al., this approach best fits in the "dance-with-God" model. The new book by Catherine Stonehouse and Scottie May, *Listening to Children on the Spiritual Journey*, describes contemplative approaches much more fully, with anecdotal (and engaging) detail.[7]

One version of a contemplative model is Godly Play, an increasingly popular approach developed over the past three decades by Jerome Berryman.[8] Berryman, an Episcopalian priest based his Godly Play materials on the original work of Maria Montessori, whose name is known in the United States primarily through the Montessori schools that utilize manipulatives and discovery approaches to learning.[9] Berryman has spent several decades adapting Montessori's and Sofia Cavalletti's[10] ideas, creating several volumes of scripts and materials that are now available from http://www.godlyplayfoundation.org.

Godly Play is a sensory-rich discovery approach, keenly focused on children experientially "entering" a story primarily via a few special but simple story props and a quietly intoned story script. This unique approach values silence and "gives children a way to confront the existential questions common to all people: aloneness, freedom, the meaning of life, and death."[11]

---

[6] Michael J. Anthony, "Children's Ministry Models," 190.

[7] Catherine Stonehouse and Scottie May, *Listening to Children on the Spiritual Journey: Guidance for Those Who Teach and Nurture* (Grand Rapids: Baker, 2010).

[8] See Jerome Berryman, *Teaching Godly Play: How to Mentor the Spiritual Development of Children* (Denver: Morehouse, 2009).

[9] See Maria Montessori and Mortimer Standing, *The Child in the Church: Essays on the Religious Education of Children and the Training of Character* (London: Sands, 1929). Though American Montessori schools are typically secular, Montessori herself was a strong Catholic and when she taught children, she always included religious lessons as well as math and other "secular" subjects.

[10] Sofia Cavalletti, *The Religious Potential of the Child: Experiencing Scripture and Liturgy with Young Children* (Mt. Ranier, MD: Catechesis of the Good Shepherd, 1983). A protégé of Montessori, Sofia Cavalletti developed one version of Montessori's ideas; this version, called Catechesis of the Good Shepherd, is used primarily in Catholic churches. Another version, Young Children and Worship, was a 1980s version of Berryman's Godly Play that he created with Sonja Stewart.

[11] Kim McPherson and Becki Stewart, *Godly Play Teacher Accreditation Training Manual* (Godly Play Teacher Accreditation, 2009), 2.

Godly Play is not primarily a cognitive approach, though Bible stories *are* told. Content questions are not usually asked; rather, wondering questions are asked. For example, in the parable of the Good Samaritan, the children are asked, "I wonder who might have been the neighbor to the robbers?" No responses to the wondering questions are required; they are simply wondering questions.

This unique approach stands in contrast particularly to the entertainment models that have become prominent in the last few decades. Some Sunday school curricula and most large group/small group models keep children busy, occupied, and moving, with every moment filled. This more contemplative approach gives children space—space to think, space to listen, space to be.

I am quite enamored with Godly Play; however, I do not see it as a comprehensive approach to children's ministry.[12] It nurtures especially the child's relationship with God; it is not primarily concerned with biblical chronology or facts *per se*, nor is it focused on a linear application of key concepts that yield measurable behaviors in children. On the

---

[12] I have been becoming increasingly familiar with this approach over the past decade. I observed my first Godly Play "lesson" in 2000 at the first International Children's Spirituality Conference in Chichester, England. There were no children present; it was simply a demonstration. I thought it was intriguing, but I clearly remember thinking that many of the children I have taught over the years would not stay attuned to such a quiet, laid-back story. I saw another demonstration at the first Children's Spirituality Conference in the United States in Chicago in 2003. Again, no children were present.

I was planning at that time to teach a course on children's spirituality in about a year, and I decided to begin purchasing materials to use in order to introduce this distinctive method to my students. I purchased scripts and materials and practiced telling the "Good Shepherd" story several times. When I presented the story in class, a young man in the class, a soccer player named Joel (and self-described "hyper" guy) announced that had that story been told when he was a child, he would have mentally checked out after two minutes. He and three other students were scheduled to teach that very lesson to a group of about ten children the following Sunday; it would be the first time they (as well as I) had seen a Godly Play story told to actual children. I admit that I expected it to fail to hold their interest. I was spectacularly wrong. The children, who began the story sitting on the floor around the story mat, so entered the story that by the end, each of the ten children had scooted back from the edge of the story mat and placed their noses at the very edge to gain close access. After the children left, the four students and I looked at each other in shocked awe, Joel stunned into dead silence.

other hand, none of the methods or approaches described here would be complete in and of themselves. Each has gaps or deficits that a second approach would supplement.

Intergenerational Small Groups

Though Anthony does not discuss this model, an intergenerational approach to ministry with children reflects the "pilgrim metaphor" that May, et al., describe.[13] Many young parents with children desire to spend intentional spiritual time with their children in the company of other families with children. However, most do not know what that might entail. For four years my family worshiped with a church that promoted intergenerational small groups every Sunday evening. We met for an hour or more with adults, children, and teens together. To open the gathering each week, every person present answered an icebreaker (e.g., What is your favorite ice cream? What are you afraid of? What do you dream about?). Old and young, we came to know each other quite well in those light-hearted responses. But each week we also prayed for every family unit present (singles, couples, families). We prayed for pregnant moms, forming babies, job situations, achievement tests, bullies, fears, hopes, futures, old relational patterns, anger issues, disappointments, losses. Also, each week we sang contemporary and traditional songs led by two different volunteers—a teen and a college student one week, a child and a mom the next, a married couple the next.

This model of "children's ministry" does not seem to fit into any type of typical children's ministry program; its focus is formation in community and thus is concerned not only with children but with the whole body of Christ. Some might say, therefore, that it does not fit into a discussion of children's ministry models. I would argue that my own children and the children of the church we worshiped with for four years were perhaps formed more authentically and more powerfully in our intergenerational small groups than in the formal children's ministry program of that church (which, by the way, I directed). Therefore, when considering ministry to children in a more holistic way, an intentional intergenerational component should

---

[13] May, et al., *Children Matter.*

be considered as an indispensable supplement to a more traditional approach.

In general, there is little published curriculum available for use in intergenerational settings. Although Desiring God Ministries out of Minneapolis has produced two sets of materials that are intentionally intergenerational,[14] perhaps the most pressing current curriculum need is for this—intergenerational curriculum.

To Purchase or to Write?

Once the planners have constructed a good understanding of their goals, that is, what they desire for their children, and have determined the one or two primary settings for which to provide curriculum, then the looming question is, Who produces curriculum that fits what is needed?

Choosing a Published Curriculum

There is a plethora of published curriculum available. The two largest curriculum producers, Group and Cook, offer several types of well-developed and well-written curricula for both Sunday school and large group/small group settings. Gospel Light, Standard, Lifeway, and other publishing houses also offer materials that are theologically attuned to particular tenets.

Seemingly hundreds of curriculum materials are also now available online, most of which are downloadable once you get a password. Some charge a fee (252 Basics), some are free. For example, MAX7 (http://www.max7.org) provides internationally compatible curriculum materials that offer some fabulous wordless videos and curricular guidelines for diverse populations.

Godly Play is the main published curriculum that fits the contemplative model.[15] As mentioned earlier there are a few curricula

---

[14] Sally Michael, *Lord, Teach Us to Pray: A Study for Children and Adults on Prayer* (Minneapolis: Desiring God Ministries, 2006); Sally Michael, *The Righteous Shall Live by Faith: A Study for Children and Adults on the Ten Commandments* (Minneapolis: Desiring God Ministries, 2005).

[15] *Catechesis of the Good Shepherd* (online: http://www.cgsusa.org) is derived from the original Montessori approach and is utilized primarily by those in

available for use in intergenerational settings. The guidelines below are especially useful for Sunday school settings and large group/small group models but can be adapted for use in intergenerational settings. Contemplative approaches require a unique, alternative approach to curriculum altogether.

It is often overwhelming to choose among the various curricula available. But one should consider the following questions:

1. Does it fit your needs? Your approach? Your size? Your purposes?
2. Does it fit you theologically? Is it biblically accurate? (Read through two to three lessons at three levels, specifically looking for biblical accuracy.)
3. Does the scope and sequence cover what you deem important? (A Scope and Sequence chart is an overview of the biblical themes and passages that are taught along with a chronology of when each is taught.)

If the answers thus far are "yes," then the next questions include:

1. Can my teachers, volunteers, and children's workers use it? Would an inexperienced teacher be overwhelmed? Can an experienced teacher easily adapt it?
2. Is it developmentally appropriate? Do the activities seem appropriate for preschoolers, early elementary, later elementary?
3. Does it take into consideration a variety of learning styles—some children love school type activities (analytical learners); some like to discuss and chat through ideas (collaborative learners); some simply want to know how they can use the material (common sense learners); and some want to move past the material and create something new and different (dynamic learners).

Catholic or Episcopalian settings; also, an earlier version of Godly Play by Jerome Berryman and Sonja Stewart can be found in *Young Children and Worship* (Louisville: WJK Press, 1990).

4. Is there plenty of movement? Are all the senses used? Does the material suggest good questions to be asked of the students—questions that move past simple recall into evaluative, affective, and/or creative realms?

Several other questions should be considered also:

1. Is there a strong emphasis on prayer?
2. Is there a strong focus on placing the Word in the heart (memory work)?
3. Are there suggestions for sensitivity to children with special needs? To those from minority cultures?

Writing Curriculum

Because it is hard to find and choose good curriculum that fits the setting, the denomination, the particular theological tenets, the ministry leaders' unique desires, and different venues, many churches are opting to create their own curriculum. The great strength of this idea is that it is a wonderful, spiritually stretching, challenging, rewarding experience for those doing the writing. On the other hand, it is an exhausting, never-ending, pressing task that can lead to burnout in just a few months.

I regularly teach a course on creating holistic curriculum for children in Christian settings. The first half of the course is spent discovering and discerning key curriculum principles (e.g., Principle #1: It is *always* about God). During the semester, students peruse about twenty print and online curricula for good and bad examples of each principle. Students are quite critical of the materials they scrutinize throughout the semester—until they begin to write their own curriculum. Ultimately the students find that creating curriculum that is theologically sound and balanced, biblically accurate, developmentally appropriate, teacher friendly, and culturally sensitive—while incorporating movement, the senses, prayer, memory work, drama, story, emotion, all the learning styles, justice issues, evangelism, and more—is much harder than they imagined. Thus, when children's ministry leaders decide to write their own curriculum, they would be well advised to start small—with a six-week series, or one age level.

These are the key principles my students must keep in mind when they write their four-part series:

Macro level

- Balanced view of God—immanent and transcendent, just and holy, yet loving and kind, Trinitarian.
- Old Testament and New Testament whole story—strong sense of the Master Story, how it all hangs together. God has been at work since the beginning, through Adam, Eve, Noah, Abraham and Sarah, Isaac and Rebekah, Esau, Jacob, Leah, Judah, Tamar, Shiphrah, Puah, Moses, Joshua, Deborah, Rahab, Ruth, Boaz, David, Bathsheba, Esther, Daniel, Mary, Joseph, Jesus—that these stories are interrelated, and that they are all about God and his work in the world on behalf of his creation.

Lesson level

1. *Does it focus on God/Christ/Holy Spirit?* (What do we learn about God in your material? Even though the story may be about Joshua, the hero of the story is not Joshua; it is always God.) Ultimately the goal is for the children to come to know God. The first evaluative task my college students must do when perusing a series is to locate 10–12 statements about God in three different levels. In one series, a student located a theme statement about God at the beginning of each preschool and elementary lesson. The following statements were typical: "God helps us get along with others." "God helps us do our best." "God helps us develop friendships." "God helps us be open and honest with friends." Though each statement was indeed about God, it was clear that in this series, the focus is on the child's needs. God is presented as a God who exists for the child. Though each individual lesson may have been true, accurate, and balanced, children dwelling in this material for years would understandably absorb the idea that the purpose of God's existence is to assist *them*; there is a fundamental flaw here—human beings exist for God, not the other way around.

2. *Is each lesson biblically accurate?* Read and re-read the biblical text and related texts; check commentaries, Bible dictionaries, and other resource materials to check on facts

and details. My students and I have found scores of biblical errors in published curricula; for example, confusing Jeroboam and Rehoboam or a statement that Joseph's *eleven* brothers sold him into slavery. The most common mistake I see and the most serious criticism I would make of the curriculum I have seen over the years is not the occasional factual inaccuracy; rather, it is the misuse of passages and stories to fit a particular focus or agenda.

Therefore, in preparing a lesson based on a certain passage, consider *why* this story or passage is in Scripture. Have you chosen it for *that* reason, or are you using it to make another point? My students have found dozens of examples of published materials using biblical stories for peripheral reasons such as the telling of Jesus feeding the five thousand to teach recycling; using the story of Lydia as a vehicle for exploring the color purple; telling the Esther story to teach purity; telling the Daniel story to promote healthy eating habits; focusing on the story of Joseph in Egypt to teach stewardship.

My best recommendation is generally to avoid topical teaching: scouring Scripture for a story that teaches sharing or perseverance often leads to misuse of Scripture. Always ask, What does this passage or story teach us about God (or Christ, or the Holy Spirit)? For example, the story of Esther is not about beauty or about purity; it is about God's work in the world on behalf of his people. God indeed used Esther's beauty for his good purposes, but the story is not essentially about beauty.

3. *Is the lesson pedagogically sound—that is, does it get where it is going?* For instance, Isa 61:1–4 is the passage in which God is described as close to the broken-hearted, the rebuilder, a restorer; therefore, a theologically, biblically congruent goal in teaching this passage would be for the children to come to know God as a healer and restorer in their lives. The pedagogical question then would be, If the children are guided through Isaiah 61 as is laid out in the curriculum, would the children indeed begin to know, feel, see God as one who heals, restores, rebuilds?

Thus, for the Isaiah 61 passage, regardless of the approach or model—a basic Sunday school approach, a large group/small group approach, a contemplative method, a cross-generational small group setting—the curricular material, to be pedagogically sound, must lead children to a deep cognitive, emotional, and spiritual understanding (in this case) of God as healer. Writing curricula that is pedagogically sound is a challenging task. Every activity should focus toward the goal.

4. *Is it usable—that is, teacher friendly?* Can inexperienced teachers follow the guidelines and design of the lesson? Is it inviting to use?

5. *Is it developmentally appropriate?* Are the preschool activities workable for four-year-olds? Are the questions for fifth graders deep enough? Does the material for first and second graders allow for the non-readers among the children? Is there occasional movement? Are the senses used frequently?

6. *Are there intentional opportunities for prayer?* Are there thoughtful questions for the teacher to ask the children? Is there designated time for placing the Word in the heart (memory work)?

Curriculum and Children's Ministry

In visioning a ministry to children that nurtures children spiritually through any model—schooling approaches, large group/small group settings, contemplative venues, or intergenerational settings—creating, or locating, good curriculum is crucial. Excellent curriculum will intentionally promote the God-child relationship through prayer, the Master Story, worship, service, and silence; choosing or writing curriculum that is theologically and biblically sound, pedagogically strong, developmentally appropriate, inviting, fun, and usable will continue to be a challenge for ministry leaders.

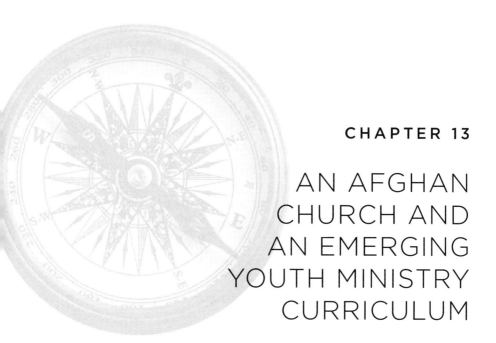

CHAPTER 13

AN AFGHAN CHURCH AND AN EMERGING YOUTH MINISTRY CURRICULUM

Mark H. Senter III

The three youth ministers got together at Newport Coffee House each week to discuss the challenges they faced in their youth ministries. Cheryl always seemed to have a stimulating question but today's zinger sounded boring at first but soon opened into a fascinating conversation: "How do you determine the curriculum you use for the high schoolers in your church?"

At first Tim thought she meant, "Do you download something or buy a book?" But it was obvious that was not where Cheryl was going.

Coming at it another way, Cheryl asked, "How far ahead do you plan what you will teach and how do the youth ministry activities tie in with the content of what they are learning?"

Tony chipped in based on his three years of experience, "Not far enough."

This baffled Tim a bit. He asked, "What do you mean?"

"My kids are either too bright or too uninterested to stitch lessons together randomly based on my current interests. I've come to the point that I need to develop a larger game plan," Tony responded. He obviously had given the question some thought.

"That's what I'm wrestling with, too," chimed in Cheryl, "I've been wondering if I shouldn't develop a plan that will take the kids all the way through high school."

"Maybe even from middle school through high school," offered Tony.

"Whoa," objected Tim, "that would never work for my kids. It sounds too much like school."

"What's wrong with that?" Cheryl probed. "Besides, I'm not sure they need to know there is such a plan. They'll see it when they look back on their years together and realize what they've learned."

"Maybe nothing is wrong with that approach," responded Tony, "as long as it goes beyond information to formation."

Tim inquired, "Did you just come up with that, or did you read it somewhere?"

Tony shrugged.

"Either way, I think you are onto something."

For the next hour the three mulled over the question, discovering a labyrinth of new questions they needed to consider. The following comments are designed to help these youth ministers frame some answers for the long-term game plan for their churches and develop a curriculum strategy. Then we will return to Cheryl, Tony, and Tim's journey into creating a youth ministry curriculum.

What Is a Curriculum?

The word "curriculum" is used in many ways. A few definitions might help our youth minister friends get a hold on how they might formulate a curriculum for their ministries. Robert Pazmiño suggests it is "the content that is made available to students or participants and their actual learning experiences guided by a teacher." The strength of the definition is the extensionality of the process. Wrapped into the learning process are the content, activities, and guidance.[1] Gary Parrett and Steve Kang remind us that "the English word [for curriculum] is derived from the Latin *currere*, which means 'to run.' Many have thus understood curriculum as a 'course to be run.' For educators, this would embrace all the elements of the design for teaching, learning, and formation."[2] I think of the cross-country coach who runs with her team in training in order to help the team members to be ready for the meet. Albert I. Oliver helps focus a youth minister's process of curriculum development by suggesting that we use "curriculum" as synonymous with "the educational program" which "consists of three basic elements: (1) the program of studies, (2) the program of activities, and (3) the program of guidance."[3] I have modified Oliver's curriculum framework to help youth ministers handle their educational task in the church (see fig. 13.1 on p. 256).

The program of studies for Christian discipleship is grounded in an understanding of the Bible, explanations of how God and people relate to each other (sometimes called the gospel), and how people have responded to God's involvement in human experience. The curricular assumption is that God has revealed himself in Scripture, in Jesus Christ, in nature, and in the church. All components are essential for people, in this case, adolescents, to encounter and know God.

The program of activities for Christian discipleship of youth is an intentional process that enables adolescents to make sense out of God's activity in their lives. The program is not just about keeping kids busy. A good curriculum is going somewhere. The activities are chosen to enable spiritual change to happen.

The program guidance includes peers and adults, including parents in roles that assist young people to grow in their faith. Some provide content, others help these students think about the implications of what

---

[1] Robert W. Pazmiño, "A Transformative Curriculum for Christian Education in the City," *Christian Education Journal* 6, no.1 (Spring 2002): 78.

[2] Gary A. Parrett and S. Steve Kang, *Teaching the Faith, Forming the Faithful* (Downers Grove: IVP, 2009), 127.

[3] Albert I. Oliver, "What Is the Meaning of Curriculum?" in *Curriculum: An Introduction to the Field*, 2nd ed., ed. James R. Gress (Berkeley, CA: McCutchan Publishing, 1988), 24.

Element	Characteristic	Time Emphasis	Question
Program of studies	Human experience with God	Past	What was God doing?
Program of activities	Pupil experience engaging God	Present	How is God changing me?
Program of guidance	Coaching and counseling services	Past, present, future	Who is helping me make sense of my journey with God?

Figure 13.1: Oliver Program Chart

they are learning; all model how life can or should be lived in the light of the discoveries being made.

What Makes a Curriculum Christian for High School Students?

When the recent research by Christian Smith and Melinda Lundquist Denton identified "Moral Therapeutic Deism" as the religious creed of teenagers in America, expressions of concern multiplied in religious circles. The researchers concluded that there was really no religious curriculum for adolescents in America, except in isolated pockets of the American religious experience.[4]

Mark DeVries places his finger on the curricular problem for youth ministry in his book, *Sustainable Youth Ministry*, when he calls for a six or seven year curriculum template that is not dependent on either a youth minister or commercial curriculum resources.[5] He calls on churches to determine the scope and sequence of that template and

---

[4] Melinda Lundquist Denton and Christian Smith, *Soul Searching: The Religious and Spiritual Lives of American Teenagers* (New York: Oxford University Press, 2009), 118–71.

[5] Mark DeVries, *Sustainable Youth Ministry* (Downers Grove: IVP, 2008), 62–63.

then select and use the specific materials that will help churches have an impact on their young people year after year.

To many people, DeVries' suggestion sounds like a step in the direction of a professionalized youth ministry, but he argues just the opposite. Instead of trying to hire their way out of a theological vacuum (like Moral Therapeutic Deism) by employing the perfect youth minister for the church, DeVries calls on a taskforce that may include a professional youth minister to determine what should be included in the middle school-high school curriculum and then work together to sustain the teaching ministry of the church to students. This is where the hard work begins.

Since church youth ministry attendance is voluntary and homework is, to say the least, uncommon, serious study of the Christian faith by middle school and high school students has become even rarer than it was in years past. There are exceptions, however.

In Smith and Denton's study of the spiritual lives of American teenagers, the religious group that bucks the trend toward laissez-faire religion is the Mormons. When questioned about what they believe, the answers of Mormon youth were far more clear and accurate to the teachings of the Latter-Day Saints than were the answers given by any other religious grouping in America to the teachings of their different faiths. A number of reasons may be suggested for why Mormon youth learn the beliefs of their church so much better than other young people, but the point that should be made is that the teaching of faith can be accomplished in the lives of young people in America.[6]

A Divinity School student who was completing his Master of Divinity program at the school at which I teach, came into my office seeking advice about the youth pastorate he would be assuming in a few weeks. He told me of his plan to raise the bar for his students and treat them like members of a Christian National Honor Society. My experience with idealistic youth pastors suggested he would have minimal success, but I wished him well. Four years later I met him on campus, and he humbly told me of the amazing results he had seen with a curriculum that was highly theological in nature. I would love to have

---

[6] Kenda Creasy Dean, *Almost Christian* (New York: Oxford, 2010), 47–50.

Christian Smith's team study his youth ministry, for it sounded as if the success was similar to that of Mormon youth.

There may have been a time when youth workers had to disguise the Christian faith in a cluster of entertaining activities in order to attract and hold middle school and high school students. While there has always been room for fun in the teaching ministry of the church, the advent of postmodern thinking has lessened the need for hiding the coin in the cupcake. As David Rahn and Terry Linhart say, meetings need to be "appropriately Christian in nature."[7] As the second decade of the twenty-first century has developed, *God* and more specifically *Jesus* has become the reason why young people are attracted to church. Scott McKnight describes the new curricular climate in *One.Life: Jesus Calls, We Follow.*[8]

J. I. Packer and Gary A. Parrett call for church leaders to build up believers the old-fashioned way, by returning to the Gospel as expressed in catechesis.[9] Parrett and Kang trace the Gospel through the entire Bible and explore the implications for thought and life as "Truth, Way, and Life": Truth—hearing and believing the gospel (creeds); Way—receiving the gospel and the Holy Spirit (Lord's Prayer); and Life—being reconciled to God and neighbor (Decalogue).[10] Their book provides a marvelous framework for developing a curriculum for middle school and high school students.

On the night of our Lord's resurrection, two disciples walked toward Emmaus trying to sort out the events of the day and the reports of his resurrection. When Jesus fell in stride with them, his identity somehow escaped them. Responding to their confusion, Jesus took them back to the Old Testament and explained how the events of this day were found as a golden cord throughout the Scriptures. Even then the two disciples did not get it. Only when Jesus sat down for dinner with them did they realize the Truth they were experiencing. To

---

[7] David Rahn and Terry Linhart, *Contagious Faith* (Loveland: Group, 2000), 75.

[8] Scott McKnight, *One.Life: Jesus Calls, We Follow* (Grand Rapids: Zondervan, 2010).

[9] J. I. Packer and Gary A. Parrett, *Grounded in the Gospel: Building Believers the Old Fashioned Way* (Grand Rapids: Baker, 2010), 21–32.

[10] Parrett and Kang, *Teaching the Faith*, 132.

develop a Christian curriculum for students, start with Jesus. Then help them discover him in every part of the Bible, but do so while on their journey and around their table.

Sustainability, Relevance, And Reliability

The curriculum must talk about Jesus, not just in a survey of the Gospels, but also in the story of Jesus from creation of the world to the end of time. For Cheryl, Tim, and Tony to be intentional about the Christian teaching ministries for adolescents in their churches, three components are essential: sustainability, relevance, and reliability.

Cheryl, Tim, and Tony already know they have a problem. There was a time when churches could rely on published curriculum to guide the church's teaching ministry but at its best, publishing houses needed economies of scale to turn a profit. The broader they cast their nets in order to attract customers, the less specific their teaching outcomes became. Methods became the selling point. The result was a Bible-lite curriculum with virtually none of the Christology that drives the gospel. These curricular pieces were interesting and to a degree relevant but not especially reliable or sustainable.

In reaction to this theological imprecision, certain smaller denominational publishing houses became highly doctrinal in their approach to curriculum publishing. Reverting to more catechism-like approaches that required memorization without much application or higher level thinking skills, with a result that these kids could not really figure out why they were learning what they were studying. These curricular pieces were to a certain degree reliable but were not relevant or sustainable.

With the coming of the youth minister in the last third of the twentieth century, the youth pastor, with the help of the Internet at the beginning of the twenty-first century, *became* the curriculum. He or she taught whatever they thought would touch the lives of the kids in their church. Themes went from month to month and sometimes from week to week. Seldom was there a larger biblical framework that directed their curriculum development. Teaching became as sustainable as the longevity of the youth minister. Often the content was highly relevant, but less often was it biblically reliable.

Unfortunately with youth ministers called on to do so many different ministry tasks, these noble people seldom had enough time to build curriculum teams who were willing to do the hard work of determining the scope and sequence for biblical teaching in youth ministry. Understanding the challenge, Cheryl, Tim, and Tony thought they would combine forces and hold each other accountable to curriculum building for Christian discipleship. Their breakthrough came nearly by accident.

Now back to our story. One morning in January, Tim exploded into their Newport Coffee House gathering with a wild idea. He seemed to be the most "week to week" person in the group, but he was also willing to look at things from a different perspective. The previous Sunday that different perspective had led him to the church boiler room. Unannounced (and without permission from the deacons), Tim took the high school group down to the church boiler room, used only a utility light, and told the students they were in Afghanistan. Tim then led the group in discussing how they would be the church in this Muslim dominated country.

To hear Tim tell it, it was the best youth ministry experience the group had ever had. What amazed him the most was how much theology the kids offered amid the clanging of steam pipes. It was as if the group had become something different merely because of where they were.

"You may be on to something," responded Cheryl.

"Boiler room?" countered Tony, "You've got to be kidding!"

"No, not the boiler room itself," opined Cheryl. "The fresh idea is asking the students to become a church. The boiler room helped to get the ball rolling, but there are a lot of other ways we might do it as well. I would never have thought of it, but the way Tim framed the boiler room experience is really an example of what some educators call problem solving. After all, why are we doing youth ministry? Isn't it to pass the faith from generation to generation? When our ministries come down to the most basic objectives, we are building the next generation church."

Energy built around the table. A second round of lattés did not hurt either. For the next two hours, the trio brainstormed how the boiler room experiment could be turned into a curriculum for middle school and high school students. Still a bit skeptical about what this problem solving thing was all about, Tony agreed to google the idea. Since Tim's young theologians had raised so many questions the previous week, he would have his hands full preparing for the next meeting of the Afghan church. This left Cheryl to explore the possibility that the idea was sustainable, relevant, and reliable.

Conditions for Learning

The Afghan church got kicked out of the boiler room by the deacons the following week. Not to be deterred, Tim moved the church to a garage behind the parish house. It was cold! The little space heater did very little to cut the chill; but with layers of clothes on, the group imagined themselves (perhaps exaggeratedly so) as suffering for Christ on the outskirts of Kandahar. The discussion centered on the sufferings of Christ and how this little church was privileged to suffer for their Lord.

When Cheryl, Tim, and Tony reconvened at the Newport Coffee House the following Tuesday, Tony had several articles from the Internet but was especially excited about a summary of Robert N. Gagné's idea of conditions for learning. Gagné identified six varieties of learning, built from simple to complex. The first was specific responding (recall type stuff), followed by chaining (linking several actions together to accomplish something more complex), then multiple discrimination (linking learning chains and sorting them out appropriately), followed by classifying (assigning functions), next rule using (like it sounds, using rules or principles to provide structure), and finally problem solving (applying rules or principles to a problem that has been identified).[11] I know it does not sound exciting now, but Tony was pumped. He had envisioned how Tim's Afghan church (or something like it) could be wed to the curricular ideas of Gagné to make learning biblical content sustainable, relevant, and reliable.

The problem, as Tony envisioned it, was how the kids in his ministry could create a church in harmony with Scripture that would be relevant to the world in which they live. Initially, it could be in Kandahar; over time they would have to bring it home.

---

[11] Robert N. Gagné, *The Conditions of Learning* (New York: Holt, Rinehart, and Wilson, 1977), 155–79.

Tony had not stolen Cheryl's assignment, just set her up for what she wanted to report. What Cheryl was most concerned about was the question of the reliability of Tim's Afghan church. It would be fairly easy for the imaginations of a bunch of high school students to soar on wings of creativity to fantasize a church half a world away but not ground it in Scripture, the historical traditions of the church, or the realities of the current challenges in a world influenced by postmodern thought.

Cheryl's research took her to the writings of Steve Kang and Gary Parrett who urged churches to return to catechesis and provided a wealth of ways to go about it. Catechesis, concluded Cheryl, was the way in which the church prepared people for Christian baptism in the pre-Christendom era. The ethos of that time, during the first three centuries of the church, was very much like the world the church faces in the twenty-first century. So she began thinking through what people in Tim's Afghan church would need to know in order to be the church.

In order to live as Christians in a non-Christian world, the people of God need to pay attention to Christian beliefs, personal Christian behavior, and vital relationships with both Christians and the rest of their neighbors. As Kang and Parrett suggest, these areas of concern can be addressed by getting inside the creeds of the church (Cheryl knew the Apostle's Creed best), the Ten Commandments (including the New Testament clarifications in the Sermon on the Mount), and the Lord's Prayer (which includes the core relational ideas of forgiveness and reconciliation). This, if properly developed, could constitute the scope of the youth ministry curriculum.

So what would be the sequence? Where would the three church youth ministers begin their discovery of the church in action and what would follow? Cheryl had outlined some thoughts for the three of them to discuss (see fig. 13.2).

By the time they finished their conversation that morning, it was nearly time for lunch. To say the least, they liked what they were stitching together, but all three sensed they needed more help.

Each youth minister knew of students, educators, and parents as well as some elders in their churches who were well-grounded in educational theory and Christian teachings. So they agreed to take a risk and see if their ideas would get shot down. In the next couple of weeks each

Seventh grade	Living freely (ten commandments and Sermon on the Mount)
Eighth grade	Thinking truly (Apostles' Creed and the gospel)
Ninth grade	Building Christian community (The Lord's Prayer)
Tenth grade	Becoming the body of Christ (Acts and Spiritual Gifts)
Eleventh grade	Engaging our neighbors (How can the world be blessed through the church?)
Twelfth grade	Implementation (Start a church somewhere)

Figure 13.2: Sample Curriculum Sequence for Youth Ministry

of the youth ministers got together with three to five people in order to see if these brainstorming sessions had any merit.

As might have been expected, Tim had the most difficulty with the process and came away feeling the discussions were a waste of time. It took Tim more time to either see the larger picture and to allow others in his church to think through what should happen in the months and years ahead. For the others, the initial conversations led to the creation of advisory groups to help guide the curriculum development process.

Making Sense of Gagné

Gagné's problem solving idea was not hard for the three to get their hands around. Tim was especially good at identifying problem situations related to the church and turning them into learning opportunities leading to a more vivid reality in church life. He was determined not to allow the church they were envisioning be similar to the boring church in which he had been raised. He was determined to make this experiment both contemporary (engaging the current middle and high school culture) and as innovative as the church in the book of Acts. He seemed to come up with ideas more instinctively than did Cheryl and Tony. Yet together, the three were amazingly balanced and holistic.

Tim's instinctive creativity often led to impatience. This came out again when Tony kept pushing Gagné's curriculum theory as a way to prepare kids to solve the problems related to planting a church, whether in Afghanistan or in the local community.

"In just about every issue related to the theology and the biblical insights necessary to understand, live, or make decisions about the church living as a Christian community, I am confident I could find a video clip on YouTube or from a movie that would frame the discussion," asserted Tim. "Throw in lyrics from contemporary music, commercials, situations from novels or even *The Simpsons*, and we have enough material to help us discuss virtually every theological issue in the Bible. After all, it seems like every book in the Bible was written to address some type of problem people of faith were facing."

"There is no doubt in my mind," responded Tony, "we could find enough problem situations in contemporary culture to fuel our discussions of what it means to be the church for the next ten years."

"So why get bogged down in Gagné?" Tim retorted.

"Because most of my kids (I don't know about yours), do not know enough about the gospel, the Bible, or theology, to plant a church based on anything better than Christian Smith's Moral Therapeutic Deism. Somehow, we and our kids' parents need to help them think Christianly."

There was a long silence at the usual Newport Coffee House table.

"Good point," Tim finally confessed.

Tony affirmed, "This is where the rest of Gagné comes in."

For the rest of their time that Tuesday morning the three youth ministers batted around what types of information from the Bible, their church's rich history, and theology, needed to be learned and recalled, connected, distinguished, and classified in order to think theologically about the problems related to being the body of Christ in a local church in the twenty-first century. Cheryl kept bringing the Ten Commandments/Sermon on the Mount, the creeds of the church (especially the Apostle's Creed) and the Lord's Prayer into the discussion. She insisted that for Christians to survive as a healthy church either in Afghanistan or down the street, they needed to know both the "what" of these theological building blocks and "why" it was important to think Christianly. The more they talked, the more all three could see a six-year curriculum emerging.

Tim and Tony began buying into Cheryl's six-year sequence. As each youth minister discussed the budding curriculum plan with their perspective advisory groups, a more holistic plan developed. Retreats, a variety of service opportunities, and mission trips came to be shaped by the question, "How will this help us be and establish a new church?" Some saw the questions as academic exercises, while others insisted that the essential function of any church should be to reproduce themselves, and who could better do it than the rising generation of believers and those they reached with the Gospel of Jesus Christ.

Initiating the Youth Ministry Curriculum

The Afghan curriculum, as it had come to be known, was too big to be pulled off by youth ministers with a couple of volunteers. Student leaders needed to buy into the idea. Advisory groups needed to become advocates among parents and church leaders. The pastor and church board needed to be fully behind the curriculum, realizing that successful implementation might mean losing parishioners to churches that were being formed.

In addition, it would be important that Cheryl, Tony, and Tim remain in their respective churches for a minimum of six more years. In order to make the three youth ministers ever more effective in implementing the curricula, the church would need to make a long term commitment to the professional and theological development of each.

To insure that students, parents, youth ministry team, church leaders, and pastoral staff were on the same page, a series of questions would need to be asked and answered on a regular basis:

1. What should a graduating Christian high school senior be capable of doing for the kingdom of God?
2. Who are the best persons/groups to influence and coach young people in their Christian development, especially in becoming a new faith community?

3. What are the books a well-developed Christian student should have read before leaving home, especially if planting a church?
4. What are the experiences a Christian student should engage in and reflect on before leaving home?
5. What should Christian students be able to explain about their Christian faith before leaving home?
6. What method should Christian students use to respond to a question they have not faced before?

These questions, when asked in the process of developing and continually revising the youth ministry curriculum, should keep the learning process focused and intentional. A youth ministry curriculum must never become static. Just as a church to remain vibrant and effective in its mission must continually engage culture, so a youth ministry needs to balance on the bleeding edge between conviction and culture. The framework proposed must be missional in nature. If taken seriously, a youth ministry curriculum such as this has the potential of sustaining the youth of the church into the next generation, when the process will start all over again.

CHAPTER 14

ALL GROWN UP
OR NOT

SHAPING ADULT EDUCATION
CURRICULUM IN THE CHURCH

Michael S. Wilder

Several years ago I had the privilege of being a part of a team that was tasked to help plant a new campus of a multi-site church. The new work was planned for an area twenty miles north in a bordering state. It seemed readily apparent there would be not only a difference in address but also a difference in the way of doing ministry. Our team was given significant freedom to make these adjustments while remaining committed to the core values of the church. Over extended meals and many cups of coffee, questions were raised related to how we would best go about discipling the people who would be reached with the gospel. These questions provoked a great deal of thought regarding effective teaching and learning, maturation of believers, and gospel living. Emerging from these conversations were three foundational assumptions:

1. The truth of the gospel transforms.
2. Communicated truth cannot be separated from lived truth.
3. Transformative learning environments reinforce gospel living.

Since that time, I have had the opportunity to express these thoughts with pastors and other church leaders who are laboring to build healthy churches. In the following pages, I would invite you into such a discussion. For the purpose of this chapter, the discussion will be limited to the curricular aspect of teaching adults. Let us begin by asking a question.

What Is Curriculum?

Though this question has been answered in previous chapters, it is helpful to address it again from a slightly different perspective. Most authors limit the definition of curriculum to the material to be taught and the methods utilized in the teaching-learning process; however, I prefer to understand curriculum in a more inclusive fashion. Curriculum is comprised of five primary components: materials selected, methods chosen, teacher involvement, learner development, and a contextualized ministry setting.

These five elements of curriculum fit nicely into the curriculum triad (see fig. 14.1).[1] This triad is composed of the *content*, the *coach*, and the *context*. If we apply the curriculum triad to adult discipleship, the content is the Christian Scriptures; the coach is the one engaged in the lives of the learners with the expressed intention of spurring them on toward conformity to the image of Christ; and the context is the learning environment intentionally developed by the coach with specific goals and methodology in mind.

Utilizing the triad, I suggest that curriculum should be thought of as the dynamic interaction of the coach and the learners moving toward maturity in Christ as they live out gospel community. This approach to curriculum is inseparable from my concept of discipleship and is driven by it. I cannot view curriculum as just the material and methods, for it includes both the people involved in the learning process and the lives

---

[1] Robert Pazmiño, *God Our Teacher: Theological Basics in Christian Education* (Grand Rapids: Baker, 2001), 141–45. I have been greatly influenced by Pazmiño regarding the teaching-learning process, and the curriculum triad in this chapter clearly finds its roots in his writings. However, here I have made a modification by discussing "coaches" as opposed to "persons" in his content-persons-context triad.

Curriculum Triad		
Content	**Coach**	**Context**
Christian Scriptures	Engaging in the lives of the learners with the expressed intention of spurring them on toward conformity to the image of Christ	Learning environment which is intentionally developed by the coach with specific goals and methodology in mind
Curriculum is the dynamic interaction of the coach and the learners moving toward maturity in Christ as they live out gospel community.		

Figure 14.1: Curriculum Triad

they are living. With the boundaries of curriculum expanded to include the dynamic interaction between content, coach, and context, I would like to probe each of these components of the curriculum triad a bit further by asking some additional questions.

Why Must Christ's Story Be the Focal Point of the Content?

I trust this question is not premature. Inherent in the question is the assumption that we agree that the Scriptures must be what our learners immerse themselves in as they pursue godliness. The second assumption is that the Scriptures have as their focal point the story of redemption through Christ Jesus. Assuming agreement, we turn our attention toward content that is characterized by five distinct markers.

The first mark of great content is that it is *narrative in nature*. This means that the scope and sequence of the curricular content is driven by the grand narrative of Scripture. The storyline of the Bible begins with God creating the world out of nothing and graciously placing our parents, Adam and Eve, in a beautiful haven amid lush provisions, giving them the responsibility to serve as his vice-regents by expanding the boundaries of Eden to the ends of the earth with their offspring. All of this is done in order to make God's glory known among the eventual nations. The story continues with man usurping his God-given boundaries and erupting into rebellion against a holy and generous God. The rebellion leads to the fall of man and the resulting curse, leaving man and creation both groaning and longing for restoration. If the story ended there we would be more than dismayed—we would be destroyed! But God promises a seed that will overcome the sting of sin and death. Generation after generation, the prophets proclaim that this seed is none other than the Son of God—Jesus, the Christ. The Gospels recount the incarnation, life, death, and resurrection of the promised seed. The good news of redemption is made clear to both Israel and the nations and is made available to our learners today as we retell the glorious story. The New Testament draws to a close in a manner similar to that of the Old Testament—the looking forward to the coming of the Messiah, but this time with the hope of consummation and complete restoration. The story—creation, fall, redemption, and consummation—is to be told and retold. It is the content we must teach. There are many reasons why it is imperative to utilize a meta-narrative approach, but most pertinent for our discussion is the fact that the majority of churched adults have never been given these simple hooks upon which salvation history is hung. This approach allows for the learner to understand where particular texts and the individual stories of the Bible fit. Ultimately, it permits the learner to develop a better understanding of specific passages they are studying.

The second mark relates to the *Christ-centered hermeneutic* that is to be utilized in examining the grand narrative.[2] I cannot tell you the number of adults who are amazed when a teacher connects the Old Testament with a gospel account. It is as if the general perception reigns true that the Old Testament is somehow not helpful for modern day believers. But we know this to be far from accurate. The issue is not irrelevance; it is the lack of seeing the Hebrew Scriptures from a Christ-centered perspective. We have the benefit of reading biblical texts on this side of the cross—which changes everything. So as teachers, we

---

[2] See Graeme Goldsworthy, *According to Plan* (Downers Grove: InterVarsity, 2001); idem, *Gospel-Centered Hermeneutics: Foundations and Principles of Evangelical Biblical Interpretation* (Downers Grove: InterVarsity, 2006), 58–66.

must help our people see the gospel from Gen 1:1 to Rev 22:21 which will aid in more faithful interpretation.

Closely related to a Christ-centered hermeneutic is the need for a strong *redemptive focus* in our teaching. The gospel must drive us as we take our learners on their redemptive journey. What this means is that our teaching must have as its primary goal to bring learners into deep relationship with and knowledge of their Creator and Savior. This is messy when put into practice because it goes way beyond behavioral applications and moves into the realm of confession and repentance— repentance and faith become our life cycle as we seek to be faithful to the full story of the gospel.

The content of adult curriculum must be *doctrinally clear,* so do not mistake the language of the content being narrative in nature to mean that doctrine is somehow relegated to the learning of the elite few. In the midst of teaching the whole of salvation history to learners, we also endeavor to dip deeper into discussions about doctrinal beliefs. This is the place where the church has gone awry at different times in her history. When we fail to teach the great doctrines of the faith proactively, we invite shallowness at best and heresy at worst.

Finally, the content needs to be *life-integrated.* This distinct marker summarizes well the previous characteristics. When content is intentionally taught in such a way that it encapsulates the whole gospel story and has a declaratively redemptive tone, then it will inevitably result in teaching which is useful for the learner in the immediate situations of life. When material is taught in the abstract, it falls short and produces knowledge but not transformation. I would say to those of you who are responsible for shaping adult curricular content in your churches, be convinced that the truth of the gospel transforms. Ensure that the content piece of the triad is firmly rooted in the whole gospel message, for indeed the gospel has the power unto salvation (Rom 1:16).

What Does a Coach Do
in the Spiritual Training Process?

Typically when we say the word *coach,* a picture of person with a logo-embroidered shirt and a dangling whistle pops into our minds. This picture often includes the coach pacing up and down the court or running down the sideline calling out instructions to various team members. So you ask, why choose the image of a coach instead of a teacher when discussing the curriculum triad? For me the answer is quite simple—teaching is only one facet of what is required for true transformation. Transformation of the learner begins and ends, of course, with the work of the Holy Spirit, but in his infinite wisdom God has called his children to live in gospel community with men and women who are wiser and more mature in their faith. These wiser and more mature not only teach the Word, but also intertwine their lives in a redemptive manner with fellow believers and God-seeking unbelievers (1 Thess 2:8). Teaching is foundational but coaches go beyond this by engaging in daily life with the learner in order to observe, instruct, and inspire on a personal level.[3] Coaches challenge learners to reach their full potential in Christ. When we talk about Christian coaching,[4] we are talking about a focused Christ-centered relationship that cultivates a person's sustained growth and action.[5] It is an incarnational relationship that intends to empower learners in their life and ministry.[6]

---

[3] Andy Stanley, *The Next Generation Leader* (Sisters, OR: Multnomah, 2003), 119.

[4] For further discussion on mentoring and coaching see Michael S. Wilder and Shane W. Parker, *TransforMission: Making Disciples through Short-term Missions* (Nashville: B&H, 2010), 181–83. Bill Hull writes in *The Complete Book of Discipleship* (Colorado Springs: NavPress, 2006), 214: "At first glance, coaching and mentoring seem to be two words that describe the same process. Yet the difference is meaningful. While coaching focuses on skills and equipping, mentoring helps others make sense of their lives. More specifically, spiritual mentoring helps an individual gain awareness of his personhood as he lives under God. A godly mentor can help us emerge from the limits of self-fulfillment and narcissism to discover the joy of living for others." In this chapter, I understand relational coaching to include the descriptors of teaching, mentoring, and coaching. Coaching goes beyond simply teaching the Word or mentoring the learner. It is more direct and finds the coach often taking strong initiative to challenge and inspire the learner. So, coaching is not less than teaching and mentoring, but is more and intends to drive the learner to a greater level of spiritual maturation and ministry involvement.

[5] Linda J. Miller and Chad W. Hall, *Coaching for Christian Leaders* (St. Louis: Chalice, 2007), 10.

[6] Steve Ogne and Tim Roehl, *TransforMissional Coaching: Empowering Leaders in a Changing Ministry World* (Nashville: B&H, 2008), 26.

So, subsumed in the term *coach* is the role of teacher, mentor, encourager, counselor, and challenger.

When I think of the committed coach, I envision one who proclaims the gospel story in such a way that the unregenerate are faced with their need for Christ's righteousness and the regenerate are challenged to daily obedience. I see a person who fosters relationships among the faith community, which reflect deep commitments toward love, discipline, and spiritual maturation. The coach models a life of service that is driven both by gratitude and obedience and results in learners' increased desire for gospel engagement in the church and society.[7] The coach is the type of person that pushes his disciples into action; provoking awareness of the overwhelming presence of societal injustice, oppression, and poverty with the intent of gospel advancement among peoples in need.[8]

The coach must also be reflective about his own life and sojourn as he leads others on their redemptive journey. May we never have someone leading and teaching who fails to recall his own sinfulness and God's gracious salvation. It is out of his redemption that the coach is able to be patient, to love, to teach, to share, to testify to the less mature believer or to the seeker. I am reminded of a fellow professor and local worship pastor who has gone to be with the Lord recently. He was a man who would often recount the parable of the Pharisee and the tax collector (Luke 18:9–14) and in the midst of it would begin to tear up because of his own sinfulness and God's redeeming work. This is the kind of person who becomes transparent and honest with his learners about his life struggles, hurts, and hopes, and then seeks to live out the truth of the gospel in everyday life. This is a coach who clearly understands that communicated truth cannot be separated from lived truth. This is a spiritual coach who will see transformation in the life of his disciples.

The committed coach knows his learners well. He knows their strengths and their struggles because he is spending time with them and is simultaneously studying them. He has a heart to know all that he can about them in order to be more effective at teaching, mentoring, and

---

[7] Pazmiño, *God Our Teacher*, 114–15.
[8] Ibid., 146–48.

challenging. I remember my first introduction to this concept of knowing the needs of the learner and employing that knowledge in the way that I teach—this is a concept that will radically change the way that you disciple.[9] As you seek to know your learners well, let me highlight two foundational facts about them.

Your Learner's Life Stage Matters[10]

When we talk about adult learners do we mean emerging adults, young adults, middle adults, or older adults? Learners in each of these age groups face different life realities. For example, emerging adults are wrestling with identity issues related to vocation and ideological commitments. The young adult is seeking out relationships that are deep and intimate. Those who are believers are trying to determine the focal point of their life—kingdom of God or kingdom of the world.[11] This is a real battle that rages among this cohort, and the Christian coach has a great opportunity to help anchor these persons in their Christian commitments. Middle adults are often reappraising their faith because they have found their beliefs and knowledge are too limited to sustain through the difficult trials. Middle adults are also considering how to invest their prime years and asking questions related to how they can have the greatest amount of positive influence on the next generation. The golden years[12] usher in a time of deep philosophical reflection and the stakes are over confidence about how life has been spent and what

---

[9] William R. Yount, *Created to Learn: A Christian Teacher's Introduction to Educational Psychology* (Nashville: B&H, 2010), 6–26.

[10] See Jeffrey Jensen Arnett, *Emerging Adulthood: The Winding Road from the Late Teens through the Twenties* (New York: Oxford University Press, 2004); Eric H. Erikson, *Identity and the Life Cycle* (Madison, CT: International Universities Press, 1959); Jean Piaget, *The Psychology of Intelligence* (New York: Routledge and Paul, 1950); Lev Vygotsky, *Educational Psychology,* trans. Robert Silverman (Boca Raton, FL: CRC Press, 1997); James Fowler, *Stages of Faith: The Psychology of Human Development and the Quest for Meaning* (New York: HarperCollins, 1981); and more recently James R. Estep and Jonathan H. Kim, *Christian Formation: Integrating Theology and Human Development* (Nashville: B&H, 2010).

[11] See Les L. Steele, *On the Way: A Practical Theology of Christian Formation* (Eugene, OR: Wipf and Stock, 1998), 155–74.

[12] See Hal Pettegrew, "Perspectives on the Spiritual Development of the 'Aging' Boomers," *Christian Education Journal* 5, no. 2 (Fall 2008): 305–20.

the future may hold. A coach can speak into these older adults' lives in such a way that they are challenged to finish well with a sense of adventure and mission.

Your Learner's Level of Spiritual Maturity Matters

Often, teachers are guilty of not discerning the spiritual maturity of their learners. They think chronological age is equivalent to spiritual maturation, but not all adults are spiritually mature. When this mistake is made, teachers employ a homogeneous approach, and learners are often stunted in their growth. This is one of those areas where the coach must accurately assess the learner and shape the content to the needs of the individual. What we are *not* doing in our small group ministry is running a factory assembly line—coaching requires a handcrafting approach. Remember that it is likely you will have a small group that includes a seeking unbeliever and a faithfully mature saint. What are you to do? You are to teach in such a way that the gospel story is simple yet deep, conflicting yet reassuring, confronting yet loving. And you are to spend face time with each participant in order to press into their lives with pinpoint accuracy as you challenge each toward conformity to Christ's perfect image.

The coaching leg of the curriculum triad is the pivotal piece. It is the component focused on deeply understanding the learner and communicating the selected content by word and deed in a way that is most effective. It is also the piece concerned with creating the right context so that spiritual transformation occurs among adults. This brings us to our last question related to the curriculum triad.

What Kind of Context Is Most Helpful for Spiritual Transformation?

The third leg of the triad is the context. Much has been written about the idea of creating the right learning context. Often these ideas revolve around the notions of having a room that "teaches" or an "attention-getting" backdrop that creates learner curiosity or making a "safe space" for sharing one's feelings. I would say that these have been helpful and have pushed us to think about more than just the preparation of the Bible study, yet they are shallow in some ways. When we consider context in relation to the curriculum triad we want to ask ourselves, what environment needs to be created in order to maximize spiritual transformation? This is a catalytic question that can spawn great conversation among small group leaders. I would suggest that the answer in part is that the coach must help create a relationally-driven, thought-provoking, life-activating, mission-oriented, and family-equipping context. Feel overwhelmed? Let us take a moment and briefly touch on these five descriptors.

Relationship-Driven

I am convinced the best teaching and learning occurs in the context of relationships. Without deep running relationships, intimacy and transparency fail to occur and gospel community proves aloof. Yount rightly includes "relating" in his discipler's model and states that when the "environment promotes freedom and openness, willingness to share with others, personal safety, and time for interactive experiences, learners have many more opportunities to connect with [other learners]."[13]

Thought-Provoking

I have sat in too many Bible studies that caused my mind to wander rather than provoking me to explore the connections of the focal text with the whole of the Scripture or to consider the personal implications for community life or gospel-living. Good teaching provokes critical reflection, so never let your teaching become mindless.

Life-Activating

The right context will act as a catalyst for the disciple, moving him toward action rather than apathy and passivity. The coach is the type of person who creates awareness of societal injustice, oppression, and poverty, and prompts redeeming action in one's own city and beyond. But life-activation is not limited to battling the woes of a fallen world; it is also sharply focused upon enacting gospel truth in one's own life. In a real sense, this is the behavioral aim that we bring to any biblical study.

---

[13] Yount, *Created to Learn*, 6–26.

Mission-Oriented

A major part of the discipleship context is the taking of the gospel to both neighbors and the nations. Coaches have a responsibility to press the concept of missional living into their disciples' way of thinking. Our learners are inundated with opportunities to make Christ known, yet they fail to see because all too often our disciples are self-consumed. Now before you agree, did you note "our disciples"? Remember that the students God has given us to disciple learn as much or more by our lifestyle as they do our teaching. So the coach must seize opportunities to develop redemptive connections in his sphere of influence as a means of obedience and as a way of modeling. We know that engagement in fulfilling the Great Commission has a transformative effect; therefore, we must engage our learners missionally.[14]

Family-Equipping[15]

This last descriptor is vital for generational discipleship. Believers are clearly instructed to pass on scriptural truth to the next generation (Deuteronomy 6; Psalm 78; Eph 6:4). Unfortunately, many have assumed that the pastors of the church are the spiritual professionals and that simply ensuring participation in church ministry is sufficient for spiritually shaping the next generation. It is not enough. Christian parents must fulfill God's expectation that they be the primary disciplers. The struggle comes when our churches fail to train and develop parents (and other adults) as generational disciplers. As a coach seeking to develop a learning context where spiritual transformation occurs, you cannot overlook this important aspect.

These five descriptors are helpful at a macro-level as they point us to the axiom—transformative learning environments reinforce gospel living—but the elephant in the room is the "how to" component. How does a coach create a context where adult learners are excited about engaging in the learning process and are experiencing radical transformation? The answer lies in understanding some simple facts about

---

[14] See Wilder and Parker, *TransforMission*.

[15] See Timothy Paul Jones, ed., *Perspectives on Family Ministry: Three Views* (Nashville: B&H, 2008).

adult learners and allowing these to shape the context. Let us list just a few:[16]

- Adult learners enter the teaching-learning process with a vast array of personal experiences through which they process the content and engage with the coach and the community of learners.
- Adult learners are life-centered in their learning orientation and therefore have a readiness to learn those things that will aid them in coping effectively with real-life situations.
- Adult learners must be actively engaged in the learning experience in order for maximum learning and growth to occur.
- Adult learners experience transformation in their way of thinking as they are challenged to reflect critically on their current life assumptions (what they believe and how they perceive the world). These challenges often come through exposure to content, conversation with fellow learners, and crisis events in the learner's life.
- Adult learners assume the role of investigator, discoverer, and doer while the coach/teacher assumes the role of stimulator and motivator (the flow of learning is not just teacher to student, but student to teacher and student to student).

There are endless books written on the subject of teaching and you are encouraged to scour them thoroughly as you try to answer this

---

[16] See Malcolm S. Knowles, Elwood F. Holton III, and Richard A. Swanson, *The Adult Learner: The Definitive Classic in Adult Education and Human Resource Development*, 5th ed. (Burlington, MA: Elsevier, 1998), 72. On the topic of critical reflection, see Jack Mezirow, *Learning as Transformation: Critical Perspectives on a Theory in Progress* (San Francisco: CA: Jossey-Bass, 2000); Stephen Brookfield, *Developing Critical Thinkers: Challenging Adults to Explore Alternative Ways of Thinking and Acting* (San Francisco: CA: Jossey-Bass, 1987). On the topic of the teaching-learning process, see David Kolb, *Experiential Learning: Experience as the Source of Learning and Development* (Upper Saddle River, NJ: Prentice-Hall, 1984); Lawrence O. Richards, *Theology of Christian Education* (Grand Rapids: Zondervan, 1979); Howard Hendricks, *Teaching to Change Lives* (Portland, OR: Multnomah, 1987); and Lawrence O. Richards and Gary L. Bredfeldt, *Creative Bible Teaching* (Chicago: Moody Press, 1998).

question of how to maximize spiritual transformation among learners. I would simply remind you that adult learning is about more than intellectual advancement; it is about seeing a radical transformation in the way learners think, perceive, feel, believe, and behave. If you gain nothing else here, be certain of two things: (1) adult learning is holistic in nature—it is not just the spirit or just the mind or just behavior—it is about a whole life change; and (2) life-transformation cannot occur without the powerful work of the Holy Spirit in the learner's life, so be diligent to create an environment where the learner's heart is prepared to respond.

Conclusion

At the beginning of our discussion, I proposed that curriculum should be thought of as the dynamic interaction of the coach and the learners moving toward maturity in Christ as they live out gospel community. This dynamic interaction is a bit hard to nail down, but it is no less than the intentional efforts of both the coach and the learner engaging one another in gospel living with the Scriptures as their guide for faith and practice. This intentional means of interaction has as its goal the displaying of God's glory among a community of believers in such a way that the gospel is accurately proclaimed and is consistently reflecting God's love and holiness and humanity's need for redemption. As you venture into developing or choosing adult curriculum for your own church, be reminded that it involves assessing the content, selecting the right coaches, and establishing a transforming context.

CHAPTER 15

FAMILY LIFE CURRICULUM

Timothy Paul Jones

H ow does family ministry look in the context of the Christian education programs in a local church? How can church leaders develop strong family life curriculum? Well, that depends on the church and on what the church sees as the purpose of family ministry. Some congregations see "family ministry" or "family life education" as a counseling program to heal troubled relationships. Other communities of faith perceive family ministry as a program to provide a roster of intergenerational events. For others, family ministry or family life education refers to how the church equips parents to be involved in their children's spiritual formation.[1]

---

[1] For the purposes of this chapter, I am using the terms "family life education" and "family ministry" interchangeably. The term "family life education" has roots in the late nineteenth and early twentieth centuries, when the informal family improvement societies of the early eighteenth century developed into formal "family life education" programs. By the mid-twentieth century, not only universities but also many states and counties featured family life education departments. See

No wonder, then, that whenever a church leader asks me how to implement family ministry, my first question is, "What do *you* mean by 'family ministry'?" What I find is that, for some ministers, family ministry describes the way that their preschool, children, and youth ministries work together. Others have no clue what they mean by "family ministry," but they have heard the term so often they are quite certain that, whatever it is, their congregation must need one—especially since the church down the street has one.

Why this disparity in definitions? Youth ministry professor Chap Clark is spot-on when he says, "Unlike other areas of ministry focus, family ministry emerged without any sort of across-the-board consensus of just what it is. . . . Because of this lack of a common perception of family ministry, people responsible for family ministry in churches are often confused and frustrated."[2]

This "lack of common perception" can make the development of family life curriculum difficult for many churches—but do not let that fact discourage you! It is possible to diminish some of these difficulties. One pathway for reducing the frustration begins with a simple question, "What do we expect our family ministry to accomplish?" Or, put in curricular terms, "What is the purpose of family ministry in our congregation?"

When I work with churches to develop ministries for families, I frequently find that congregational leaders have never discussed precisely what they expect family ministry to achieve in their church. Even when they have discussed their vision for family ministry, the primary points of consensus may center on the problems that they expect family ministry to solve. For some, the perceived problem may be parental disengagement from the discipleship of children. For others, the dilemma

---

Margaret E. Arcus, et al., "The Nature of Family Life Education," in *Handbook of Family Life Education*, ed. Margaret E. Arcus, Jay D. Schvaneveldt, and J. Joel Moss (Newbury Park, CA: Sage, 1993). Soon, denominations and congregations were establishing family life education departments as well. In the late twentieth and early twenty-first centuries, the older practices of family life education were subsumed within the burgeoning family ministry movement, with the result that the functions of the two terms began to be less distinguishable.

[2] Chap Clark, *The Youth Worker's Handbook to Family Ministry* (Grand Rapids: Zondervan, 1997), 13.

is the separation of generations from one another. Still others see the primary issue as the failure of students' faith to persist past their freshman year of college.

In each instance, what these well-intended leaders lack is a clear positive vision for what their future family ministry should accomplish. They are operating with conflicting goals without even knowing it, and that is a problem, especially when it comes to curriculum development. Curriculum requires clear objectives, and objectives are built on shared goals and purposes. Unless church leaders reach consensus on the purpose of family ministry, confusion and lack of clarity will obscure the church's curriculum for families. That is why, before guiding you through a process to develop family life curriculum, I want to help you clarify your purpose.

Clarifying the Purpose of Your Church's Family Ministry

The precise curriculum for family ministry will vary from one congregation to the next. Although some common threads will characterize different curricula, a resource that works well in one church could result in dismal failure elsewhere. That is simply because families in different contexts can have very different needs. Both the intergenerational congregation of seventy people and the mega-church where every event is generationally-segmented need family ministry—but the curricula and the required changes in these two congregations will be radically different. There is no cookie-cutter curriculum for family ministry that will work perfectly in every congregation.

When it comes to the purpose of family ministry, however, there can be far more common ground. The perceived purposes for family ministry tend to fall into three primary categories. All three categories are thoroughly biblical, and your church will not necessarily need to develop a written curriculum for each of these purposes. In fact, many congregations practice these patterns in their communities of faith without any planned curricula at all! The "family life curriculum" in these churches is a natural rhythm of living life together that has been intertwined over time into the congregational culture.

Regardless of your church's unique needs and culture, here is one foundational observation that is easy to overlook. Some aspects of each purpose will overlap, but a single curriculum is unlikely to fulfill every purpose. That is why, before developing a family life curriculum, it is essential to clarify which purpose you intend your curriculum to accomplish.[3]

Church-as-Guardrail: The Purpose of Rescuing Relationships Through Counseling

When the purpose for family ministry falls into the category of church-as-guardrail, the goal is to strengthen healthy households and to heal strained or shattered family relationships. The church provides a guardrail—often in the form of counseling—to keep families from falling apart. At best, this form of family ministry draws from a range of Scripture-tested resources ("all wisdom," Col 3:16) to apply the gospel in the context of household relationships.

Although this form of family ministry is certainly needed, church-as-guardrail ministry does not typically require the development of a common curriculum for the entire church. The family counselor's "curriculum" tends to be customized and contextualized to fit each family's needs. As a result, while recognizing the value of church-as-guardrail ministry, this chapter will not focus on developing curriculum for family counseling. The intersection of the gospel with people's sins and struggles *is* the curriculum for church-as-guardrail ministry. Although the content of the gospel never changes, the precise implications of this intersection will shift from one counseling session to another. Church-as-guardrail ministry belongs in a distinct category that rarely requires a church-wide curriculum.

Church-as-Family: The Purpose of Making the Church More Like a Family

When a church's purpose for family ministry falls into the category of church-as-family, the goal is to help God's people to relate to one another more like a family. What this means is that the church nurtures members within a rich matrix of multi-generational relationships.

---

[3] Although these categories are my own, my development of them has been influenced by modes that Chap Clark proposes in *The Youth Worker's Handbook to Family Ministry*.

Children and teenagers whose parents are not believers find their lives intertwined with mature men and women who become spiritual parents and grandparents. Married couples mentor singles. New parents learn child-rearing from empty nesters. The entire congregation works together to meet the needs of widows and orphans (Jas 1:27). Church-as-family ministry clearly recognizes that, inasmuch as I am a follower of Jesus, my family includes anyone who does the will of my heavenly Father (Mark 3:35).

In church-as-family ministry, every gathering of the church brings people together in a multi-generational family reunion, except that the purpose of this reunion is far greater than enduring a picnic with people we cannot stand for the sake of pleasing our earthly parents. What church-as-family ministry recognizes is that social or generational similarities are *not* what define Christian fellowship. The people of God are unified and defined by Jesus himself. Jesus has bonded believers together by breaking the barriers between them on the basis of his own blood (Eph 2:14–15). As a result, those who rub shoulders in the shadow of the cross should be precisely the people that the world would never dream of mingling together—brothers, sisters, fathers, and mothers from different nations, social strata, and generations. That is why the Holy Spirit of God, speaking through the words of Scripture, specifically calls for close multi-generational connections among God's people (Titus 2:1–5). These are not issues of preference or convenience. They are issues of faithfulness to God's design for his people, and they are rooted in the gospel itself.

So why might churches need a planned curriculum to bring people together in this way? Many churches have so thoroughly segmented their structures that Christians from different generations rarely interact with one another. Each demographic cluster in the church gathers separately for worship and studies Scripture in age-segmented small groups. Yet, if a church completely segregates the generations, how will youth learn to see older men as their fathers in the faith (1 Tim 5:1)? When will mature women train younger women (Titus 2:3–5)? How can the younger generation learn to glimpse God's glory in the faces of the elderly (Lev 19:32)? Church-as-family ministry reconnects the generations to reflect more faithfully God's multi-generational vision for his church.

Family-as-Church: The Goal of Helping Each Family to Become a Little Church

When the purpose for family ministry falls into the category of family-as-church, the goal is to equip parents to disciple their children in the context of their daily lives together. What this means is that Christian households become living microcosms of the larger community of faith as families learn and live God's Word together. Great Awakening pastor Jonathan Edwards describes the Christian household as "a little church" and declares that "the head of the family has more advantage in his little community to promote religion than ministers have in the congregation."[4] The thought that parents must be primary disciple-makers in their children's lives did not, however, originate in the Great Awakening! This expectation is woven deeply throughout the pages of Scripture.

Paul commands fathers to nurture their offspring in the "discipline and instruction" that comes from the Lord (Eph 6:4 ESV). In other contexts, Paul applies these same terms—"discipline" and "instruction"—to patterns that characterized the development of disciples (see 1 Cor 10:11; 2 Tim 3:16; Titus 3:10). Such texts strongly suggest that Paul expected parents, and particularly fathers, to engage personally in discipling their children. This engagement includes planned instruction in the form of regular teaching of God's Word as well as unplanned elements, where the truths of God are discussed in the context of everyday life together.

When Paul penned these words, he was drawing from a Scripture-saturated legacy that had already shaped the Hebrew people for centuries. This heritage of songs, statutes, and ceremonies foreshadowed the coming of Jesus and explicitly recognized the primacy of parents in the formation of children's faith. When Moses received the law of God, he passed on precise instructions regarding how the people must preserve these precepts: "You shall teach them diligently to your children" (Deut 6:6–7 ESV; cf. Exod 12:25–28; Deut 11:1–12). Even in the songs of Israel, parents were called to impress on their children the

---

[4] Jonathan Edwards, "Living to Christ," in *Sermons and Discourses, 1720–1723, Volume 10: The Works of Jonathan Edwards*, ed. W. H. Kimnach (New Haven: Yale University, 1992), 577.

stories of God's works. A songwriter named Asaph put it this way: "I will utter dark sayings . . . that our fathers have told us. We will not hide them from their children. . . . [They will] arise and tell them to their children, so that they should set their hope in God" (Ps 78:1–7 ESV).

If Scripture so clearly calls parents to train their children in God's ways, why might churches need curriculum to equip parents for such practices? In many churches, church leaders have not equipped or even acknowledged parents as primary disciple-makers in their children's lives.[5] Packed rosters of age-segmented activities (an "implicit curriculum") coupled with silence regarding parents' responsibility to disciple their children ("null curriculum") have contributed to the unspoken assumption that the Christian training of children is best left to professional ministers. As a result, Christian parents need focused guidance ("explicit curriculum") to respond in obedience to God's commands. Family-as-church ministry contributes to this reorientation by calling parents to function as primary disciple-makers in their children's lives.

Focusing Your Family Life Curriculum

Two of the primary purposes for family ministry—church-as-family and family-as-church—frequently require some sort of curriculum. But which of these purposes should your congregation embrace? Church-as-family or family-as-church? The answer, of course, is *both*.

This twofold approach is the foundation for "comprehensive-coordinative family ministry"—ministry that coordinates the God-ordained function of the Christian household with the church's role

---

[5] In recent research, nearly seventy percent of parents in evangelical churches stated that no leader in their church had made any contact with them in the past year regarding how parents might be involved in their children's Christian formation. In another survey, conducted by Barna Research Group, 81 percent of churched parents placed themselves in a similar category. See Timothy Paul Jones, *Family Ministry Field Guide* (Indianapolis, Indiana: WPH, 2011), chap. 8; and "Parents Accept Responsibility for Their Child's Spiritual Development But Struggle With Effectiveness," Barna Research Group, n.p. [cited 13 December, 2010]. Online: http://www.barna.org/barna-update/article/5-barna-update/120-parents-accept-responsibility-for-their-childs-spiritual-development-but-struggle-with-effectiveness.

Church-as-Family Ministry	Comprehensive-Coordinative Family Ministry
Equipping parents to disciple children: No	Equipping parents to disciple children: Yes
Developing family-like relationships in the church: Yes	Developing family-like relationships in the church: Yes
Could include a church-as-guardrail ministry	Could include a church-as-guardrail ministry
Challenge: Without specific and intentional encouragement to become primary disciple-makers in their children's lives, parents may assume that it is the task of the church to disciple their children.	Challenge: After decades of segmented-programmatic ministry, many churches find it difficult to make the transition to a comprehensive-coordinative approach.
	The three primary models of comprehensive-coordinative family ministry are family-equipping, family-integrated, and family-based. For more information on these models, see Timothy Paul Jones, ed., *Perspectives on Family Ministry* (Nashville: B&H Academic, 2009).

Segmented-Programmatic Ministry	Family-as-Church Ministry
Equipping parents to disciple children: No	Equipping parents to disciple children: Yes
Developing family-like relationships in the church: No	Developing family-like relationships in the church: No
Could include a church-as-guardrail ministry	Could include a church-as-guardrail ministry
Challenge: With the church's entire range of programming segregated into age-segmented "silos" with separate ministers, family ministry is, at most, a church-as-guardrail counseling program. Parents tend to relinquish their children's discipleship to paid professionals at church, and spiritual formation occurs almost exclusively in peer groups. Neither of these patterns reflects God's perfect design for his people.	Challenge: Without an emphasis on developing relationships with a multi-generational matrix of persons from different backgrounds, church families may become ingrown, focusing only on discipleship within their own households.

Figure 15.1: Family Ministry Purposes and Practices

as a Christian's first family (see fig. 15.1).[6] Why is all of this so significant for curriculum development? It is because a single curriculum is unlikely to move your congregation toward both goals. The two purposes support and connect with one another. Yet each purpose represents a distinct trajectory and will likely require a distinct curriculum.

So how can congregations develop curricula that will guide church members toward these two purposes? The first step is to recognize that curriculum is *not* the answer. If you have trusted Jesus, God has already equipped you with his Spirit, his Word, and his people (John 16:12–14; Eph 4:11–16; 2 Tim 3:16–17; Heb 13:21)—everything you could ever need to follow Jesus! At the same time, the wisdom of God's people can sometimes be systematized in written resources that remind us how God's truth applies to our daily lives. The goal when creating family life curriculum is not to supplement God's work; the work that God has accomplished through Jesus needs no supplement (Gal 1:6–12). Family life curriculum is a tool to develop habits of life that will help Christians to embrace the sufficiency of Christ's work in their lives at home and in church.

Developing Comprehensive-Coordinative Curricula for Family Life Education

In the 1960s, an educator named William Frankena developed a conceptual model for the purpose of analyzing educational philosophies (see fig. 15.2).

I am fairly certain that Frankena never intended his model to provide a flowchart for creating a family ministry curriculum. Nevertheless, as I have worked with churches, his model has proven to be an effective tool to guide the formation of discipleship strategies. The final pages of this chapter will work through Frankena's model in

---

[6] Bryan Nelson, "The Problem with Family Ministry," in *Trained in the Fear of God*, ed. Randy Stinson (Grand Rapids: Kregel, 2011). For the term "church as first family," see Rodney Clapp, *Families at the Crossroads* (Downers Grove: InterVarsity, 1993), chap. 4. For the idea of church as family in the first century AD, see Joseph Hellerman, *When the Church Was a Family* (Nashville: B&H, 2009).

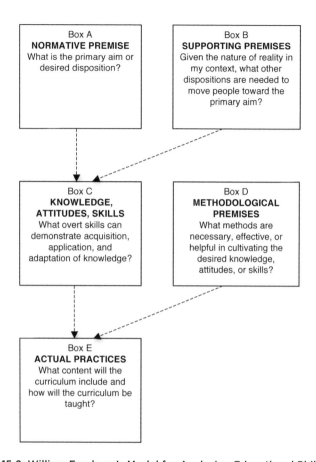

Figure 15.2: William Frankena's Model for Analyzing Educational Philosophy[7]

four steps to equip you with a framework for developing family ministry curricula for your congregation.

Step 1: Begin with Transcendent Principles, Not with Temporary Problems

Family ministries frequently begin with the goal of fixing some particular problem. Perhaps one too many recent high school graduates have

---

[7] Adapted from William Frankena, "A Model for Analyzing a Philosophy of Education," *The High School Journal* 50, no. 1 (October 1966): 9–12.

walked away from the faith during their first few months of college. Maybe it has become apparent that too few parents in the church are actively guiding their children's spiritual growth. It could even be that the Holy Spirit has led a church leader to see that segregation of the generations fails to reflect God's perfect design. All of these problems represent valid concerns. Yet the development of a family ministry curriculum must be driven by motivations that run deeper than problem-centered reactions. Otherwise, family ministry becomes perceived as a programmatic panacea to fix the church's problems instead of a Scripture-driven reorientation of the church's priorities.

It is at this point that Frankena's model becomes especially helpful. His model begins by asking, "What primary disposition do we desire to cultivate?" (see the first box in fig. 15.2). Or, to ask the same question in a way that focuses specifically on curriculum development, "What is the primary aim that will drive this curriculum?" For those of us who view Scripture as God's eternal Word, this first question helps us to focus our curriculum development on transcendent truth instead of temporary problems. If you are developing a church-as-family curriculum, your answer to the first question might run something like this: "Because we desire to pursue more faithfully God's design for Christian community, our aim is to develop multi-generational practices of discipleship that demonstrate how Jesus has broken down the barriers between us" (see Eph 2:14–15).

A curriculum that is intended to strengthen the family-as-church aspect of family ministry would begin with a quite different answer. An aim similar to this one could provide a foundation for family-as-church curriculum: "Recognizing that God designed parents to be primary disciple-makers in their children's lives, we desire parents to engage actively and intentionally in guiding their children to conform every part of their lives to Jesus Christ" (see Rom 8:29; Eph 6:4). If the fathers in your congregation have disengaged from their children's spiritual development, your aim might be a bit more specific: "God has called Christian fathers to reflect the sacrificial leadership of Christ in their homes; our aim is for every father to become a Christlike leader in the discipleship of his wife and children" (see Eph 5:25–33; Col 3:21). Whatever the particular wording, root your answer in the truth of God's Word and in the transforming power of the gospel.

The next box in Frankena's model contains the premises that support your primary aim (see the second box in fig. 15.2). These premises focus on the particular realities and challenges in your local church; they are likely to be somewhat unique to your context. When developing these premises, you will be asking, "Given the nature of reality in my church and community, what specific dispositions are needed to move people toward the central aim?"

If the purpose of your curriculum is to develop deeper church-as-family relationships, some of these dispositions could include a desire to connect "spiritual orphans" with believing families. Church-as-family curriculum might also seek to cultivate recognition among the youth that they need Christ-centered relationships with senior citizens. If you are focusing your curriculum on family-as-church, these premises will probably focus on parents. One of your desired dispositions might include a church-wide recognition of the parents' role as primary disciple-makers. Another desired disposition might be that fathers would view themselves as spiritual leaders in their families. This box could also contain some desired patterns of life such as family devotional times or parents praying with their children.

Step 2: Choose Your Target

Once you have stated your principles and premises, you are ready to develop objectives for your family life curriculum (see the third box in fig. 15.2). These objectives will provide leaders and learners with a clear target for their learning experience. At this point, it is important to state specific, measurable actions! Another way of expressing this same idea draws from Robert Mager's classic book on curriculum design: Base your objectives on *overt performance* not *covert performance*.[8] For example, do not simply suggest in your objectives that parents should desire to disciple their children. That is a hidden attitude that will be almost impossible to assess. State specifically *what* parents will be able to do as well as *how* you will know whether parents have gained this skill.

I am not suggesting, of course, that outward actions are the final goal for your family ministry curriculum. What we desire ultimately is

---

[8] Robert F. Mager, *Preparing Instructional Objectives*, 3rd ed. (Atlanta: Center for Effective Performance, 1997).

not the cultivation of external habits but the transformation of people's hearts. Outward skill without inward renovation is likely to result in the same self-righteousness that Jesus condemned in the scribes and Pharisees (Matt 23:25–28).

At the same time, Scripture is clear that outward actions can demonstrate the inward reception of God's Word: "Be doers of the word and not hearers only, deceiving yourselves," James admonishes first-century believers. "The one who looks intently into the perfect law of freedom and perseveres in it, and is not a forgetful hearer but a doer who acts—this person will be blessed in what he does" (Jas 1:22,25 HCSB). The development of outward skills can help persons to solidify inner changes as well as providing a catalyst for changes yet to come.

So how can you develop clear objectives that emphasize overt skills in your family ministry curriculum? Here is an example how this process could look as you work from the identification of your purpose to the crafting of your objectives:

1. Select a disposition	Prayerfully select specific dispositions that your curriculum could influence in the lives of participants. You will probably draw these dispositions from the first two boxes in Frankena's model.
2. Identify supporting skills	For each disposition, identify overt skills that could support the development of this disposition. If possible, formulate three overt skills for each disposition—one skill for each of the following categories: acknowledge, apply, and adapt.
3. Develop assessments	For each overt skill, come up with a specific way that this skill will be assessed under specified conditions.
4. Craft objectives	Craft a simple, one-sentence objective that summarizes each overt skill, condition, and assessment.

Figure 15.3: Creating Objectives for Family Life Curriculum

Purpose of family ministry	Examples of possible desired dispositions	Examples of possible learning objectives
Church-as-family	Because we desire to pursue more faithfully God's design for Christian community, our aim is to develop multi-generational practices of discipleship that demonstrate how the death of Jesus has broken down the barriers between different generations of believers.	*Acknowledge:* Based on what they learn in this study, youth will paraphrase for their context three specified biblical texts that point to the need for multi-generational interaction and appreciation. *Apply:* Based on what they learn in this study, youth will plan a mission outreach that includes youth and senior adults. *Adapt:* Following the mission outreach, youth and senior adults will evaluate the experience together and make recommendations for future joint projects.
Family-as-church	Recognizing that God designed parents to be primary disciple-makers in their children's lives, we desire parents to engage actively and intentionally in guiding their children to conform every part of their lives to Jesus.	*Acknowledge:* Given a worksheet at the end of this study, parents will be able to match five verses related to parental discipleship with verse references. *Apply:* Prior to the final class session, each parent will outline—in a small group with other parents—a three-month plan for family faith-talks. *Adapt:* After practicing family faith-talks by role-playing with other class participants, parents will lead their families in a faith-talk at home before the next meeting.

Table 15.4: Examples of How Learning Objectives Can Be Developed for a Family Life Curriculum

Acknowledge (Remember and understand)	Apply (Apply and analyze)	Adapt (Evaluate and create)
Memorize biblical text.	Practice leading a family faith-talk.	Based on a brief Bible study outline, formulate a twenty-minute family devotion customized for your family.
Locate a specified Scripture based on one key phrase from the text.	Share salvation testimony with an individual from a different generation.	
Identify one primary meaning of a specified biblical text.	Plan twelve weeks of family faith-talks.	Design rite-of-passage experiences for each of your children, from baby dedication through graduation from high school.
Paraphrase biblical text.	Distinguish between faith-talk activities that would be appropriate for preschoolers, children, and teenagers.	Appraise the strengths and weaknesses in the ways that you are currently discipling your children.
Describe three ways that parents can disciple their children.	Prepare a list of discussion questions to consider after watching a movie with a teenager.	Role-play how older adults and young adults seem to interact in contemporary culture; critique this perceived pattern from a biblical perspective.

Figure 15.5: Examples of Overt Skills for Learning Objectives[9]

---

9 This chart represents my simplified adaptation of components related to the cognitive domain of Lorin Anderson, et al., eds., *A Taxonomy for Learning, Teaching, and Assessing: A Revision of Bloom's Taxonomy of Educational Objectives* (New York: Addison Wesley Longman, 2001).

Step 3: Be the Missionary in Your Culture

The fourth box in Frankena's framework (fig. 15.2) focuses on the question, "What methods will be most effective in my context?" Because of this emphasis on your particular context, it is at this point that your family ministry curriculum will begin to diverge most radically from that of the church down the street.

Formulating your answer to this question could require administering a survey to families in your community of faith. You might need to research what has been effective in churches that are similar to yours. Conversations with key leaders in your congregation could be helpful as well. Become a missionary in your church and community, considering carefully what is needed and what is most likely to be effective in your context. Throughout these contextual considerations, do not forget that God defines "effectiveness" not by numbers on a ledger sheet but by faithfulness to his Word.

Suppose the purpose of your projected curriculum is to equip families to function as microcosms of the church. Your research might reveal that even though Christian parents sense their responsibility to disciple their children, they are uncertain what to do. It could also become clear that many families are already too busy; so, adding another class for parents at church would be counterproductive. One solution might be to develop a curriculum for family faith-talks coordinated with the pastor's messages; this curriculum would be mentioned and provided to parents in printed form each Sunday morning. Curriculum of this sort may require two levels of objectives. The first level includes the learning that you intend children to experience in their homes; the second level has to do with the habits of family discipleship that you are developing in the parents.

Another possibility could be to write a curriculum that trains fathers to engage in faith-walks and faith-talks with their children; this study might replace your usual small-group studies for a few weeks, or it could be used in a monthly men's meeting. In other churches, you might choose to develop a parent-equipping curriculum that coordinates with youth or children's events that are already on the calendar.

Notice that a family-as-church curriculum can take many different forms, including some that do not even occur in classroom settings. This same pattern characterizes church-as-family curriculum as well.

Often, the best context for developing multi-generational relationships is not on your church campus. For example, bringing the generations together for mission trips or other service opportunities may be far more effective church-as-family activities than any formal class in the educational wing.

Even church-as-family activities that *do* occur on your church campus may happen outside the context of a formal class. These activities could include a youth prayer time that places senior adults and teenagers together. It may be a "families-in-faith" program that matches believing families with spiritual orphans. No matter how your church chooses to bring the generations together, a clear curriculum will help leaders and learners alike to develop deeper connections as a family in Christ.

Step 4: Develop the Content

Once your objectives are clear and you know what is needed in your context, you are ready to begin writing the content for the curriculum. The format and the number of learning sessions will vary from one context to another. The content, however, must be rooted in the gospel in such a way that it turns the attention of every participant toward the vast and beautiful story of how God has worked with humanity through creation and fall, redemption and consummation. Connect your content with your objectives, and take the time to evaluate whether participants are actually achieving the objectives.

The development of family life curriculum is a radically countercultural process. Particularly in Western culture, people cluster together according to peer groups and personal interests, so church-as-family does not happen easily or naturally. Parents tend to turn over the shaping of their children's souls to trained professionals, so family-as-church does not come easily either. But efficiency and ease are not the goal of gospel-motivated ministry. Conformity to the character of Jesus Christ—the one through whom the first family was formed in Eden and the one who is bringing together a new family even now on the basis of his own blood—is our purpose and ultimate goal.

CHAPTER 16

PURCHASING READY-TO-USE CURRICULUM

Bret Robbe

Your family wants a vacation! You consider going through the trouble of planning out an excursion all on your own. Visiting websites, calling for information, checking on flights and rentals, searching for housing . . . and eventually deciding it is not worth the trouble. On the other hand, you could decide to take a vacation and call your local travel agent. Travel agents have prepackaged travel plans with options designed to fit your family's size, budget, and interests. You can pick up the pamphlets, talk to an agent, and select the right vacation package that suits you. You get to enjoy the vacation without the hassle of doing it all yourself. In the next few pages, we will examine the value of ready-to-use curriculum, your pre-packaged trip arrangements, and look at ways to overcome perceived weaknesses and identify factors to consider in selecting the ready-to-use curriculum that is right for a church.

Frees Leaders to Lead and Minister

Vacations take time to plan, but a travel agent makes the planning easier. A church that purchases ready-to-use curriculum rather than creating its own adds the equivalent of a staff member to its leadership team. Using a minister's time to produce curriculum takes precious hours away from time that could be spent with members of the church family. Nothing can minister better than flesh-and-blood presence. Nothing can replace staff members who are available to invest in the lives of people. The incarnation of Christ, who came and dwelled among us, sets the standard for what pastoral ministry should look like.

If a staff member takes on the task of developing quality Bible study resources, time that would have been dedicated to other more important work has to be cut. Developing relationships, equipping others (Eph 4:11–12), casting a vision, providing direction, and responding to needs become secondary. Choosing a ready-to-use curriculum frees church leaders' schedules from the massive amounts of time required to produce Bible studies. That time can be used more deliberately to lead the church and minister to people.

Makes Members A Priority

The main destination or goal of Bible study is discipleship. In spite of their efforts to reach this goal, leaders find themselves in a quandary because members choose to straddle the fence, live according to the flesh, or take a nonchalant view of God and his Word. Just as you value the comfort and safety of your family, church leaders see the members of Bible study classes as incredibly important to the church. These are "travelers" ministry leaders must lead step-by-step to spiritual maturity.

Ready-to-use curriculum includes an essential tool for class members. This tool is often called a learner guide. Addressing the educational and learning needs of members, the learner guide is a vital component for the spiritual development of members in Bible study. A personal learner guide benefits class members for several reasons.

First, each lesson in the learner guide provides an essential step in moving members toward spiritual maturity and discipleship. A believer matures as the Holy Spirit helps him or her apply scriptural truth to life, and the learner guide contains biblical truths God uses in this transformational process. Members will not get all they need at church or from a single handout. The learner guide becomes a companion to the Bible that members can use for personal study.

Second, the learner guide combats biblical illiteracy, an alarming trend in churches today. Believers of all ages are faltering because they lack knowledge of God's Word. The learner guide provides significant biblical content that can help to reverse the trend of biblical illiteracy in three significant ways:

1. *Preparation for group time.* Biblical literacy and life-changing discipleship do not happen through a one-hour information dump on Sunday mornings. The best discipleship happens when the learner prepares before the class session. When used as intended, the learner guide prepares believers' hearts and minds to receive the teaching that takes place during the class session. Without preparation, the learner may absorb only a small amount of the biblical content presented during the class session. With preparation, believers allow the Holy Spirit to cultivate their hearts so that God's Word can be readily planted deep. Designed by experts in education and group dynamics, the learner guide begins to connect learners to the lesson before the group meets.

2. *Biblical focus during group time.* During group time, the learner guide keeps the discussion from straying into topics unrelated to the lesson or from focusing on participants' feelings and opinions. Everyone in the group is literally on the same page. The learner guide helps keep the class centered on God's Word, diminishing the possibility of chasing topics that are not part of the Bible study. A good learner guide, used by a trained teacher, leads members to find true biblical solutions to questions and avoids everyone doing what is right in his own eyes (see Judg 21:25; Deut 12:8). This discipleship model differs substantively from the common practice of discussing eight to ten questions related to the pastor's sermon. A Bible-centered learner guide, used appropriately, takes learners much deeper into a study of

God's Word and helps them grow and mature in their relationship with God.

3. *Continued learning after group time.* After group time a quality learner guide reinforces what has been learned. Many
learner guides include daily readings that help learners
continue to apply what they learned during group time and
discussion. Learners can continue to absorb biblical truth
each day throughout the week.

Third, the learner guide provides content that challenges worldly
perspective. Every day we receive cultural messages that shape our
thinking. Many people, even believers, succumb to this powerful influence. Our ideals and worldviews are shaped by the culture in which we
live. A learner guide helps church members develop a biblical worldview. A church that provides sound learner guides communicates to
each member, "We believe the Bible is essential in shaping the way you
think, act, and feel during the week." Learners need to grow in their
understanding of the biblical text in order to interpret reality correctly
and then apply Scripture to life needs within a culture that draws them
away from God. Answering a few questions about a sermon or giving
personal opinions in a small group does not lead to a change in worldview. If true biblical answers are not the outcome of the discussion,
the group or the learner will never understand more than they already
know. The only way a biblical worldview can develop is through members' interaction with biblical content. The learner guide is just that:
a guide that helps learners stay in the Word day after day, week after
week.

Utilizes the Experience and Knowledge of Experts

A quality, ready-to-use curriculum enables churches to benefit from
the experience and expertise of countless educators and professionals.
Most churches will never have access to the kinds of experts and scholars employed by a publisher of Christian curriculum. Companies like
LifeWay are able to pull together a team of twenty or more experts from
different fields and backgrounds to develop a single Bible study lesson.
Age-group ministers, theologians, professors, and archaeologists are

involved in some aspect of the creation of biblically centered studies. Most churches cannot consistently draw from that pool of experts.

Car manufacturers would not think of creating a car without utilizing a team of experts. Why do churches believe a single minister can successfully create Bible studies week after week that include all of the resources teachers need to teach the lesson effectively? A person skilled in biblical exposition sometimes lacks knowledge in application or educational theory. A person strong in teaching methodology might be useful in instruction but may fall short in delivering biblical exposition. The diverse disciplines and skills required to create a complete, satisfying, and balanced lesson are most likely found in a team setting, not in one person.

A good curriculum for Christian education in the local church has at least seven characteristics:

1. Biblical and theological soundness, so that what is taught in the curriculum is biblically accurate
2. Relevance, so that the teaching is suited to the nature and needs of the learners in their current situation
3. Comprehensiveness, so that the scope of the curriculum includes the essential components that lead to the development of well-rounded Christians
4. Balance, so that the curriculum neither underemphasizes nor overemphasizes key Christian truths
5. Sequence, so that the presentation of topics is in the best order for learning
6. Flexibility, so that the curriculum is adaptable to the individual differences of the learners, to churches of different types, and to the varying abilities of leaders and teachers
7. Correlation, so that each part relates properly to the total curriculum plan[1]

Another benefit of ready-to-use curriculum is age specificity. Most of us find it easier to teach one age group. The needs of preschoolers are vastly different from those of a sixth grader or a high-school senior.

---

[1] See Howard P. Colson and Raymond M. Rigdon, *Understanding Your Church's Curriculum* (Nashville: Baptist Sunday School Board, 1981), 50.

People spend their entire lives trying to understand better how to teach one age group. Expecting church leaders to develop quality resources for multiple age groups is setting them up for failure.

One way to illustrate the importance of the experts is seen in the creation of the Experiencing God resources. Dr. Henry Blackaby had led conferences and presented the content before the first workbook was ever published. He was teamed with a group of editors and educators who complemented his skill set. Because of that partnership, what was once a compelling presentation became a life-changing movement that has made a dramatic impact on churches and individuals from all walks of life.

By having as many as twenty individuals working to create an individual lesson or set of lessons, each individual can contribute from his strengths in the collaborative process. A team is assembled from different fields and is composed of people with different skill sets. You want people from different backgrounds working together to build your car. Each inspector looks at the project from a different angle, resulting in a better-finished vehicle. You want the engineer with the most extensive knowledge of brakes to design the ones for your car. You want a tire expert to select your tires. You want the paint job to last for the lifetime of the vehicle. We could talk about every part of the car—fabrics for the seats, dashboards that look good and do not rattle, metal that withstands road salt and does not corrode.

We all teach or preach from a unique point of view based on our specific experiences, study, and personality. If we are the only one who engineers a curriculum, then over time the people using that curriculum run the risk of developing a limited perspective. There is a reason God used more than forty different individuals to write the Bible. They each brought a different perspective, and each perspective is one that God knew we would need.

Ensures More Hands and Eyes

Ready-to-use curriculum providers usually follow steps in a production process focused on quality control. Proofreaders, doctrinal readers, editors, production specialists, and printers are parts of these multiple eyes and hands. Doctrine and biblical integrity matter!

Typically, when a church creates its own curriculum, fewer people look over the resource. Time constraints may limit the process to only one read-through. Choosing a ready-to-use curriculum significantly decreases the chance that biblical error will slip into a lesson. You would not want a car that had been inspected by only one quality-control technician who faced a thirty-minute deadline. Even with all of the extra eyes and hands examining a ready-to-use curriculum, some things will slip by—but not nearly as many as if fewer eyes had looked over the content. Henry Ford stated that nothing is "particularly hard if you divide it into small jobs."[2] Ford understood the value of many hands and eyes. Each week church leaders trust a team of teachers to help disciple their church members, and this discipleship takes place most effectively when they put resources into their hands that help them teach the Bible in a way that is scripturally sound and doctrinally correct.

Provides for Balanced Results

A by-product of having many experts who design and create curriculum is the issue of balance. The next time you sit behind your steering wheel, take a careful look at the dash. You see gauges that tell you important information like speed, water temperature, and amount of fuel in the vehicle. Just as important are the controls for the air-conditioning system! These things all have a practical function in the operation of your car, and they are also designed for your comfort. You will likely see circles, ovals, squares, rectangles, triangles and a host of other shapes that make the dash more appealing, interesting, or functional. When designing that dash, the designer was aware of the need for a balance between style and function.

Quality, ready-to-use Bible study curriculum is created with balance in mind. Balancing the amount of exposition against the amount of application, balance among different teaching methods, and balance among different teaching outcomes are all considered. Many publishers have adopted approaches that also help their customers

---

[2] Henry Ford, as quoted in Fred R. Shapiro, ed., *Yale Book of Quotations* (New Haven: Yale University Press, 2006), 282.

move toward balanced spiritual growth. For example, LifeWay uses the LifeSpan strategy as a filter for this type of balance.[3] A balance of multiple spiritual disciplines enhances healthy spiritual growth and transformation.

The word curriculum refers to the course, track, or path on which a person runs. Curriculum is similar to running a race toward a finish line, much as the author of Hebrews encourages his readers to "run with endurance the race that lies before us" (Heb 12:1 HCSB). Choosing a Bible study curriculum means pursuing the course the Bible sets for life—Christlikeness, transformation into the image of Christ (see Rom 8:28–29; 2 Cor 3:18). Sunday school curriculum is the continuous course, process, or system Bible study groups can use to guide unbelievers toward faith in Christ and believers toward Christlikeness through the transforming power of the Holy Spirit.

Sometimes curriculum can resemble a sprint, a course that is finished quickly like a six- or eight-week study. Ultimately, however, curriculum should be viewed as a marathon, something that takes place over a long period of time. There are two aspects of curriculum: the curriculum plan and the curriculum resources. The curriculum plan sets the agenda for what is studied. The curriculum resources contain the curriculum plan and set forth how to study it.

Gives You a Comprehensive Plan

A curriculum plan or curriculum map, as some call it, is an orderly arrangement of Bible study content organized so that Sunday School leaders can engage learners in the study of God's Word in a balanced, systematic way.[4] Months of planning were required before the frame of your car was manufactured. Comprehensive concept drawings, testing, spec sheets, machine orders, timing of delivery, and a host of other elements were planned so that your car would roll off the assembly

---

[3] For more information about the LifeSpan strategy, see "LifeSpan transforming people from birth to heaven," n.p. [cited 31 January 2012]. Online: http: lifeway.com/Article/Why-Lifespan-can-make-a-difference-for-your-church.

[4] Adapted from Bill L. Taylor and Louis B. Hanks, *Sunday School for a New Century* (Nashville: LifeWay Press, 1999), 162. Used by permission.

line complete and ready to drive. When the manufacturer began the process, the production team knew exactly what it was attempting to do and what it would need to do to get the job done. Ready-to-use curriculum is usually based on a comprehensive plan. That plan may call for a curriculum to take three to ten years to complete. This kind of detailed planning is invaluable to churches and teachers. One of the biggest struggles in developing any curriculum is determining what will be studied and when it will be studied (scope and sequence). Creating the scope and sequence is nitty-gritty work that takes hours of consideration and thinking. The developers of ready-to-use curriculum have already completed this most difficult task for churches by planning the scope and sequence of Bible studies. This frees church staff from days of planning meetings to determine the scope and sequence of materials they might produce, which in turn frees them to do what God called them to do—lead the church.

When considering a curriculum plan, choose one that covers all of the Bible's content, not just selected or favorite parts. "All Scripture," Paul writes, "is . . . profitable for teaching, for rebuking, for correcting, for training in righteousness" (2 Tim 3:16 HCSB). Make sure the curriculum plan is comprehensive enough to cover the entire Bible and all life concerns that people face over a specified length of time. Second, choose a plan that has a balance of biblical content, Bible study approaches, and life issues. For example, the plan should contain a balance of Old Testament studies, the life of Christ, and New Testament epistles. The plan should contain a balance of approaches to studying the Bible, such as studying through a book of the Bible, a character in the Bible, or a topic or life issue in the Bible.

Why not just allow groups to study whatever they want or whatever the hot topic or felt need is? By following a systematic, comprehensive plan, ongoing Bible study repeatedly points to the fact that the Bible, not developmental life needs and human issues, must guide and shape believers' lives. If a Sunday school leader selects studies that address only age group needs and issues, the leader risks supplanting the Bible's goal for believers with contemporary perceptions of age group needs and issues. Occasional topical, issue-oriented studies are necessary and included in ongoing curriculum plans, but the ultimate goal of the Bible and Sunday school curriculum is to lead people toward faith in

Christ and transformation toward Christlikeness through an encounter with the truth of God's Word.

Although Jesus was responsive to immediate physical, emotional, and spiritual needs, He did not always teach on subjects the people wanted—their felt needs. Jesus was aware of the deeper issues of the human heart that went beyond the current issues of the day, such as ceremonial washing of the hands, observing Sabbath laws, and getting caught in adultery. Jesus' curriculum plan focused on redemption; the cross; and the transformation of human lives, beginning with the heart. A balanced curriculum plan not only addresses hot topics and felt needs but also places people on the track toward mature biblical faith by considering doctrines such as union with Christ, the person and work of the Holy Spirit, evangelism, compassion for a lost world, and a biblical worldview.[5]

If a group is left to determine its own course of study, there will be significant consequences. Sunday school classes will not receive the whole counsel of God without a balanced approach to studying Scripture from both the Old and New Testaments. If classes are not going to study the entire Bible over a period of time, adult learners will learn only a small percentage of the Bible. No one would be satisfied to read half a book, but that is what some Sunday school classes are getting—half the Book. They are not receiving instruction in the entire Bible because a poor curriculum strategy was adopted.

Pet topics can dominate the discussion. Prophecy, the book of Revelation, or a particular doctrine—each one is a potential focal point for a Sunday school class over an extended period of time if it is a topic either the teacher or the learners feel passionate about. I heard one minister of education ask, "Who am I to tell him he can't teach the topic he wants to?" This was said in regard to a Sunday school teacher who held that God told him to lead the class in a particular pet study. Pet topics increase the likelihood of imbalance in the study of God's Word. If you turn children loose in a buffet line, they will eat all the macaroni and cheese, pizza, and cookies you let them eat. If you turn teachers loose to study whatever topic is near and dear to their hearts, class members will have a similar buffet experience: they will study the

---

[5] Taylor and Hanks, *Sunday School for a New Century*, 162–63.

same topics over and over again. The result will be spiritually imbalanced, unhealthy believers.

A lack of strategy is perhaps the most glaring weakness of all when curriculum is chosen that does not provide a balanced approach to studying God's Word. Sunday schools need curriculum that strategically develops learners who are spiritually balanced and are being transformed by the power of God's Word. The LifeSpan strategy addresses this need head-on. LifeSpan is a promise backed by a plan. LifeSpan, a strategy developed by LifeWay Christian Resources, provides a strategic, coordinated approach to study God's Word from birth to heaven. LifeSpan promises a balanced study of God's Word over the lifetime of the individual. Preschoolers are taught eight foundational biblical concepts, and additional biblical concepts are added during the childhood and student years. Finally, adults of all ages study fifteen biblical concepts. Special care is given to the development of the scope and sequence of each curriculum line so that learners experience a balanced diet of Old and New Testament studies.[6]

The curriculum plan must be properly sequenced so that learners can build on what they already know. A systematic approach to Bible study facilitates the integration of biblical truth into the learner's life as a lifelong process. Jesus built on what his hearers already knew and took them to a new level when he said, "You have heard that it was said . . . But I tell you . . ." (Matt 5:43–44 HCSB). Remember that spiritual transformation into Christlikeness is a lifelong process.

Because curriculum is best viewed from the perspective of a marathon, the appropriate repetition of biblical content and life concerns in different ways and at different times strengthens learners, much as a cup of fresh water reinvigorates a marathon runner. The Heb 12:1 principle of the perseverance of believers applies here. At the same time, open Bible study groups (groups that expect new people to attend each week) will always have new people joining the curriculum race—new learners who need the basics the veteran learners could help teach. Do a quick survey of Jesus' teaching in the Gospels, and you will discover

---

[6] For more information about the LifeSpan strategy, go to lifeway.com/lifespan; lifeway.com/adultstrategy; lifeway.com/studentstrategy; lifeway.com/kidspromise

how frequently he repeated themes—and how slowly his disciples caught on. A properly sequenced Bible study plan is an expression of the principle of renewing the mind found in Rom 12:2. One ministry of the Holy Spirit is to help believers recall what Jesus taught, to help believers become experts in living and bearing witness for Christ. Curriculum can support your goals for transformational Bible study.

A planned, ongoing Bible study strategy creates a ministry environment that fosters strong relationships and challenges members to regularly invite the lost to become Christ followers. Ongoing groups have a fixed organizational structure that provides stable leadership over a long period of time. With regard to curriculum planning or curriculum mapping, God knows the timeliness of any study for an individual's life, as well as for a congregation's time and circumstances. The Holy Spirit can work in the hearts of curriculum planners months and years in advance to design studies that will be used by God at a particular time.[7]

A ready-to-use curriculum can be an essential tool for setting a recognized standard for the Bible study organization in churches. Church leaders can use the scope and sequence behind the chosen curriculum to communicate what they want to happen in the lives of people. Providing well-developed resources for both leaders and group members also creates a standard for accountability. Leaders are expected to use the resource, and group members are expected to prepare. In fact, by providing every group member with a study guide, leaders communicate that they expect members to do some type of personal Bible study outside their group experiences.

Maturity does not happen in a six-week study or even over a two-year period. Curriculum is designed to lead people toward spiritual maturity and transformation. Frequently changing curriculum means members would miss the balance that comes from a well-planned design. Allowing every class to study whatever they want introduces the risk of missing essential Bible stories and core doctrines. Good leadership involves knowing where you are leading your people. When you choose a ready-to-use curriculum that gives attention to the whole counsel of God, you are leading your people toward a solid biblical foundation.

---

[7] See Taylor and Hanks, *Sunday School for a New Century*, 163–64.

Addressing Perceived Weaknesses

Curriculum will never replace trained teachers. Trained teachers can make bad or mediocre curriculum good, and they can make good or great curriculum superior. But an untrained teacher can find a multitude of ways to misdirect even the best curriculum. Curriculum alone will not solve our need for more teachers or for more quality teachers.

There are no shortcuts when it comes to training teachers. Willing teachers are handed a ready-to-use curriculum resource and told to use it. But how do they use it? How do the parts relate to one another? What is required of them to use the resource the way it was designed? Every teacher requires and deserves training, regardless of the type of curriculum being used.

No matter what curriculum church leaders use, they still need to maintain the organization. As with any organization, Bible study groups and the supporting organization will die if leaders fail to nurture and cultivate it. More leaders, new groups, upgrades to equipment, and attention to ministry involvement are just a few of the tasks required to maintain a quality Bible study organization. Ready-to-use curriculum was never intended to replace regular evaluation and refinement of the Bible study groups using the resources. However, ready-to-use curriculum can free leaders to do the things required to keep their Bible study groups healthy and vibrant.

Ready-to-use curriculum is developed for the masses. Leaders need to help their teachers customize the content to the needs of their groups. Most ready-to-use curriculum provides tools beyond the basics that will help make the teachers' jobs easier and will help them customize the material. Teachers who receive extra resources for their preparation will naturally be more confident when facing the group. Extra resources provided to teachers can enhance the group experience and can make it easier for them to have a satisfying Bible study week after week. No matter how good a curriculum resource may be, teachers will need to make changes to make it their own, and they should.

When incorporating ready-to-use curriculum, church leaders must be comfortable using someone else's scope and sequence—someone else's directions to the desired destination. Leaders must be willing to trust a prescribed path even when they may wonder about a particular leg of the journey. A ready-to-use curriculum allows leaders time to lead and shepherd the congregation, but the cost of that freedom is releasing control over the scope and sequence of the Bible study. The good news is that leaders can select from different curriculum options at the onset, finding the scope and sequence that best fit their needs.

Choosing the right curriculum is an important decision that will impact the church family for years. Church leaders should not expect to flip through the pages of catalogs and make their decision in a few minutes. This decision should not be based on the hottest fad or the latest trend. This is a decision about multiplying disciples of Jesus Christ. In order to evaluate curriculum, churches need to spend time getting familiar with the format, the feel, and the theology directing that curriculum. The time leaders invest in the decision will most likely save them time in the future. Making a hasty decision now will usually cost them in the long run. Doctrinal direction and educational philosophy should be at the top of the list as these decisions are made.

A stark reality to keep in mind when working with a travel agent is that the vacation will cost more if each piece is customized individually than if purchased as a package deal. The cost to create curriculum is similar to buying the individual parts of a major vacation separately. Most of us forget to calculate some of the fixed costs when thinking about what it costs to take the full trip. These are the costs that will be spent no matter what it costs to reach the destination. Fixed costs are usually seen in salaries, benefits, equipment, software, and reference materials (commentaries and other resources the creator/writer may need to complete the task). In contrast, variable costs are those that can fluctuate, such as paper, ink, color, and amount of graphic design. Be aware that we are not talking about creating five discussion questions and calling that a curriculum. We are talking about providing a resource set that offers sound Bible exposition, key insights, teaching plans, and resources that help teachers approach their task confidently and help class members prepare for transformational Bible study. Such a curriculum is more likely to result in quality Bible study experiences in small groups that will help people move toward Christlikeness.

Conclusion

"I'm going to plan my own vacation! It'll save bundles of cash!" That's the paradox of ready-to-use curriculum versus "write-your-own" curriculum. People think they are saving money, but they are not; they are paying more and often getting less. Fortunately, savvy church leaders have learned this lesson. They are swapping curriculum-writing time for hands-on ministry time with their people with confidence they are making the right choice.

CONTRIBUTORS

Editors

James Riley Estep Jr. is Professor of Christian Education at Lincoln Christian University. He has edited many books, including *Christian Formation: Integrating Theology and Human Development* (B&H, 2010) and *A Theology for Christian Education* (B&H, 2008).

Karen Lynn Estep is Associate Professor of Professional Education at Lincoln Christian University.

M. Roger White is Professor in the Departments of Graduate Ministry as well as University Libraries at Azusa Pacific University. He is a contributor to the *Evangelical Dictionary of Christian Education* (Baker, 2001).

Contributors

Holly Allen is Professor of Christian Ministries and Director of the Child and Family Studies Program at John Brown University. She is the editor of *Nurturing Children's Spirituality: Christian Perspectives and Best Practices* (Cascade, 2008).

Timothy Paul Jones is Associate Professor of Leadership and Church Ministry and editor of *The Journal for Family Ministry* at The Southern

Baptist Theological Seminary. He is the author or editor of many books, including *Trained in the Fear of God* (Kregel, 2011) and *Perspectives on Family Ministry* (B&H, 2010).

Bret Robbe is Director of Leadership and Adult Publishing at LifeWay Christian Resources.

Mark Senter is Chair of the Educational Ministries Department and Professor of Educational Ministries at Trinity Evangelical Divinity School. He is the editor of *Four Views of Youth Ministry and the Church* (Zondervan, 2001)

Michael S. Wilder is Assistant Professor of Leadership and Church Ministry and Associate Dean for Doctoral Studies at The Southern Baptist Theological Seminary. He is the author of *TransforMission: Making Disciples through Short-Term Missions* (B&H, 2010).

NAME INDEX

SUBJECT INDEX

Read before Jan 25   Intro; Ch 1   ✓

   Done

☑   Feb 4   c. 2, 3

☑   feb 11   c. 4, 5

☑   feb 18   c. 6, 7

☑   feb 25   c. 8, 9

☑   Mar 4   e. 10, 1)

☐   Mar 11   c. 12, 3

☐   Mar 18   c. 14, 15

☐   April 1   c. 16

———————————

1. interact on moodle.
2. Project due April 5th
3. Paper due April 30th.